Industry Agglomerations and Regional Development in Hungary

Schriften zur Wirtschaftstheorie und Wirtschaftspolitik

Herausgegeben von
Klaus Beckmann, Michael Berlemann, Rolf Hasse,
Jörn Kruse, Franco Reither, Wolf Schäfer,
Thomas Straubhaar und Klaus W. Zimmermann

Band 42

PETER LANG
Frankfurt am Main · Berlin · Bern · Bruxelles · New York · Oxford · Wien

Cordula Wandel

Industry Agglomerations and Regional Development in Hungary

Economic Processes during European Integration

PETER LANG
Internationaler Verlag der Wissenschaften

Bibliografische Information der Deutschen Nationalbibliothek
Die Deutsche Nationalbibliothek verzeichnet diese Publikation in der Deutschen Nationalbibliografie; detaillierte bibliografische Daten sind im Internet über http://dnb.d-nb.de abrufbar.

Zugl.: Hamburg, Univ., Diss., 2009

Gedruckt auf alterungsbeständigem, säurefreiem Papier.

D 18
ISSN 1433-1519
ISBN 978-3-631-60091-7

www.peterlang.de

This book is dedicated
to my mother, Ingrid Hantke,
and to the memory of my father,
Otto Heinrich Hantke,
and my father-in-law,
Dr. Karl Wandel.

Acknowledgements

The inspiration for this research originated from my work for the European Commission in Brussels as an assistant to the Commissioner for regional policy, Dr. Monika Wulf-Matthies. During a study on the interpenetration of trade between the CEECs and the EU conducted under director Dr. Horst Reichenbach at the DG Economic and Financial Affairs of the European Commission, Hungary struck me as a forerunner on the way to a market economy. This research has benefited from the experience I gained in practical policy making in Brussels.

Professor Dr. Thomas Straubhaar, Director of the Hamburg Institute of International Economics (HWWI), gave me the opportunity to carry out this project. I am grateful to him for his support of my doctorate. My thanks also go to Professor Dr. Thomas Eger for assuming the co-referate. I would also like to acknowledge the help of Dr. Silvia Stiller of the HWWI in providing useful comments and suggestions for the manuscript. This research was accepted as dissertation by the University of Hamburg on 2nd of December 2009.

Above all, I want to thank my husband, Dr. Hans-Ulrich Wandel, for his encouragement and support of my endeavour to achieve the doctorate in economics. My thanks also go to my three children Celia, Reinhold and Jacqueline, who were born during the research of this project, for going joyfully to kindergarten enabling me to complete this dissertation.

Hamburg, in February 2010 Cordula Wandel

Table of Contents

Index of Figures

Index of Tables

List of Abbreviations

BCE	Border regions with Central and East European countries
BEU	Border regions with member states of the European Union
BEX	Border regions with external countries
CEECs	Central and East European countries
CMEA	Council of Mutual Economic Assistance
DG	Directorate General (of the European Commission)
EC	European Community
EU	European Union
Eurostat	European Statistical Office
FDI	Foreign Direct Investment
GDP	Gross Domestic Product
HCSO	Hungarian Central Statistical Office
HUF	Hungarian Forint
INTERREG	Interregional cooperation community initiative
ISPA	Instrument for Structural Policy in the pre-accession period (until 2004)
ICT	Information and communication technologies
ISIC	International Standard Industrial Classification of All Economic Activities
N.A.	Not available
NACE	Statistical Classification of Economic Activities in the European Union
NEG	New economic geography
NTBs	Non-tariff barriers
NUTS	Nomenclature des Unités Territoriales Statistiques
PPS	Purchasing Power Standards
R&D	Research and Development
SMEs	Small and medium-sized enterprises
SIC	Standard Industrial Classification
SITC	Standard International Trade Classification
TEÁOR	Hungarian Standard Classification of Economic Activities

1. Introduction

In context with the Eastern enlargement of the European Union (EU), this research deals with the effects of pre-enlargement integration policies on industry agglomeration and regional development in Hungary. Without the fall of the Berlin Wall and the people-induced processes which led to it, no Eastern enlargement of the EU and no German unification would have been possible. Hungary played a major role in this unprecedented political and economic process in Europe, undergoing subsequently the successful transition to a market economy and a pluralistic democracy governed by the rule of law. The profound processes part of the transition to a market economy affected the industrial set-up and regional economic structure to an unprecedented extent until about 1995, entailing a decline in industry output and employment by one third. In the almost two decades analysed by this research, Hungary's share of exports to the EU market rose from one third to over 80%. The institution of the European agreement which governed the lion share of the period played an important role in this development. During the 5 years since the Eastern enlargement of the EU in 2004, trade volumes have tripled in the enlarged EU from 175 billion Euro to 500 billion, and Central and East European countries (CEECs) now trade 5 times as much with each other than prior to their EU accession.

Hungary was chosen for this research for several reasons. Firstly, Hungary used to be the show case among CEECs when this research project was started. Having embarked on economic reforms towards a market economy much earlier than other CEECs, already during the mid-1980s, the country was economically well off. The highest stock of foreign direct investment (FDI) in any of the CEECs endorsed the attractiveness as a location for investors, due to favourable conditions regarding productivity, training of the workforce, the legislative framework, as well as the geographic location of the country functioning as a hub for reaching neighbouring markets in the area. By spring 2009, the economy had fallen behind among CEECs because Hungarians had lived beyond their means for years, the general government - as manifested in mounting public debt - as well as the people.[1] The current world economic crisis hit Hungary harder than most of its neighbours.[2] Austerity and fiscal policy measures taken by the new

1 Many people in Hungary have financed their housing mainly in debts denominated in foreign currencies; the serving of this debt consumes a rising share of their disposable income now due to the devaluation of the Hungarian forint in which their income is denominated.

2 The decline in Hungary's GDP forecast for 2009 is -6.3%, according to the *European Commission (2009a)*.

Hungarian government in office since April 2009[3] are to contribute to the economic recovery. Secondly, as this research is interested in economic effects of the EU's pre- and post-accession integration policies, Hungary seemed particularly suitable as a small open economy.[4] The early political orientation towards the West entailed that Hungary was among the first beneficiaries of the PHARE aid programme and the first to negotiate a Europe agreement with the EU, whilst the application for full membership followed in 1994. The manufacturing industry - the sector based on which agglomeration is analysed and which was at the core of trade liberalisation by the Europe agreement - is more important in Hungary in terms of employment, exports and output than for example in Poland where the agricultural employment was over 26% prior to EU accession. Hungarian government policies such as the free-trade zones and industrial parks policy contributed to the spur in exports towards the EU's market. And thirdly, the regional structure of Hungary and the availability of data also played a role in the choice. A sufficient number of regions at the Nuts-3 level and the good availability of reliable data from the national statistical office from 1992 onwards and in English were additional arguments.[5]

The theories of the new economic geography (NEG) make certain predictions about the formation and development of agglomeration as well as about regional specialization during integration processes. Integration processes are mainly modelled by a reduction in transport costs, which the European context can be taken to comprise costs for transportation, for non-tariff barriers (NTBs) and for administrative formalities due to the passing of national borders.[6] Empirical proof for one of the key propositions of NEG, namely that trade induces agglomeration, is scarce so far and has been called for.[7] Overall, the results of this research on manufacturing agglomeration and regional specialization in Hungary contribute to bringing such an empirical confirmation.

---

3 Recent austerity measures include the elimination of the 13th monthly pension and the 13th monthly salary for public civil servants paid out last for 2009.

4 Hungary's exports to the world set in relation to GDP were 80% in 2007, according to the Economic forecast of spring 2009, *European Commission (2009a), p. 85.*

5 The availability and reliability of data for Poland is much worse until the time of finishing this research. No data were published by Eurostat for Poland's regional disparities at Nuts-3 level, measured in terms of GDP per capita relative to the EU average, at the time of writing (7th of May 2009).

6 In the EU, where customs duties and quotas have been eliminated decades ago - the customs union had been completed among the initial 6 EU member states in 1968 - and between Hungary and the EU by the Europe agreement since the early 1990s, NTBs have played the dominant role ever since. NTBs can take multiple forms such as different national rules, norms and product standards as well as regulations for market access including professional degrees and accreditations.

7 For example by *Head & Mayer (2004)* in their article: "The Empirics of Agglomeration and Trade".

This research analyses three dimensions of industry agglomeration: (i) the degree of concentration per manufacturing sector and the development over time - strong or relatively weak concentration, and was there a pattern in the development? (ii) Where in space did agglomerations form? And (iii) which influences played a role - industry-specific factors or integration factors or regional characteristics? Similarly, the multiple dimensions of regional specialization are examined: the degree and development of specialization for the Hungarian regions during the phases of economic integration - was there a common pattern for groups of regions? And which influences played a role, region-specific factors or integration variables?

A particular feature of this research is that it combines concrete empirical research with policy relevance in light of practical work-experience of the author gained in European policy making.[8] Further, Hungary as a transformation economy and the profound economic processes entailed are examined in context with European integration over the time span of almost two decades, much longer than previous studies on transition countries. With respect to the empirical analysis of industry agglomeration, the present research uses regional-level data to analyse agglomeration for Hungary, whereas most previous research was based on country-level data for a group of countries (EU or CEECs). With reference to the tools, a special contribution of this research is that it applies six different concentration indices to the same set of manufacturing employment data, thereby allowing for a comparative analysis. Regression analysis on the influences working onto industry concentration and in particular on regional specialization has rarely been performed before nor been based on data from Central and Eastern Europe.

The empirical results regarding the effects of pre- and post accession policies on Hungarian manufacturing industries and regional development have certain policy implications. Conclusions will be drawn for the role which agglomerations - industrial agglomerations, networks of towns and cities - can play in fostering economic growth at the country-level. The option of strategic specialization for a region will be discussed as a possible road towards fostering regional economic development. In the face of the new challenges after Eastern enlargement in Hungary, and probably to a similar extent in the other CEEC, proposals for the next reform of European regional policy will be discussed, taking into account the current debate at the academic and political level. Finally, the pre-accession policy perspective will be opened towards current enlargement candidates of the EU such as Croatia in the nearer future and Ukraine further away on the horizon.

---

8 *Cordula Wandel* worked in the Cabinet of Commissioner Dr. Monika Wulf-Mathies in Brussels from 1997 until 1999, in DG Consumer Policy until 2000, and perviously in the DG Economic and Financial Affairs of the European Commission from 1993 until 1995.

The remainder of this research is structured as follows: Chapter 2 will introduce the theoretical framework of models chosen for this research and give an overview of previous empirical research regarding agglomeration and regional specialization, leading to the formulation of the hypothesis for this research. In an empirical descriptive analysis, chapter 3 will look at the main elements playing a role in Hungary's trade structure with the EU, manufacturing industries, and foreign direct investment, at the one hand, and the regional set-up and main characteristics of the regions including economic development and inter-regional net migration, on the other hand. This is done with a view to identifying indications for the ensuing econometric analysis. The development of agglomeration in Hungary's manufacturing industries will be analysed in chapter 4, using as a tool six different concentration measures, thereby allowing for the comparative analysis of these indices. The development of regional specialization will be analysed in chapter 5. The pattern during different phases of the integration process will also be examined for various groups of regions. Chapter 6 presents the results of an econometric analysis based on panel regressions regarding influences playing a role for an industry's concentration - integration factors and/or industry-specific characteristics - as well as separately regarding factors playing a role for a region's specialization. Chapter 7 will summarize the main empirical findings of this research. Policy implications regarding the future shape of European regional policy will be inferred from the different degree of adjustments and challenges among Hungary's regions in the light of the current academic and political debate. The role which agglomerations can play in national growth strategies and the option of using specialization as a tool in regional development will be discussed. This research concludes by giving a perspective on policies for future EU accession countries with a view to the economic geography of an ever wider Europe.

2. Literature Overview

In this chapter, the topic of this research "Agglomerations and regional development in Hungary" shall be positioned in a theoretical and literature context. The appropriate analytical framework will be selected and suitable models will be identified in section 2.1. The new research contribution of this research will be shown against the background of previous empirical studies reviewed in section 2.2. The aim is to infer hypotheses for this research, more concretely on how integration with the EU has influenced industry structure and regional development in Hungary during the period 1992 to 2008 and whether there were direct effects measurable in Hungary's agglomeration and regional specialization pattern. The hypotheses will be formulated in section 2.3. These will include questions like the following: How has agglomeration of manufacturing industries developed over the period? Which effects could be observed with respect to specialization for the regions in Hungary? And thirdly, where in space have manufacturing concentration processes and certain specialization pattern taken place?

Further, the Europe agreement - which was the main pre-accession policy of the EU and was in force for 12 years of the period encompassed by this research - shall be presented in its main elements in section 2.3, as the regulatory framework is deemed to have shaped economic relations between the EU and Hungary to a large extent. The hypotheses posed by this dissertation shall be formulated in detail towards the end of this chapter in section 2.4. Finally, the data available as a basis for this research shall be presented in section 2.5.

2.1 Theoretical background

In the choice of a stream of theory, it has been taken into consideration what this research is interested in, namely to explain to which extent regional industry structures in Hungary and the degree of agglomeration is influenced by economic integration with the EU. While liberalisation of trade and falling transport costs are certainly important factors playing a role in economic integration, free capital flows (FDI) and technological progress - expressed in advances such as higher productivity due to newer production facilities and fresh know-how in production processes[9] - also play a role. As the Europe agreement had a concrete influence on

9 A number of empirical studies prove the benefits of FDI brought about directly or by spill-over effects on the efficiency of production and improvements in competitiveness.

trade volumes and on investors' location decisions with respect to FDI, theories on trade and location have been looked at as a basis.

This theoretical section is structured as follows: section 2.1.1 explains in an overview the choice of theory, while section 2.1.2 contains various models of the NEG. In that part, section 2.1.2.1 presents the basic *Krugman (1991a)* model, section 2.1.2.2 modifications to the *Krugman* model, including the one by Livas-Elizondo & Krugman (1996), section 2.1.2.3 the model by *Ludema & Wooton* (1997), and section 2.1.2.4 the models by *Krugman & Venables (1996)* and by *Puga (1999)*.

2.1.1 Selection of a stream of theory

The subject of this section is to explain the choice of a stream of theory used as a theoretical framework for this research. To this end, the main theories taken into consideration have been summarized in form of a table. Table 1gives an overview of theories involving trade and making a statement on the location of industry, generally speaking, or more concretely on industry agglomeration or regional specialization in the context of trade and economic integration.

The three steams of theory which have been examined are: Neo-classical theory, the New Trade Theory, and the NEG.

The distinguishing features of the three schools of theory are as follows:

(i) *Neo-classical Theory*

The *neo-classical theory* is based on *Ricardo, Heckscher* and *Ohlin.* It is characterised by homogeneous products and constant returns to scale. Location is determined exogenously, given spatial distributions of natural endowments, technologies and factors. Economic activity is spread or concentrated over space according to the spread or concentration of these underlying features. For basic literature, please see the overview in **Table 1**.

The dominating location pattern is inter-industry specialization: sectors settle in locations with a matching comparative advantage. In this framework, with the assumption of zero trade costs, the spatial distribution of demand affects the pattern of trade, but not the location of production. At prohibitively high trade costs, perfect dispersion of industries producing non-traded goods follows the geographical distribution of demand.

Thus, the neo-classical theory is not judged a suitable framework for this research due to the lack of statements on the regional distribution of industries within a

Table 1: Overview of trade theories making statements on industry agglomeration or on specialization

	Neo-classical Theory	New Trade Theory	New Economic Geography
Basic Literature	Ricardo, Heckscher, Ohlin[a] (1933), Balassa (1964, 1985), Samuelson (1948, 1964)	Krugman (1980), Helpman & Krugman (1985), Grubel & Lloyd (1975), Brülhart & Torstensson (1998)	Krugman (1991a, 91b, 1992, 93, 94), Venables (1996), Krugman & Venables (1996), Puga (1999), Head & Mayer (2004), Fujita &Thisse (2002)
Market structure	Perfect competition on all markets	Monopolistic competition	Monopolistic competition on industrial markets
Other assumptions	Constant economies to scale, homogenous products, full rents to factor owners, growth through capital accumulation, inter-industry trade	New: intra- and inter-industry trade (globalisation, integration areas); aggregate scale effects due to local spillovers; size of home market (exogenous)	New: existence of transport costs (transport, transaction and trade costs, including NTBs); internal economies of scale; product differentiation; backward-forward linkages
Determinants of location	Natural resource endowments, or factor endowments and intensities; technological differences	Degree of plant-level increasing returns; substitutability of differentiated goods	The level of transport costs; Pecuniary externalities (labour markets, input-output linkages, migration-induced demand linkages); strength of centripetal and centrifugal forces; technological externalities (in some models)
Welfare effects of trade liberalisation	Net welfare gain; all countries gain; owners of scarce factors lose	Net welfare gains; large countries benefit more than small ones; possibly all factor owners gain	Net welfare gains; "u-curve"[b] of real wage relation of two regions during falling transport costs; periphery versus core can lose at intermediate or advanced stages of integration
Whether suitable for this research	**No**: lack of statements on the regional distribution of industries within a country; "Balassa-Samuelson effect" is of certain interest for CEEC-EU context	**No** (only in part, not ideal): lack of explicit statements on regional location of agglomeration and on the degree of specialization over time	**Yes**: Formalisation of mechanisms by which even *a priori* very similar regions can end up with very different production structures; agglomeration and specialization explicitly dealt with; with factor mobility regional industry structures emerge endogenously (static total industry)

Source: Own summary. Notes: a) For a discussion of *Ohlin* in the light of NEG, see *Krugman's* essay "Was it all in Ohlin?" *(Krugman 1999).*
b) For an explanation of the u-curve, see the text at the end of section 2.1.2.1.

country. The so-called "Balassa-Samuelson effect" is nevertheless interesting for explaining certain broad developments in the CEEC-EU context (see in chapter 3, section 3.2.1).

(ii) *New Trade Theory*:

The models of the New Trade Theory take as exogenous only market size, while the other elements are no longer taken as exogenous. Market size is determined primarily by the size of the labour force in a country, and labour is immobile internationally. For industrial products, these models introduce imperfect competition, differentiated products and increasing returns to scale. The typical outcome is inter-industry specialization of countries, with sectors clustering near large product markets, as well as intra-industry specialization across firms producing a different variety of good each. As long as some firms are left in the smaller market, intra-industry trade will prevail. As trade costs fall towards zero, all increasing returns activity will tend to concentrate near the core market, and intra-industry trade between the core and the periphery vanishes.

New Trade Theory is not fully suitable as a framework for this research, as it lacks explicit statements on regional location of agglomeration and on the degree of specialization over time.

As the existence of increasing returns to scale plays a role in *New Trade Theory* as well as in the models of the *NEG*, an overview on these scale economies shall be given here, which is based on the survey by *Pratten (1988)* conducted in context with the Single Market programme. The author categorised different types of economies of scale. *Pratten* defined economies of scale as "reductions in average unit costs attributable to increases in the scale of output". Based on estimations of the importance of scale economies in the EU by means of engineering estimates, he concluded that the apparently lower degree to which manufacturing firms in Europe seem to exploit economies of scale in comparison to their Japanese or US counterparts, when judging from their size, should be a cause for concern. The dimensions of economies and diseconomies of scale are summarized in **Table 2**.

(iii) *New Economic Geography*:

In the models of the *New Economic Geography (NEG)*, the location of industry becomes entirely endogenous. As production factors and firms are mobile, even market size is explained within the model. In a set-up with two or three regions over which labour and output of industry is uniformly distributed at the start, externalities, input-output linkages and other factors produce self-reinforcing agglomeration processes. The economy will tend towards new locational equilibria in the medium-term.

In NEG models there are many possible and locally stable equilibria, i.e. of the distributions of industry and workers over a given regional space which remain constant as such over a certain period. Which pattern is attained depends on the initial distribution of workers and industry, on various industry characteristics, and on the assumptions regarding the mobility of workers. The strength of centripetal and centrifugal forces - forces attracting workers and firms towards the centre, or in the latter case, inciting them to relocate in the periphery - will shape the form of the equilibrium attained.

Table 2: Overview of economies and diseconomies of scale

Economies of scale exist in

1) Production:

- the total output of particular products over time,
- the duration of production runs,
- the rate of production of particular products per unit of time (incl. the size of batches),
- the extent of standardization of components and products,
- the capacity of units of production lines or of individual plants,
- the overall size of plants at one site, and
- the extent of vertical integration;

2) Selling and distribution costs:

- sales to each customer,
- the geographic concentration of customers, and
- the size of consignments to customers;

3) Overall dimensions of scale:

- the size of firms,
- the scale of an industry, and
- the scale of a national economy.

Diseconomies of scale include

1) A fixed supply of a production factor, or **increasing cost of a factor** as demand rises:

- the labour supply in an area,
- the space available at one site for a factory,
- the supply of water which can be taken from a river for cooling a plant, and
- the size of a ship which can dock at a port;

2) The **efficiency in the use of factors of production may decline** with increases in scale due to:

- technical forces,
- management,

Source: Own summary based on *Pratten (1988)*.

The level of trade costs or transport costs over time - in the course of integration processes - plays a decisive role. NEG models make certain predictions about the location of industry and the degree of regional specialization during economic integration processes. While trade costs were falling between countries due to the measures implied by a customs union and technological progress in the transport industry, they are also falling between regions within a country, not only due to the latter, but also due to infrastructure improvements such as those implied for beneficiaries of the European regional policy and the respective pre-accession instruments[10].

During European economic integration in particular, trade costs between member states in the form of tariffs and quotas had been eliminated by 1968 when the customs union formed among the six founding member states had been completed und subsequently widened to the member states acceding to the EU in various EU enlargements. Since then, trade costs in the form of non-tariff barriers (NTBs), border controls and customs formalities, as well as transport costs played the dominant role. NTBs comprise these national rules and regulations regarding safety and health standards, packaging and labelling requirements, national certifications, norms and standards, to name just a view. Where later in this research the word of declining *"transport costs"* is used to describe the process of economic integration, this is meant to comprise all of these aspects, i.e. it is used synonymous to the notion of *"trade costs"*.

NTBs have played a prominent role as trade impediments during European integration between member states since 1968. In its jurisdiction, the European Court of Justice and the European Commission have tried to combat them based on rulings such as the famous "Cassis de Dijon" case.[11] Furthermore, in an effort to enhance competition and further trade liberalisation with respect to these NTBs, the European Single Act of 1986 has explicitly attacked NTBs and national product market regulations as well as the mutual recognition of professional and university diploma with the Single Market programme.

NEG is chosen here as the suitable stream of theory. With factor mobility, regional industry structures are emerging endogenously, given a static total of industry. NEG contains the formalisation of mechanisms by which even a priori very similar regions can end up with very different production structures.

---

10 In the case of Hungary and the other CEECs, this was called ISPA.

11 Official Journal of the European Communities, Series L 120/78 (Rewe/ Bundesmonopolverwaltung für Branntwein), Jurisdiction No. 1979. Subsquently, the European Commission sent the new interpretation of the articles 30-36 of the Treaty on the European Economic Community, which was based on this ruling, to all member states, and established a supervision by the Commission in this area.

Regional effects of economic integration can be deducted from the models, and the location of industry in space can be predicted over time. The processes of the formation of industry agglomerations and of the specialization of regions are explicitly dealt with in NEG.

2.1.2 NEG models

This section will now look at important models of NEG, and in particular at those models thought of potential relevance for explaining the actual development of industry agglomeration and regional specialization in Hungary in the context of European integration since 1992.

Economic integration processes are constructed in NEG models via transport costs falling over time. Transportation of goods is subject to "iceberg" transport costs as first modelled by Samuelson: rather than modelling a separate transportation sector, it is supposed that a fraction of a good shipped simply melts away or evaporates in transit (*Fujita et al. 1999*). For 1 unit from region 1 to reach its destination in region 2, $n = 1+\tau$ units must be shipped, where $n > 1$. τ is meant to include trade barriers (tariffs, quotas and NTBs) as well as ordinary transportation costs. This is then manifested in higher prices for industrial goods imported from another region (or country) as compared to the locally produced industrial goods.

The basic *Krugman (1991a)* model is described in its main elements in section 2.1.2.1, as are some variants of that model, such as those extending to more than two regions (section 2.1.2.2), and in particular the model by *Livas-Elizondo & Krugman (1996)* which models the effects of trade liberalisation on the internal economic geography of a country. The model by *Ludema & Wooton (1997)* - see section 2.1.2.3 - which allows for partial agglomeration and partial inter-regional migration of workers - is described in more detail than the *Krugman* model, as that model is of particular interest for the empirical research on industry agglomeration in Hungary under the Europe agreement. Finally, the model by *Puga (1999)* is described in section 2.1.2.4 as it makes explicit statements on agglomeration and specialization during integration processes, as is the model by *Krugman & Venables (1996)* for that same reason.

2.1.2.1 The basic Krugman model

The model by *Krugman (1991a)* which was the starting point of the new wave of models and theoretical approaches called "*New Economic Geography*" set out in an effort to explain the relatively persisting shape of manufacturing in the U.S.A..

Krugman[12] considered the formation of the US manufacturing belt during the industrial revolution and the continued relevance of that concentration of manufacturing industry, with the location of one third of the U.S. population today still in the original 13 states, as well as with the formation of a new industrial centre to the West in the Silicon Valley. He sees a long shadow cast by *history* coupled with what he calls "accident" over the location of production. The view by *McCarty (1940)* that "outside the manufacturing belt, cities exist to serve the farms; inside, farms exist to serve the cities"[13] must have enticed *Krugman* to the stylized facts which his NEG model is based on.

In his model, *Krugman (1991a and 1991b)* considers an economy with two sectors, manufacturing and agriculture. The agricultural sector produces a single homogeneous good under perfect competition; the total quantity is C_A, whilst the manufacturing sector is characterized by monopolistic competition. A large number of potential firms can each produce one differentiated product; products are symmetric in the sense that consumers do not prefer one product to another; consumers have, however, preference for variety. The behavioural assumptions are as follows: consumers maximize their utility functions U (C_A, C_M) given their budget constraints.[14] There is free entry for firms; and firms maximize profits.

Further, it is assumed that the only production factor in the economy is labour, more concretely two types of labour: workers who produce the manufactured goods, and farmers who produce the agricultural good. The agricultural sector works with constant returns to scale, while each variety of manufacturing goods is produced with increasing returns to scale.

Geography enters in *Krugman's* basic model in the way that the economy consists of two distinct regions, East and West. The transportation of manufactured goods between regions is costly; exogenously given transport costs in the iceberg form are incurred, i.e. he assumes that a certain fraction of the goods does not reach its destination.[15] Transport costs for agricultural goods are assumed to be non-existent. And the initial distribution of manufacturing firms is taken as given by some historic factors which are, however, difficult to grasp or explain logically.

---

12 *Paul Krugman* was granted the Nobel Prize in Economics for his work in 2008, including for the articles which started the stream of theory now referred to as "New Economic Geography".

13 See *Krugman (1991)*, p. 13.

14 Consumers' utility function is described more in detail in context of the *Ludema & Wooton* model in section 2.1.1.3.

15 *Iceberg* transport costs are explained more in detail in context of the Ludema & Wooton model in section 2.1.1.3.

With regards to the mobility of labour, *Krugman (1991a)* assumes that agricultural labour continues to be immobile, while manufacturing labour always moves to the region which offers the higher present real wage. More concretely, the population of manufacturing workers moves to the high wage location at a speed that is proportional to the present wage differential. In equilibrium, both regions must either offer the same manufacturing wage (symmetric situation), or the (complete) manufacturing population must be concentrated in the region offering the higher real wage. The latter is the case of (complete) industry agglomeration in one region. In Krugman's model, *agglomeration* becomes *irreversible.* For such a constellation to be robust, no firm must have an incentive to build a plant in the periphery. For an illustration, please see **Figure 1**.

Figure 1: Centripetal and centrifugal forces acting on the firm in the centre-periphery equilibrium with agglomeration according to the *Krugman* (1991a) model

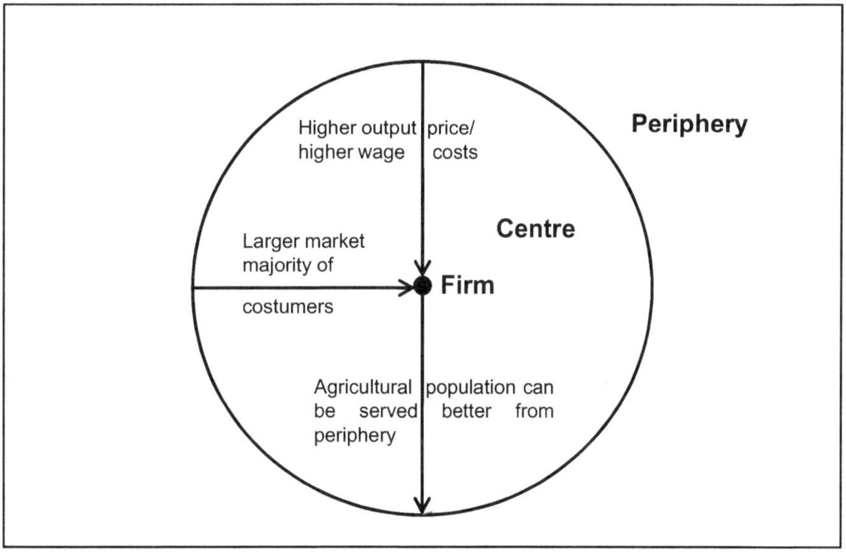

Source: Own graphical illustration based on *Krugman (1991a)*.

Figure 1 shows the centripetal and centrifugal forces working on the firm in the Krugman model for the equilibrium with agglomeration. The first *centripetal* force is that one acting on firms in the centre, i.e. in the agglomeration. A firm wanting to move to the periphery would need to induce manufacturing workers to move to the periphery. As they will have to import most consumption goods from the centre, the costs of living are higher in the periphery. As a result, the firm would need to pay higher wages in the periphery, which drives up the output price.

The second *centripetal* force is the fact that the majority of the firm's customers live in the centre. Serving them from the periphery would involve transportation costs making the product more expensive, thus another reason to stay in the centre.

The third is a *centrifugal* force, namely the agricultural population in the periphery could be served cheaper if the firm produces in the periphery. Basically, an agglomeration equilibrium in the *Krugman (1991a)* model - with complete agglomeration of manufacturing industry in one of the two regions - results when the last, centrifugal, effect is small relative to the first two, centripetal effects.

The *Ludema & Wooton* model, which is described in section 2.1.2.3, will add further assumptions to the location of firms and workers between centre and periphery during regional integration.

2.1.2.2 Modifications to the Krugman model

While the basic model by *Krugman (1991a and 1991b)* captures important aspects of regional patterns of location of industry and agriculture, it relies on a number of assumptions which have a high level of abstraction. More complex model variants change the results of this model only slightly, as the interactions between agglomerating forces and centrifugal forces remain valid, according to *Fujita et al. (1999)*. The relation between transportation costs, scale economies and agglomeration patterns, and the role of history for the formation of agglomeration in a region will not be altered in their basic statements by model modifications. If some of these assumptions are relaxed, however, the modified model scenario may lead to additional insights on the spatial pattern. This section shall give an overview of some of these further developments.

The assumptions in the basic *Krugman* model which were relaxed in subsequent literature are:

(1) There are no negative externalities between firms, such as due to pollution or congestion;

Schmutzler (1999) pointed to a paper by *Brakman et al. (1994)* which modified the *Krugman* model by introducing negative technological externalities in a multi-region version, adding the assumption that the fixed and marginal costs associated with production of an industrial good depend positively on the number of firms in the location, thus capturing a congestion effect. Those negative congestion externalities make production in the dominant manufacturing region excessively costly. This leads to an equilibrium where agglomeration is usually *not* complete, and where some firms will find it profitable to move to the less congested periphery.

(2) No market for housing and land; both regions offering identical wages;

Further, a modified version of a 3-region set-up is the more recent paper by *Brülhart et al. (2004)* produced in the perspective of further enlargement of the EU to the East. They use that model to stipulate that an Eastern enlargement of the EU by Croatia or other countries in the Balkans would benefit Greece economically. *Livas-Elizondo & Krugman (1996)* introduced urban land rents and commuting costs, which add a centrifugal force. This model is very interesting for this research, as it explicitly models the effect of trade liberalisation on the internal geography of a nation. It will be described more in detail under point (4). When farming and housing are space-consuming activities, agglomerations have to offer higher wages to compensate for commuting costs and land rents. This additional centrifugal effect will reduce both the likelihood of an agglomeration and its size.

(3) There are only two regions;

In the basic *Krugman* model, there are only two locations, East and West. As *Schmutzler (1999)* points out, however, the main insights generated in the two region framework about history, the relation between transportation costs, scale cconomics and agglomcration pattcrns arc robust to thc rclaxation of this assumption. With many potential locations, however, agglomeration and decentralization are not the only possible equilibria. In particular, *multiple agglomerations* in different regions are conceivable as equilibria.

Krugman himself modified his basic model *(in 1992, 1993, and 1994)* to introduce more regions, namely 12 equidistant regions. Given various initial distributions of manufacturing in these regions and an appropriate generalisation of the process of adjustment to regional wage differentials, a great number of equilibrium constellations exist. The typical equilibrium in such a set-up involves *agglomeration in more than one region*, mostly either in two locations or sometimes in three. This is an interesting outcome which could be useful for explaining the shape of industry agglomerations in Hungary and its 20 regions during the research period. To give a slight hint already at this point of what is analysed in more detail in chapters 3, 4, 5, Hungary has developed two agglom-eration centres during the later 1990s and early 2000s, namely in the centre of Hungary around Budapest, and in the West near the border with the EU-15.

(4) Trade liberalisation between countries is not modelled, in particular the effects on the internal geography of a country;

A very interesting variant of the *Krugman* model is the multi-region model by *Livas-Elizondo & Krugman (1996)* aimed at modelling the *effects of trade liberalization* on the internal geography of a nation. They take a three-region model, where two regions can be regarded as different regions within the boundaries of one country integrating with each other, while the third region may be a different country, or the rest of the world. The assumption of relatively low transportation costs between the first two regions within the same country can then be interpreted as the absence of trade barriers. Labour is perfectly mobile between domestic regions, but not between domestic regions and the rest of the world. Transportation of goods is subject to "iceberg" transport costs, however of different size, one for transports within the country, the other - higher one - for imports. This second one includes trade barriers (tariffs, quotas and NTBs) as well as ordinary transportation costs. The fraction of manufacturing goods provided by the rest of the world is exogenous in the model. Regions are modelled to capture the centrifugal forces including due to land rents and commuting costs in agglomerations.

In such a framework, one can investigate how trade barriers affect the manufacturing pattern (within countries). *Livas-Elizondo & Krugman (1996)* aim at explaining the emergence of many of the world's largest cities (metropolis) in Third World countries. As a possible explanation for this, they state that there is a negative relation between geographical concentration within a country and the degree of trade liberalization of this country. Namely, at very high international transportation costs, there will be no international trade. If an agglomeration exists within the two-region country, then it will be the only supplier of manufacturing goods for consumption in the country, and the local demand for the cheaper goods will be higher.

A significant reduction of trade barriers reduces the importance of these centripetal forces: as the economy becomes more dependent on international markets, local demand is less important. In the region with the agglomeration, land rents and commuting costs are high. Firms will be attracted to the other region because they can pay lower wages there. Numerical simulations of the authors showed that for very low international transportation costs, only the decentralized equilibrium will be sustainable, while for intermediate ranges, there are multiple stable equilibria: agglomerations in both regions and the decentralized equilibrium, where manufacturing is spread evenly across regions. *Schmutzler (1999)* points out that this outcome is not inconsistent with the basic *Krugman* model, as the reduction of transportation costs between two regions could lead to complete agglomeration in one region, whereas in this three region model, they are considering transportation costs between the two regions and the rest of the world; so as the set-up is different, the resulting effect can well be different.

In the latter case, namely very low international transportation costs, *Livas-Elizondo & Krugman (1996)* show that trade liberalisation tends to break up geographical concentration within an economy, i.e. enabling agglomerations in both regions, or the decentralized equilibrium. This implies that with falling trade costs, regional specialization will first rise, then fall again as geographical concentration of industry is breaking up.

This could be an interesting idea for the context of industry agglomeration in Hungary during the trade liberalisation period of the Europe agreement. As a caveat, it shall be mentioned here that it is difficult to have data for the falling level of international transport costs. While some figures for international transport costs *per se* are shown in section 2.2.3 of this chapter, the EU keeps data on the level of tariffs and quotas between the EU and Hungary after the start of the Europe agreement confidential.[16]

2.1.2.3 The model by Ludema & Wooton

The model by *Ludema & Wooton (1997)* differs from the basic model by *Krugman (1991a)*, who assumes complete mobility of manufacturing workers, in that it takes additionally account of *partial immobility* of workers. Due to this assumption, the model is able to explain regional structures in which industry is spread unequally in space, yet not fully concentrated in only one region. These somewhat more realistic scenarios regarding agglomeration may be of interest for the interpretation of the empirical results on agglomeration of the manufacturing industry in the 20 regions in Hungary (see chapters 4 and 5). A large part of NEG-models based on the basic model by *Krugman* does not allow for such a spread of industry, but only for complete agglomeration of industry in one region or an equal spread over both regions, which diminishes the political relevance of those models. The model by *Ludema & Wooton (1997)* has been discussed by various authors before, such as *Schmutzler (1999),* and by *Lammers & Stiller (2000)* in the context of suitable regional policy goals for the EU.

In the following, the *Ludema & Wooton* model shall be described more in detail with a view to an interpretation of the empirical results obtained for industry

16 Those were not even made available to Commission internal authors, such as John Sheehy from DG Economics and Financial Affairs writing in 1993 and 1994. I have found data on the level of tariffs and quotas between the EU and Hungary only for the years 1989, 1990 and 1991, in: *European Commission (1994).*

agglomeration and regional development in Hungary under the Europe agreement in this research. The model starts out with the following assumptions:

- There are two homogenous regions, North and South.
- There are two production sectors:
  - the agricultural sector production homogenous agricultural goods, at constant economies of scale, and
  - the industrial sector producing differentiated industrial products, with increasing economies of scale.
- All individuals have preferences for product diversity, according to their utility function:

(1) $$U = C_M^{\mu} * C_A^{1-\mu}$$

where C_A is the consumption of the agricultural goods, C_M the consumption of an aggregate of industrial goods, and μ the share of spending on industrial goods. With c_i as consumption of the product variant i, the aggregate of industrial goods C_M is defined as:

(2) $$C_M = \left[\sum_{i=1}^{k} c_i^{\frac{(\sigma-1)}{\sigma}}\right]^{\frac{\sigma}{(\sigma-1)}} \quad \text{with} \quad \sigma > 1$$

where k is the number of potentially producible industrial goods and σ is the elasticity of substitution between industrial goods, which are close but not perfect substitutes.

The next set of assumptions concerns the production factors:

- full employment of the production factors prevails at all times;
- agricultural workers are producing the agricultural goods, and industrial workers producing the industrial goods;
- agricultural workers cannot become industrial workers and not vice versa either;
- the number of industrial workers and agricultural workers is given exogenously;
- agricultural workers are completely immobile and equally distributed over both regions;
- industrial workers, however, are mobile to a differentiated extent due to regional preferences: It is assumed that workers prefer either of the regions as a personal preference, independently of the income level, as their place of work and living. *Ludema & Wooton* take account of the different individual extent of those regional preferences by introducing a "discount

factor" applied to the income of the other region, which enters into the decision making of the industrial workers.[17]

The assumptions made regarding transport costs are:

- the transport of agricultural goods between the two regions is assumed to be free of cost. Therefore, the price of the agricultural goods and the income of agricultural workers are equal in both regions.
- the transport of industrial goods between the two regions, however, is subject to transport costs in the "iceberg form" described by Samuelson: rather than modelling a separate transportation sector, it is supposed that a fraction of a good shipped simply melts away or evaporates in transit (*Fujita et al. 1999*). In order for consumers in the target region to receive 1 unit of industrial goods, $\tau > 1$ units have to be shipped. This is manifested in higher prices for the imported industrial goods as compared to the locally produced industrial goods.

Assumptions regarding industrial firms and the regional distribution of industrial goods:

- all industrial goods are produced with increasing returns to scale;
- in equilibrium, production costs equal sales revenue due to the assumption of free market entry (i.e. zero profits);
- each firm produces one product variant, each firm a different one. The number of product varieties is therefore equal to the number of firms;
- each product variant is either produced in region North or in region South;
- the number of firms in a region is proportional to the number of workers in a region:
- consumers always want to buy all product variants, such that they must be transported between the regions.

Thus in the *Ludema & Wooton* model, there are 3 exogenous influences on the equal distribution of industrial goods producers (industrial workers and firms):

1. the size of transport costs - τ,
2. the part of expenditure spent on industrial goods in the utility function - μ, and
3. the elasticity of substitution between industrial goods - σ.

17 The higher the regional attachment of the industrial worker, the higher the discount factor, and thus the lower is the interregional mobility of industrial workers *(Ludema & Wooton 1997)*.

Endogenous to the model is the determination of the distribution of workers and firms between the two regions North and South, as are the regional wages (nominal and real wages). Those in turn are determined by the decisions of firms and industrial workers, which depend on the strength of agglomerating and centrifugal forces:

- A centripetal force is the aim of firms to locate near the largest market, i.e. in the region with more workers (as agricultural workers are equally distributed). For industrial workers, it is advantageous to live also in that region, as their real income is higher there due to the larger choice of product variants available locally. These two forces both reinforce a process of geographic agglomeration.
- The centrifugal force is the following: in the region with less industrial workers, called the "periphery", the demand for industrial goods by the immobile agricultural workers and the (small) number of industrial workers is an interesting location for firms seeking less intensity in competition, as less firms are located in this region. Thus for firms, there is a trade-off between being close to the larger market in the agglomeration and benefiting of less intense competition in the periphery (also according to *Krugman 1991b).*

The regional real wages, resulting from a combination of regional price index and nominal wages, differ in a situation of unequal regional division of industrial workers and firms for 3 reasons:

- due to *the home-market effect*: nominal wages are *ceteris paribus* the higher, the larger the local market;
- due to the *price index effect*: the price index is lower in the region with the larger market, this is due to the transport costs for imported goods as the greater number of (cheaper) local product variants is available there;
- due to the *competition effect*: in the smaller market, the intensity of competition is weaker and the profit maximizing price under certain conditions higher; the firms in the region with less industry will then pay higher nominal wages due to the zero profit assumption for firms.

The home-market effect and the price index effect tend to work as centripetal forces reinforcing agglomeration, while the lower competition in the smaller market tends to work as a centrifugal force. Which effect of these three is dominant in the *Ludema & Wooton* model, depends on the level of transport costs (thus the price difference between imported and locally produced industrial goods) and on the strength of regional preferences of workers.

Ludema & Wooton (1997) distinguished the following transport costs:

- Relatively high τ: the real wage is higher in the region with fewer industrial firms;
- Medium τ: the real wage is higher or lower in the region with fewer industrial firms;
- Relatively low τ: the real wage is higher in the region with more industrial firms (in the agglomeration);
- Very low τ: the real wage is higher in the region with more industrial firms (in the agglomeration).

Long-term *equilibrium* is characterized by the non-existence of incentives to migrate. As industrial workers do have a regional preference, real wage differentials may exist even in equilibrium in the *Ludema & Wooton* model. The interregional difference in real wages, which will trigger the decision to migrate of the industrial worker, depends on the strength of the individual's regional preference.

Table 3: Possible equilibria depending on the level of mobility of industrial workers and on the level of transport costs

	Low mobility of industrial workers (= strong regional preference)	**High mobility of industrial workers** (= low regional preference)
Relatively high or medium transport costs	**Case 1** Symmetric equilibrium; no regional income differentials	**Case 4** Symmetric equilibrium; no regional income differentials
Relatively low transport costs	**Case 2** Symmetric equilibrium; no regional income differentials	**Case 5** Asymmetrical equilibrium; regional income differences prevail; "u-shaped" relationship between transport costs and the relation of real wages
Very low transport costs	**Case 3** Symmetric equilibrium; no regional income differentials	**Case 6** Symmetric equilibrium; no regional income differentials

Source: Summary based on *Ludema & Wooton (1997)* and *Lammers & Stiller (2000).*

Depending on the level of transport costs and the preference to migrate, different equilibria can form in the *Ludema & Wooton* model. A symmetric equilibrium is defined as an equal distribution of industry over both regions. In five cases, a symmetric equilibrium will come about in which no regional income differentials prevail. This is namely the case for relatively high or medium level transport costs, and for very low transport costs, both no matter the strength of regional preference of industrial workers; it is also the case for relatively low transport costs combined with low mobility of industrial workers.

Table 3 gives an overview of these 6 cases, where a small change in transport costs in the course of proceeding integration may have a decisive influence on the regional equilibrium and the distribution of economic activity (industrial firms and industrial workers). Falling transport costs from medium to relatively low levels will initially strengthen agglomerating forces, and when falling even further, will weaken them, reversing into a centrifugal force (due to external diseconomies[18]).

The interesting case of this model is **case 5**, the asymmetric equilibrium which will come about when relatively low transport costs are combined with a high mobility of industrial workers. In this asymmetric equilibrium, both regions have some industry, however to a different extent. In the larger region, higher real wages prevail; some workers, however, will never migrate to the larger region due to their regional preference for the other region. Thus, a complete agglomeration of industry in one region, leaving the other region void of industry - as in the *Krugman (1991a)* model where the agglomeration is even irreversible - will never come about in the *Ludema & Wooton* model.

Reading Table 3 column-wise from top to bottom and staying in the right column, thus with a high mobility of industrial workers, economic integration associated with falling transport costs will start by an equal spread of industry over both regions, then at relatively low transport costs, pass through an equilibrium with agglomeration of most industry in one of the regions **(case 5)**; at this stage, regional specialization will be highest. And finally, with still falling transport costs to very low levels, set about a re-location of firms and industrial workers from the centre back into the periphery. In this latter process, real wages in the periphery will rise and attract industrial workers and firms until a symmetric equilibrium with equal distribution of industry and no differences in real wages has come about. This will entail a falling degree of regional specialization.

This process just discussed in the proceeding paragraph is of interest in analysing the empirical findings for industrial agglomeration and regional development (per capita income) in Hungary during the period of this research. Namely, it will be interesting to view industry agglomeration, the inter-regional migration of

18 For concrete examples of external diseconomies, see my overview of *Pratten (1988)* on the subject of scale economies, in section 2.2.1.

workers, the development of industrial wages and the degree of regional specialization in the light of predictions on equilibria cases 4, 5 and 6 of the *Ludema & Wooton* model. This would take as a premise that the inter-regional mobility in Hungary was that of industrial workers and could be categorized as "relatively high" (for empirical data on the inter-regional mobility in Hungary, see chapter 3 section 3.5).

2.1.2.4 The models by Krugman & Venables and by Puga

For the sake of completeness of this overview of relevant NEG models, the article by *Venables (1996)* shall be mentioned first. *Venables* introduced backward-forward linkages in an international trade context into the set-up of an NEG model in order to deal with the effects of decreasing trade costs on economic geography. Notably, he considered two monopolistically competitive industries (instead of one as in the *Krugman* model) which are in an upstream-downstream relationship. He assumed that labour is immobile. Nevertheless, concentration of the sales of manufacturing industry in one of the two initially identical regions may result: upstream firms benefit from being in locations with many downstream firms since they can serve customers more cheaply; and downstream firms benefit from being in a location with many upstream firms because this decreases their input costs. The region with the concentration of manufacturing industry sales becomes specialised in that respect.

In that setting by *Venables*, the effects of integration on the likelihood of agglomeration are non-monotone. As trade costs decrease from very high to medium level, clustering forces come to dominate, and industrial agglomeration is likely to form, giving rise to regional wage differentials. At very low trade costs, however, such wage differentials are not sustainable: industry relocates in response to wage differences, so that a dispersed pattern of production re-emerges as the equilibrium.

In a more recent paper, *Overman et al. (2008)* build on the assumption of backward-forward linkages and combine the framework of the NEG models with some aspects of the urban systems literature. They aim to explain why the impact of a positive shock is in some sense shared between regions when they are in a complementary relationship with each other, but when they are in a competitive relationship instead, the positive shock to one region has a negative impact elsewhere. Their explanations depend on what they call three relationships: the earnings-employment relationship which captures the supply side of the economy (increasing or decreasing returns to expanding employment in a region); the "cost-of-living" relationship capturing the effects of the employment level on prices of goods and assets; and third the "migration" relationship linking population movements between regions. They produce a specific diagrammatic framework to explain the different potential outcomes for those regional set-ups based on the strength of forces in the three relationships, which is, however, not directly applicable in the context of this research.

Krugman & Venables (1996) ask the question whether increasing integration will make countries more or less similar in their industry structure, i.e. on the degree of specialization. This model is interesting, as this research will deal with the question of specialization of regions in Hungary in chapter 5. Their model is a variant of the *Venables (1996)* model, in that two monopolistically competitive industries are no longer in a clear upstream-downstream relationship, but instead, the product of each industry can be used either for consumption or as an input. Each industry uses inputs from the other sector as well from its own. Crucially, such intra-industry linkages are assumed to be more important than inter-industry linkages. Labour is assumed to be internationally immobile, but can move between different sectors as a response to the sector offering the higher present real wage.

The outcome with respect to agglomeration is the following: at high levels of transport costs, there is never agglomeration. There is a range of transport costs - medium level - for which agglomeration may, but need not occur. And at sufficiently low transport costs, only agglomerated equilibria are stable. Therefore, economic integration in this model first makes agglomeration possible, and then, if transport costs become low enough, makes it necessary. This outcome is subject to the condition that input-output links and the consequent cost and demand linkages are stronger within each of the industries than between them. If that condition is reversed, however, each location will always have some of each industry, as firms then derive more benefit from proximity to firms in the other industry than their own.

With respect to (country) specialization, *Krugman & Venables (1996)* predict that in the process of proceeding economic integration and declining transport costs, each country will develop agglomerated industrial districts. Specialization will take place in the way that each country will lose its presence in one of the industries. This will initially cause adjustment problems, as workers of that industry will suffer a loss of real wages. In the end result of this process, however, real incomes will rise, and in addition to the usual benefits from integration, cost savings will be realized from the benefits of agglomeration.

In a different model by *Puga (1999)*, the effects of regional integration and regional differences in production structures and income levels are analysed with respect to agglomeration and regional specialization. This model is of particular interest for this research, as it describes the process of industry concentration during integration when depicted graphically as an Ω-shaped relationship. To give a hint at this point, this is very close to the actual findings of manufacturing industry concentration in Hungary during European integration, as will be analysed in detail in chapter 4.

Figure 2: The „u-curve“ for industry shares in two regions' economic integration processes

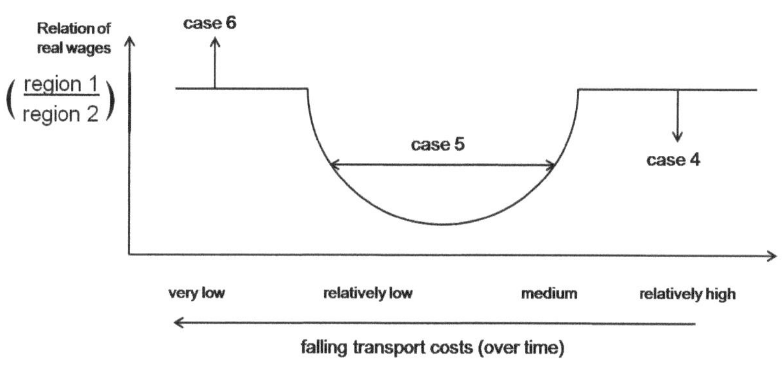

Source: Graphical illustration based on the *Ludema & Wooton (1997)* model and on *Lammers & Stiller (2000)*.

Before going into detail, the notion of the so-called *"u-curve"* of NEG models shall be explained here. The "u-curve"[19] has been formalised in a three-country setting with regional integration by *Puga & Venables (1997)*.[20] The graphic illustration of the relationship between the level of transport costs during

19 A different "u-curve" exists in models of business administration. That u-curve by *Michael Porter (1990)* describes the relationship between a firm's profitability and market share: high profitability for the specialised firms with small market shares and also for the generalists with large market shares, low profitability for those "stuck in the middle".

20 Their model allows for input-output linkages and for factor price changes in response to complete specialization in the production of the increasing-returns to scale industry. Countries are identical in endowments and size, but at a critical threshold of regional integration, agglomeration forces endogenously trigger a discrete formation of a core-periphery division among participating regions of the country (as production factors are internationally immobile). Further integration leads to a gradual re-dispersion of the increasing returns-to-scale activity within the integrating area.

integration and the relation of real wages in the two integrating regions takes the shape of a "u" and is therefore called the "u-curve". This is shown in **Figure 2**.

In addition, *Puga & Venables (1997)* showed that locational changes of industry along a "u-curve" can have considerable welfare implications, since welfare gains accrue disproportionally to the core or centre, while the periphery can suffer absolute declines in welfare in an intermediate interval of trade costs. The "u-curve" hypothesis has been used in the *Ludema & Wooton (1997)* model and by *Puga (1999)*. The latter considers it of empirical relevance based on the findings by *Hanson (1998)* in the context of US-Mexican integration in the NAFTA setting, and by *Brülhart & Torstensson (1998)* in the EU context (for details of that empirical work, see section 2.2.3).

Now turning towards the details of the model by *Puga (1999)*, he assumed that the world is populated by L workers, consists of two regions, region 1 and region 2,[21] which are endowed with K_1 and K_2 units of arable land. Each region can produce both agricultural and industrial output. Land is used only by the agricultural sector. The industrial sector produces differentiated products under increasing returns to scale. Labour is used by both sectors and is assumed to be perfectly mobile between sectors within each region, and immobile between regions. Agglomeration without labour migration across regions takes each region's labour endowment as fixed. The requirement that in equilibrium real wages must be equalised across regions is dropped.

For agglomeration without inter-regional migration, as a first stage with high trade costs, when firms concentrate in a region, they must draw workers solely from the agricultural sector in the same region, and this drives up local wages. Higher wage costs tend to discourage firms from clustering together. Yet the agglomeration of industry can still be an equilibrium if firms more than make up for higher wages by being close to other firms, thus avoiding trade costs on purchases of intermediates and sales to other firms. Secondly, at intermediate trade costs, agglomeration forms, which is a partial agglomeration in Puga's model. One region attracts more industry due to demand and cost linkages than the other. Regional specialization is rising to its highest level then.

At trade costs still falling to very low levels, starting from the equilibrium with (partial) agglomeration, industry will spread out across regions again. Concentration will decrease, and so will regional specialization. This is because then the cost saving of firms from being able to buy intermediates locally instead of having

21 In an appendix, *Puga (1999)* also derives some of the main results for any number of regions; however, that generalisation adds little to the two region case as long as trade costs change symmetrically.

to import them falls with trade costs, but the wage gap between regions remains. At some point, a firm finds it worthwhile to re-locate to the de-industrialised region, and combine imported intermediates with cheaper local labour. In this case, relocation to the de-industrialised region will continue until symmetry between regions is re-established. This is associated with the lowest regional specialization levels.

Depicted graphically, the above process results in what Puga calls *"an Ω-shaped relationship"* between the concentration of industry and falling trade costs. This is illustrated in Figure 3.

Figure 3: Industry shares in the two regions during a gradual process of integration without inter-regional migration: Ω-shaped relationship

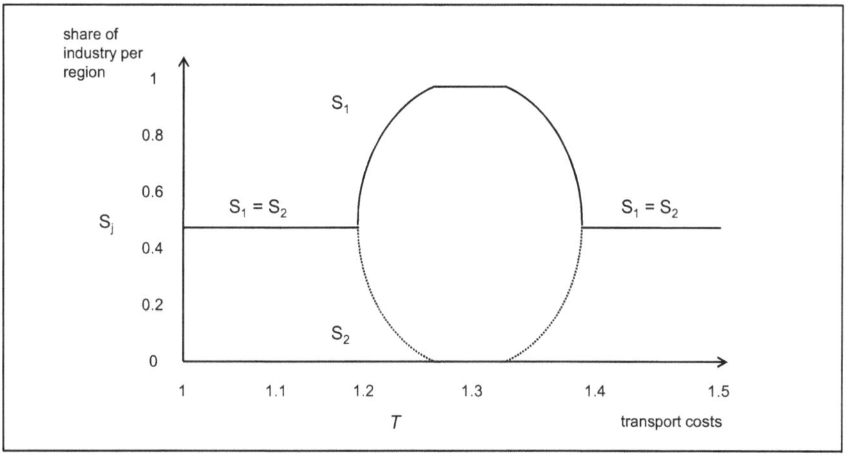

Source: Own graphical illustration, based on *Puga (1999)*.

The graph in **Figure 3** shows the Ω-shaped relationship for industry concentration or agglomeration to happen in one region and falling trade costs as described by the *Puga (1999)* model[22]. At high trade costs, firms want to be where final demand is, so they split between the regions (symmetric equilibrium). As trade costs fall below some critical level at which the symmetric equilibriumbecomes unstable, the share of industry in one of the two regions rises gradually until it absorbs all firms (complete agglomeration). Thus at intermediate levels of trade costs, firms cluster in one region to exploit cost and demand linkages. Without

22 *Puga (1999)* describes this *Ω-shaped relationship* for a gradual process of integration. He adds, however, that whether there is discontinuous or gradual change in trade costs, the relationship between regional integration and agglomeration is the same.

inter-regional labour mobility, however, agglomeration opens up wage differences. Further integration and even lower levels of trade costs lead to a gradual fall in this region's share of industry, until symmetry between regions is re-established. This is so as at low levels of trade costs, firms want to be where immobile factors are cheaper, so they spread across regions again.

With respect to regional specialization, *Puga (1999)* states that regional specialization is increasing to its highest point at medium levels of trade costs. This is the situation where agglomeration of industry has formed in only one of the two regions. With trade costs further falling to low levels, specialization of the regions is decreasing again.

With the actual empirical findings for agglomeration and concentration in Hungary in mind (see chapters 4 and 5), I would like to make the following summary statement regarding the appropriateness of two of these theoretical models: If the actual level of inter-regional migration[23] in Hungary can be judged "high", then the use of the *Ludema & Wooton* model - the right column of Table 3 - seems appropriate as the theoretical interpretation. If, however, the inter-regional migration levels in Hungary would be judged to be "low", then rather the use of the *Puga (1999)* model with the Ω-shaped development of industry concentration in the course of European integration seems appropriate (low inter-regional migration is then approached by the assumption of no migration).

This concludes the overview of a suitable theoretical framework for my research. The next section 2.2 will deal with previous empirical work in related areas and of potential interest for the subject of this research.

2.2 Previous empirical studies

In this second part of chapter 2, an overview shall be given with respect to previous empirical studies in fields of interest for the topic of this research, which is on industry agglomeration and regional development in Hungary under the Europe agreement.

The word "agglomeration" will be understood in this context in the narrow sense meaning industry agglomeration, not in the sense denoting mere urban areas of high population density. The focus shall further be on empirical work on Europe, although some studies on the US and Japan are also mentioned. Most studies on

23 The inter-regional migration in Hungary is analysed in detail in Chapter 3, sections 3.5.1, 3.5.2, and 3.5.3.

related topics existed for the EU-15 or selected member states, yet very rarely on the EU-25 or even EU-27[24] due to the short time span passed since the Eastern enlargement. Relevant studies on the CEECs where they include Hungary will also be reviewed. Previous empirical work on certain economic or regional aspects in Hungary with relevance for this research will also be described. Where studies touch on various topics, they are described in all relevant aspects under the heading which covers most of the contents. Empirical studies on regional development, including the most recent cohesion report and reviews by the European Commission, will be dealt with in chapter 7, as they are the basis for any economic policy discussion involving the regions.

The remainder of this overview of previous empirical studies is organised as follows: section 2.2.1 reviews empirical research on industry agglomeration and concentration. Section 2.2.2 looks at empirical work on industry specialization of countries or - where rarely available - of regions. Section 2.2.3 summarizes where previous empirical papers found results regarding the effects of trade on industry location and also quotes estimates on the magnitude of trade costs in the manufacturing sector. Section 2.2.4 will look at relevant studies of the influences of FDI and of local labour markets on industry location. The final section of this part - section 2.2.5 - will discuss studies on various CEECs and on Hungary regarding industrial developments during the transition period and in the years around the Eastern enlargement of the EU.

2.2.1 Industry agglomeration and concentration

Industry agglomeration and concentration are both expressions for the same phenomenon. They describe how concentrated or dispersed an industry is over the space looked at, for example a country or the EU. Industry agglomeration further describes areas of high density of industries, often coupled with a high share of industry employment in local employment. These areas are characterized by various spill-over effects, economies of scale play a role, and sometimes dis-economies are also starting to skew the balance of benefits and disadvantages of such agglomeration centres.

In a report on the location of European industry commissioned by European Commission, *Midelfart-Knarvik et al. (2000)* analysed production data for 13 EU countries and 36 industries from 1970 to 1997 using OECD data. They found that the industrial production structures of countries grew in their difference from each other over that period. Using Gini coefficients as concentration measure, they observed a slight decrease in average industry concentration from 1970 to 1985,

24 The Eastern enlargement of the EU has come to a halt in 2007 with the accession of Bulgaria and Romania as 26th and 27th member state on 1st of January 2007.

followed by a slight increase to the early 1990s and a reverse thereafter. Among industries initially concentrated and dispersing over time were beverages and tobacco, machinery & equipment. Dispersed industries concentrating over the period were textiles, wearing apparel, leather and fur products, furniture, and transport equipment.

As a complement to traditional concentration indices, the authors proposed an index of spatial separation giving a production-weighted sum of all bilateral distances between countries. They found this to first rise for manufacturing as a whole, then falling from 1991 onwards. Interestingly, the high-technology industries were the least separated throughout the entire period. This included drugs and medicines, office and computing, radio, television and communication, electrical apparatus, and professional instruments.

The authors also looked at country specialization using the Krugman specialization index for the period 1970 to 1997. They found that average specialization was lowest for the period 1980 to 1983 and then rose up to 1997. Grouping countries by their date of EU accession, they found that the 1973 and 1981 entrants exhibit an increase from the early 1980s, whilst the 1986 entrants show increasing Krugman specialization from around 1992 onwards.[25]

In an analysis of manufacturing industries with respect to the Single Market, *Brülhart (2001a)* looked at 32 manufacturing sectors of an OECD data base for 13 EU-15 countries over the period 1972 to 1996, using locational Gini indices based on employment data.[26] He found that concentration increased continuously over the period in employment terms, while remaining roughly unchanged in export terms. On average, increases in concentration were stronger in the period up to the launch of the Single Market programme than afterwards. The sectors most sensitive to the Single Market, however, showed an acceleration in concentration after 1986. He also found evidence that low-tech industries were the most strongly concentrated. This is the contrary of the results by *Midelfart-Knarvik et al. (2000)* based on their spatial separation index. Finally, *Brülhart* concluded that centre-periphery gradients across countries were losing importance for industrial location in the EU-15 over that period.

Brülhart & Traeger (2003) described the distribution of 7 broad economic sectors across 17 West European countries and regions over the period 1975 to 2000.

25 EU-accessions: 1973 UK, Ireland, Denmark; 1981 Greece; 1986 Spain, Portugal. The study from 2000 does not examine the effects on the 1995 entrants Austria, Sweden, and Finland.

26 *Brülhart (2001a)* also analysed country level specialization using the same data base, see summary in section 2.2.2.

Based on a Cambridge Econometric data base of employment at a country and Nuts-3 regional level, they applied entropy indices as measure of concentration and associated bootstrap tests for de-composing geographic concentration into within-country and between-country components. With regards to manufacturing industry, they found that manufacturing has become gradually more concentrated. Further, the accession of a country to the EU during the period was associated with an increasing tendency for manufacturing activity to locate in countries' peripheral regions.[27] It will be interesting to see which tendency prevailed in Hungary during the period analysed in this research which spans until 5 years after EU accession.

Ellison & Glaeser (1997) introduced a new kind of concentration index to measure industry concentration at the plant level, while controlling for the size of geographic areas for which data are available. Their index is intended to also capture the co-agglomeration of related industries, i.e. the additional agglomeration caused by localized industry-specific spill-overs and natural advantages. In their further research, *Ellison & Glaeser (1999)* applied their index to US 2-digit industry data in order to answer the question whether natural advantage can explain agglomeration.[28] Their empirical results explain about 20% of the observed geographic concentration by a small set of such advantages.

Giacinto & Pagnini (2008) analysed agglomeration within and between regions in Italy using Italian census data for 103 manufacturing and service industries for the year 1996. Their idea was to find out whether agglomeration forces stop at regional administrative boundaries or not. The authors chose a firm-level concentration index and use Monte Carlo simulation techniques. They concluded from their analysis that between-regions spill-overs existed in Italy. They found, however, that Ellison-Glaeser type indices, which require firm-level data, are not sufficient to measure the intensity of spatial clustering forces when such between regions-linkages exist.

In an analysis of structural developments in the manufacturing sector of ten CEECs, *Hildebrandt & Wörz (2004)* examined industrial concentration for the years 1993 to 2000. This was done with country-level data on output and

---

27 The within-country concentration of agriculture and construction were not affected by accession to the EU. Market services relocated increasingly towards central regions in context with EU accession.

28 In their formula defining the probability of a "crucial spill-over" between each pair of plants, *Ellison & Glaeser (1999)* interestingly also built in the Herfindahl index in the nominator and denominator, but applied to the plants' shares of industry employment. In my research (see Chapter 4, Section 4.5), the Herfindahl index is applied to an industry sector per region and the share in manufacturing employment. Plant level data were not available for Hungary, making it impossible for me to use an Ellison-Glaeser index.

employment for 13 industries using a database of their research institute, the wiiw. In terms of the one indicator chosen, the authors observed an increase in concentration of industrial activity both in output and employment terms, to higher levels and by a higher percentage than in the EU during the "pre-Single market period".

Using panel estimation techniques, the authors further found output concentration to be strongly influenced by differences in technology, differences in FDI levels, and the location of domestic demand, while concentration of the labour force was strongly related to productivity differentials only. In their model, the variables designed to capture explicitly NEG explanations - scale economies, trade costs, and input-output linkages - remained insignificant. The variable for export orientation to the EU was significant or highly significant for 3 of 6 industries with high increases in concentration between 1993 and 2000, while the variable for imports from the EU was relevant for only two industries. This hints towards inter-industry trade with inputs sourced from different countries than those where output is sold to. For those three industries - wood, pulp and paper, and electronics-, the authors conclude that export re-orientation of the CEECs towards the EU-15 had an impact on increasing concentration and industrial re-structuring in CEECs. For Hungary, however, the concentration trend in the electronics industry was, according to the authors, certainly policy driven to a great extent. *Hildebrandt & Wörz* called for further research of concentration and specialization patterns in CEECs and for the EU-25 as a whole, as the concentration levels in the EU-15 were falling during the period 1993 to 2000 due to the Single Market programme, while those in the 10 CEECs were rising during the pre-accession period. This research is one contribution in that field.

In an article on the Single market and geographic concentration in Europe, *Aiginger & Pfaffermayr (2004)* analysed the development of industry concentration for 99 Eurostat 3-digit industries for the years 1985, 1992 and 1998. Their analysis of three concentration measures is based on value added data for the country-level of 14 EU member states. They found a highly significant difference in concentration trends in the pre- and post-Single market period. While concentration was rising before 1986, a decline was observed after the start of the Single Market programme. Interestingly, the authors acknowledged that while this is an important political and economic result, countries are not the ideal unit for studying regional concentration of industries. This seems to confirm the need to perform such an analysis based on regional level data - as is realised for Hungary in this research.

Stirböck (2001) looked at possible agglomeration tendencies of capital in seven EU-15 countries.[29] She was interested in relative concentration of capital in industry from 1985 to 1994. She applied standardised Gini coefficients and Lorenz-Münzner coefficients to data on direct investment and gross fixed capital formation for 11 industries at the Nuts-2 regional level (instead of employment, production or value added data which are used by most other studies on agglomeration). Concentration was found to have increased in Belgium by 18%, Denmark (by 21%) and Ireland, while the UK had decreasing concentration (by 8%). On the national level, absolute concentration was calculated also for employment data; this resulted in a level of concentration lower than for capital. *Stirböck* concluded that employment is more uniformly allocated than capital, possibly due to the lower mobility of employment. This is an interesting statement, which allows the inference that the empirical results on industry concentration and regional specialization in Hungary of chapters 4 and 5 of this research - which are obtained based on employment data - can be judged as "more conservative" than they would have been with capital data.

Brülhart et al. (2008) looked at the influence of tax differentials on agglomeration. Drawing on a firm-level dataset for Switzerland and employing fixed-effects estimation techniques, they found that firm births on average react negatively to corporate tax burdens, but that the deterrent effect of taxes was weaker in sectors that were more spatially concentrated. Those findings – according to the authors - support the validity of recent theoretical results, suggesting that agglomeration economies can reduce the importance of tax differentials for firms' location choices and thereby lessen the intensity of corporate tax competition, even if technological and administrative barriers to capital mobility are low.

Finally, in a study on concentration in the services sector, *Stierle-von Schütz & Stierle (2004)* looked at concentration in the services sector for 14 EU member states and the 10 CEEC candidate countries from 1995 to 2000. They calculated three of the measures used by *Hallet (2000)*[30] for 11 NACE services sectors with Eurostat data of gross value added per region. They found that concentration of financial intermediation slightly increased for the 25 countries over the period, with a high in 1997, while that of public administration hardly changed at all. They also found that hotels and restaurants were more likely to be found in peripheral regions, while financial intermediation and real estate businesses tended to concentrate in the centre. Overall, they admit that the period analysed - 1995 to 2000 - was comparatively short for finding general results.

---

29 These seven countries were: B, DK, F, Irl, I, Lux, and the UK.

30 For a summary and details of *Hallet (2000),* please see in section 2.2.2.

2.2.2 Industrial specialization of countries or regions

Related to the topic of agglomeration of industries is the notion of specialization of countries or regions. Specialization looks at a geographic area and determines - by means of a selected measure - whether that area is specialised in certain industries, or whether it is well diversified, or whether the industrial structure is just equal to the average of a greater space. This section summarizes relevant findings on this topic in fields related to the subject of this research.

In a working paper on the competitiveness of European industry done for DG Enterprise of the European Commission *(European Commission 1999)*, a group of authors analysed industrial specialization of 14 EU countries with regard to exports and production at the country level. They found that export specialization - as measured by the Balassa index for revealed comparative advantage - declined for 3-digit NACE industries during 1988 to 1998, and that specialization in production[31] increased weakly from 1985 to 1998.

Amiti (1999) analysed country specialization for 65 manufacturing industries in 5 EU-15 countries for selected years from 1976 to 1989 using - despite certain disadvantages[32] - the Gini index. She found increasing specialization from 1980 to 1989 both in the richer "core" EU countries France and Germany as well as in the poorer "peripheral" EU countries Spain and Portugal.

In an analysis of specialization trends in 32 manufacturing industries across 13 EU-15 countries, *Brülhart (2001b)* analysed country-level specialization using OECD employment data with locational Gini indices for 1972 to 1996. He found an increase of specialization and of the dissimilarity of industrial structures in the sample countries. Specialization was found to be most pronounced in resource- and labour-intensive sectors. Increasing clustering was found in technology-intensive industries since the mid-1980s. Specialization of exports, whilst decreasing on average, was stronger than specialization of employment.

Hallet (2000) used Eurostat data of gross value added for 17 Nace manufacturing branches for 119 regions in order to examine regional specialization and concentration in the EU from 1980 to 1995. On average, he found a very moderate decline in regional specialization over the period.[33] 34 regions had become more

---

31 The authors measure specialization at the country level based on output for which they take value added at factor costs calculated with the Herfindahl index.

32 See discussion in Chapter 5, Section 5.1 for details.

33 Regional specialization by *Hallet (2000)* is measured as the coefficient of variation of sectoral GVA composition in a region in % of the coefficient of variation of sectoral composition of total GVA of EU-15.

specialised, while 85 regions had become less specialised. In 1995, Southern peripheral regions tended to be higher specialised due to their smaller economic base. Several core regions along the "blue banana" also tended to be highly specialised.

In looking at concentration in the EU-15, *Hallet (2000)* used four measures, a concentration measure based on a coefficient of variation, a clustering measure based on a gravity model summing up distance-weighted production of all pairs of regions, a centrality measure expressing whether production is located in the centre or the periphery of the EU, and an income measure capturing the GDP per capita of the regions. For the year 1995, he found that only transport equipment, paper and printing products were spatially highly concentrated. By means of the clustering measure for data of 1995, he found that for metal products, transport equipment, and chemical products the values indicated that production took place in regions close to each other. Tested for the centrality measure in 1995, most branches followed the centre-periphery pattern of GDP, except for banking and insurance services on the high end and textiles on the low side. The income measure showed in 1995 that the more traditional labour-intensive branches - food, beverages and tobacco, mineral products, and textiles and clothing - tended to be located in peripheral regions with lower income.

In a paper on industrial activity in accession countries, *Traistaru et al. (2002)* analyzed relative employment specialization in selected accession countries for the period 1990 to 1999. Using data collected in a private data base and relative concentration at Nuts-2 or Nuts-3 level, they stated that Hungary had no region with high specialization and 5 regions with low specialization. Overall, they suggested that industries in accession countries tend to locate where production factors are abundant, e.g. labour intensive industries in regions where labour is abundant, and research-oriented industries in regions with higher shares of researchers in employment. And larger regions tended to have larger shares of manufacturing activity than smaller regions.

Finally, in their empirical research on the existence and importance of economic geography effects, *Davis & Weinstein (1999)* investigated production structure for a sample of regions in Japan in the year 1985. They included factors such as absolute market size, backward-forward linkages and "real-world" geography in their model. They found that for 8 of 19 manufacturing sectors, among them transport equipment, electrical machinery, and chemicals, these factors did play a role in determining the structure of production.

2.2.3 The effects of trade and the magnitude of trade costs

As the Europe agreement with Hungary as a legal framework for economic integration consisted to an important extent of trade provisions, and this research is interested in seeing whether there was an influence of bilateral trade and integration on agglomerations and regional development in Hungary, this section will review previous research on trade in its effects on industry location. As trade costs play an important role in the models of NEG dealing with economic integration, studies with empirical estimates on the magnitude of trade costs will also be included.

A report commissioned by the *European Commission (1994*) analysed the economic interpenetration in foreign trade between the EU-12 and Eastern Europe. For the period 1988 to 1993, the authors found that Hungary's export strength to the EU tended to be in labour-intensive products requiring medium-skill level labour input. The progress of more R&D as well as skill-intensive industries in the early 1990s showed that the dominance of rather simple labour intensive exports may have been characterizing the pre-transition and early transition phase only. The authors also calculated an index measuring the change of trade pattern with the EU. With respect to exports and imports, that index was lowest for Hungary among the 5 CEECs which were part of that study during the five-year period 1988 to 1993. This means that Hungary's trade pattern with the EU countries had changed much less than that of the other CEECs during that re-orientation phase. This could be explained by the fact that in 1988, Hungary was the most market-oriented CEEC by some distance, having already started down the path of reform some time before.[34]

The authors of *European Commission (1994)* also looked at trade barriers at the NACE 3-digit industry facing Hungarian exports into the European Community level during 1988 to 1992. Almost all sectors were subject to a most-favoured nation rate of duty not equal to zero, of on average 7.1%, ranging from about 1% up to 18% in 1988. About a quarter of all import sectors was subject to quota regimes, encompassing in some cases almost 100% of the EU imports of the product from Hungary, equal to 26.8% on average over all sectors. Further, about one fifth of imports from Hungary were subject to other non-tariff barriers; this encompassed on average 14.2% of the EU imports from Hungary in 1988.[35] The 30 most protected EU sectors were also listed in that publication. These sectors were encompassing a cumulated export share of 51.4%, among them many food

34 More details on economic reforms in Hungary will be given in chapter 3, section 3.1, section 3.2.3, and section 3.8.

35 This figure is certainly at the low side, the actual figure must be much higher in my view, given the multiple potential obstacles on the NTB side.

and textiles products, steel tubes and radio and television equipment. Those findings were broadly confirmed in the "Trade Policy Review" of Hungary by the *World Trade Organization (1998)*.

In studies by *Landesmann & Stehrer (2002* and *2008)* on several CEECs, the authors analysed the evolution of competitiveness, industry and trade specialization. While one set of countries remained locked into a rather traditional pattern of trade and industry specialization (in low-skill, labour-intensive branches), others - among them Hungary - showed a much more dynamic pattern of integration into the European division of labour. Different countries in the region had succeeded to different degrees in the qualitative nature of their structural transformation and in developing their position in cross-European trade structures. This differentiation was likely to have, according to the authors, a bearing on how they would cope with the additional adjustments required by the accession process itself and on what footing they would be able to participate in the integrated structures of the enlarged European economy. This also has implications for the instruments required to deal with the problems of cohesion once they are members of the EU (on this latter aspect, see the policy conclusions of this research in chapter 7, section 7.2).

Brülhart & Torstensson (1998) analysed the role of intra-industry trade during European integration on the location of European industry. They used Eurostat data on the country level for 12 EU-15 countries. They were interested in the role of scale economies and the level of intra-industry trade during increasing European integration. The authors also included in their analysis the role of NTBs for the sample of 98 industries for 6 selected years between 1961 and 1990. They found that intra-industry trade (IIT) was highest for industries with low scale economies and low NTBs, lower for high scale economies and high NTBs, and lowest for high scale economies, low NTBs. Over the time span from 1961 to 1990, IIT had risen for all of these categories. From 1977 and 1990, the level of IIT remained more or less the same. Whether NTBs were high or low only mattered for industries with high scale economies in producing different levels of IIT, and not noticeably for industries with low scale economies.

In a paper on trade-induced adjustments in industry, *Azhar & Elliott (2003)* applied a so-called S-index[36] to industry level data in the United Kingdom (UK). Their aim was to identify increases in inter-industry trade, which mean that import and export changes were unmatched and thus induced a re-allocation of resources from industries contracting to those expanding. Those adjustments follow the rule: the greater are the factor requirement differences between

36 The S-index is a modified measure for adjustment costs, belonging to the family of marginal indices measuring intra-industry trade.

industries and the more geographically dispersed is the production, the more severe are the adjustment implications. If increases in trade are intra-industry in nature, however, the smooth adjustment hypothesis should hold, i.e. the adjustment costs will be less because resource transfers as a result of sectorally matched increases in imports and exports can be contained within individual industries or possibly firms.

Applying the S-index to 80 SIC 3-digit manufacturing industries' trade of the UK with the rest of the world from 1979 to 1991, *Azhar & Elliott* found differentiated results. The textiles industry experienced the most severe contraction due to trade induced adjustment pressures, as did the extraction and manufacture of minerals. The largest adjustment costs associated with expanding sectors were found in mechanical engineering, food processing, manufacture of motor vehicles, and the manufacture of office machinery. The application of that S-index is judged not to be appropriate for this research' analysis of industry agglomeration and regional development in Hungary, as it describes intra-industry trade at the country-level between countries only and makes no predictions for the regional level.

The phenomenon of outward processing trade (OPT) which played a role for most CEECs in the 1990s was analysed by *Tajoli (2003)*. Looking at EU-CEEC trade structures during the transition period, the author calculated shares of outward processing trade (OPT) in total trade for the years 1989 to 2000. For Hungary, the OPT had its main importance in the early years of that period; its influence declined rapidly from 1997 onwards. In 1989, the share of OPT in total trade was at 16.3%, in 1992 and 1993 both above 20%, 1994 still high at 17.5%; then the gradual decline started with 13% in the following two years, 10% in 1997, and down to a mere 4% by the year 2000. In comparison with other large CEECs, Hungary had the second highest share of OPT in total trade, second only after Romania. Poland, the Czech Republic and Slovakia experienced a similar relative decline over time as Hungary did. Only for the Baltic countries, OPT played an increasing role during the later 1990s, however declining from 1998 onwards as well. The reason behind the end of this phenomenon of OPT in Europe is that processes in the textiles industry were subject to globalisation. While labour costs in CEECs had been gradually increasing, international trade costs were falling and quality standards were improving slowly in China, it became economically more attractive for the textiles sector to shift production completely to countries in the Far East, such as India and the largest share to China.

The next set of empirical studies deals with the magnitude and importance of trade costs. With respect to borders and international trade, the *World Bank (2008a)* states that the number of international borders has increased from 100 to more than 600 since 1900. What matters for economic growth is the "thickness" of economic borders, which depends on the restrictions on the flow of goods, capital, people, and ideas. That report stated that borders between the member states of the EU were only about one-forth as thick as those in Western Africa. Further, while stating that prosperity demands mobile people[37], the role of falling transport costs is recognised explicitly. Falling transport costs encourage specialization and trade between economies at similar stages of development. Intra-industry trade is now half of global trade, up from about a quarter in the 1960s. Because this trade is especially sensitive to transport costs, East Asia, North America, and Western Europe account for much of it.

In an analysis of the magnitude and causes of market fragmentation in the EU-15, *Head & Mayer (2000)* applied a monopolistic competition model of trade to estimate border effects for 120 NACE 3-digit industries for the period 1975 to 1987, including also Eurostat Comext trade data and information on NTBs[38]. They found on average smaller border effects in Europe than those estimated for the Canada-US border. For the average industry in 1985, Europeans purchased 14 times more from domestic producers than from equally distant foreign ones. The tariff equivalent of the border was 36% for 1984-1986, as indicated by the most conservative estimation method. Where countries had a common language, however, the border impediment effect was only around 5%. *Brenton et al. (2001)* pointed out the importance of NTBs for accession countries, in context with their integration into the European Common market and their taking over the Acquis Communautaire in the field.

Head & Mayer (2000) further decomposed border effects into a part due to government actions impeding trade, i.e. NTBs, and into consumer preferences for domestically-made products, i.e. home bias. While the impact of borders has declined over time during the process of European integration, the reductions began at least a decade before the launch of the Single Market programme. Their results provide indirect evidence for a consumer bias as explanation of border effects.

Niebuhr & Schlitte (2008) based themselves on estimates by *Bröcker (1998)* and other authors and used travel time equivalents instead to measure the impediment effect of a border. This means that for them, travel time between the CEECs and EU-15 countries includes waiting times at border crossings, which are added as a

---

37 The USA, the world's largest economy, is also among the most mobile, with about 35 million people changing their places of residence every year *(World Bank 2008a)*. This corresponds to 12.0% of the population. The figure is not inter-state mobility, but counts any internal mobility.

38 See also a study of the European Commission by *Buigues et al. (1990)* on NTBs in the EU.

time penalty to raw travel times. Proceeding economic integration is then modelled by reducing the time penalties. The authors assumed that the accession of the CEECs to the EU corresponds to a decline of this time penalty from the start level of 60 minutes - when crossing from a CEEC to an EU-15 country - and 100 minutes in the case of crossing from one CEEC to another CEEC. By these estimates, they generated data for the purpose of evaluating improvements in market access due to Eastern enlargement of the EU, based on GVA and consumption data.

In a discussion paper on the economic geography of trade, *Overman et al. (2001)* looked at transport costs estimates in literature. They stated that there exists a wide dispersion of transport costs (here in the narrow sense, i.e. not including NTBs) across commodities and across countries. For the US in 1994, freight expenditure was only 3.8% of the value of imports according to customs data, while the equivalent numbers for Brazil and land-locked Paraguay were 7.3% and 13.3% respectively. These data incorporate the fact that most trade is with countries that are close, and in goods with low transport costs. Looking at transport costs unweighted by trade volumes gives much higher numbers.[39] The median cif/fob ratio, across all country pairs for which data was available, was 1.28 - implying 28% transport and insurance costs. Sharing a common border substantially reduces transport costs. Finally, overland distance is around 7 times more expensive than sea distance: being landlocked increases transport costs by approximately 50%.[40]

A further empirical study on trade costs is that by *Hummels (2001)* who estimated the cost of time in transit and also looked specifically at manufactured goods. He used data on some 25 million observations of shipments into the US, some by air and some by sea. The cost of an extra day's travel is around 0.3% of the value shipped. For manufacturing sectors, the number goes up to 0.5%. Remarkably, these costs are around 30 times larger than the interest charge on the value of goods. The share of US imports going by air freight rose from 0 to 30% between 1959 and 1998.

Estimates by *Hummels* also indicate that each additional day spent in transport reduces the probability that the US will source from that country by 1 - 1.5%. For manufactured goods, each day saved in shipping time is worth 0.8% ad-valorem. The advent of fast transport (air shipping, containerization and faster ocean vessels) is equivalent to reducing tariffs on manufactured goods from 32% to 9%

---

39 Looking across commodities, an unweighted average of freight rates is typically 2 to 3 times higher than the trade weighted average rate, according to *Overman et al. (2001)*.

40 Whilst being landlocked is the case for Hungary, the value should probably be lower than 50%, as Hungary uses the Danube waterway advantageously for shipment of goods.

between 1950 and 1998. That gives a reduction in average shipping times of 26 days over 50 years, equivalent to a shipping cost reduction worth 12 - 13% of the value of goods traded. This analysis shows that even without the effects of economic integration, trade costs have fallen over time due to technological progress and probably also due to the simplification of customs formalities.

2.2.4 Foreign Direct Investment (FDI) and local labour markets

Foreign direct investment (FDI) can also play a role in directing industry location and the formation of agglomerations. Local labour markets bear an influence on the location or relocation decision of firms or industries as well. The findings of empirical studies on Hungary relevant for this research shall be summarized in this section.

In a paper on the labour market in Hungary during the transition period 1993 to 2000, the Hungarian author *Fazekas (2003)* analysed the effects of foreign direct investment and other influences on the performance of local labour markets. He described that during the first phases of the transition to a market economy, more than 1.5 million jobs disappeared in Hungary; new jobs were created elsewhere, namely in developed urban agglomerations. He saw the observed polarisation of local labour markets in Hungary as mainly driven by employment changes as a consequence of agglomeration forces in transition economies. *Fazekas* further found that unit labour costs were lower in regions with low unemployment due to higher productivity prevailing there. He called the internal migration flows observed in the years 1996 and 2001 "quite modest", yet acknowledged that they did react to economic incentives to some extent. By means of regression analysis, the author found that the industrial past of the regions, the proximity to Western borders, and the education level of the local labour force had a positive impact on attracting foreign direct investment to a region. Finally, an increasing density of firms with FDI was found to have a significant positive effect on the productivity of domestic firms. According to the author, this could be one of the explanations of the increasing regional productivity gap between firms settled in good and bad regions.

Csengodi et al. (2003) did research on foreign takeovers and wages in Hungary during the period 1992 to 2001. Using private firm level data from Hungary, they found that wage levels for FDI-target firms tended to be about 9% higher than those of indigenous firms, and this already prior to the ownership change - which they saw as confirmation towards the "picking the winner" hypothesis.

Békés (2005) analysed Hungarian FDI data from a firm level data base for the period 1993 to 2002. His question was whether there existed agglomeration effects strong enough to explain the co-location of firms. He analysed two-digit sectors by means of a model including input-output linkages, wage level data for labour costs, but disregarding market structure and competition, one of the main weaknesses of that model. He found it difficult to disentangle various agglomeration forces within an industry. He concluded that most of the industries do have a strong tendency to settle where other similar firms have already settled, and that subsidies tended to attract large firms. He suggests that improving the relationships between suppliers and multinationals would probably foster more investment.

In a study on agglomeration economies and location choice for FDI, *Boudier-Bensebaa (2005)* developed a panel model of the location determinants of FDI. She estimated this based on FDI stocks for the 7 Nuts-2 regions in Hungary from 1990 to 2000. The author concluded that countries with higher labour availability, greater industrial demand and higher manufacturing density attract more FDI. Surprisingly, higher unit labour costs were found to attract FDI - as in the research by *Csengodi et al. (2003)*. The causation should rather be vice-versa in my view: That firms with FDI tend to pay a wage premium. In addition, inter-industrial agglomeration economies and infrastructure availability were found to be important in that article.

2.2.5 Studies on the CEECs and on Hungary

This section looks at studies comprising several CEECs or Hungary directly during the transition period and the pre-accession phase, where such studies looked at regional development during integration or at some aspects of industry location. Literature since the EU accession of Hungary is hardly available so far due to lack of recent data.

In an analysis of regional development in Poland, Hungary and the Czech Republic, *Dreyhaupt-von Speicher (2002)* investigated the influence of various factors on regional welfare and growth. That study comprised data for 77 regions in the 3 countries for the years 1996 and 1999. Factors included were the unemployment rate, the activity rate, employees in industry, gross wages in industry, gross production investment, and some welfare indicators like doctors and the availability of certain services. Using cluster analysis, four types of regions were identified with respect to their per-capita-GDP and welfare. For Hungary, the relative position of Central Hungary had advanced from the third to the most dynamic group between 1996 and 1999. No catching-up of the economically weaker regions in Hungary was noticeable from 1996 to 1999.

In a regression analysis of influences on regional development, *Dreyhaupt-von Speicher* found a positive correlation of housing conditions and the availability of passenger cars with regional per-capita-income. The state of the transformation process to a market economy, infrastructure endowments, human capital disposition, and geographical factors such as the distance to the national capital or to economic centres of the EU were also found relevant. As a policy strategy for EU regional policy, the author recommended to grant transition countries more national autonomy in the allocation of funds, such that they could foster growth regions and put more means into the improvement of national labour mobility and the housing infrastructure.

In a study on the emerging economic geography in EU accession countries, *Traistaru et al.* (editors, *2003)* gave an overview of the economic situation in 5 CEECs[41] in the 1990s in view of their expected EU accession. The research used a private data base comprising the years 1990 to 1999, for Slovenia only from 1994 onwards. The authors stated that border regions with the EU-15 countries benefited most in terms of growth of per-capita-income, employment rates and FDI, while regions bordering external countries proceeded with their decline. The study found declining wages in more peripheral regions as compared to the capital region for all countries. A catching-up had started only towards the end of the decade, but could not be directly related to trade integration with the EU according to the data base of these authors.

Regarding geographic concentration of manufacturing, the study found that this had not changed significantly in Estonia, Hungary, Slovenia and Romania during the 1990s. Higher regional specialization tended to be associated with inferior economic performance, while regions with lower specialization performed better than the national average. This finding was not confirmed, by the results drawn from the Hungary chapter, however, where the Western regions were found to be more specialised than the rest of the country and economically better off also.

In a publication called "Change of course", the *Hungarian Central Statistical Office (2005)* provided an overview of developments in the broad sectors of Hungary's economy based on the statistics of HCSO. This broad summary allowed to analyse the effects of the transition phase on the situation of the economy and of the population. To give an example, while GDP declined in real terms from 1989 to 1998 when it reached again its pre-transition level, real income per capita declined with a lag of about 3 years and only reached its 1989 level in the year 2001. Other figures from that publication will be referred to in chapter 3 to put my own findings into context.

---

41 The five CEECs were Bulgaria, Estonia, Hungary (that chapter was written by *Mafioli 2003)*, Romania, and Slovenia.

Rechnitzer (2000) analysed Hungary's regions during the transition period. Based on 11 indicators, he identified similarities between Nuts-2 regions and showed how the regional system in Hungary had changed from 1991, at the start of the transition, to 1995, which he called near the end of it. Whilst in the first year, he noticed seven clearly separated groups, by 1995, more homogenous blocks with similar growth courses had formed, linked by apparent routes of development.

In his contribution to a book by *Petrakos et al. (2000), Nemes-Nagy (2000)* looked at the new regional structure in Hungary after the transition to a market economy. For the year 1996, he stated that around 40% of Hungary's population of about 10 million was living in different types of settlements part of "winner" regions, 19.3% in so-called "starting-up" (the catching-up) regions, 17.8% in stagnating regions, and 22.8% in "loser" regions. Based on micro-regions, he further identified two areas of economic potential, one broadly around the capital, the other near the Western border with the EU.

In a chapter contained in the book edited by *Hajdú (1999)* on regional processes and spatial structures in Hungary in the 1990s, *Faragó (1999)* analysed regional economic development in a historical perspective.[42] He described territorial development axes in Hungary in the 1990s. He pointed out that the development watershed of the socialist era had been an axis reaching from the North-East of Hungary - with heavy industry and mining - to the South-West, crossing through Budapest.[43] In the later 1990s, the new development shed was between a prospering Western part and a declining Eastern part, notably a North-South axis starting at the Northern border of Central Hungary and passing through Budapest to the Southern border.[44] According to this line, 13 regions are in the Western part and 7 of the 20 Nuts-3 planning-statistical regions make up the Eastern part of Hungary. *Faragó* further identified winner and loser regions based on 1996-data. He called the former industrial centres as well as the Eastern-most region Szabolcs-Szatmár-Bereg "the main losers" in the 1990s, for those regions have not been capable of coping with the structural transformations.

---

42 According to *Fazekas (1999)*, in the Roman age the river Danube separated the civilization of the Roman Empire from the "barbaric territories". Under Turkish rule, the Great Plain lost a significant part of its population. Urbanisation, the development of the bourgeois middle class was a significantly faster process in the North (mainly in the areas that today belong to Slovakia) and in the Western part of the country, where conditions were also more favourable for industrialisation.

43 In terms of Nuts-2 regions, the socialist era development axis would reach from Northern Hungary to Southern Transdanubia, and passing through Central Hungary.

44 That axis starts in the North-Centre, passing along Pest and Budapest regions, Bács-Kiskun and in the South along Csongrád region's border.

Hantke (1995)[45] analysed trade relations of Hungary with the countries of the EU at the start of the Europe agreement and immediately prior to it. After an overview of the main trade provisions of the Europe agreement, the reorientation of Hungary's foreign trade flows which took place from 1988 to 1994 is looked into by means of trade statistics. Trade frictions which occurred in sensitive sectors in the first years of application of the Europe agreement were investigated from a political economy point of view, and actual developments were evaluated in the light of the predictions made by gravity models and discussed in view of EU trade and pre-accession policies. The results showed that Hungary's exports to the EU increased by over 40% from 1988 to the end of 1992, the first year of being in force of the Europe agreement, and the share of the EU countries in total exports had increased from 23% in 1988 to 50% by 1992. The commodity composition started to change by 1993, from primarily agricultural towards manufactured products due to the scope of the trade provisions of the Europe agreement. Furthermore, *Hantke (1995)* assessed Hungary as being not yet well prepared to cope with the full impact of EU membership on its economy and predicted that this would be the case between 2000 and 2005. This has been a realistic prediction with hindsight, given that the actual EU accession date of Hungary was 1st of May 2004.

De Sousa & Disdier (2002) looked at the importance of the legal framework as a trade barrier in 3 CEECs, using data for 17 ISIC sectors during the 4-year period 1995 to 1998. With respect to Hungary, they found that legal trade barriers did play a significant role in reducing international trade. The trade impediments worked both on the importers as well as on the exporters. In order of magnitude, border effects were found to be highest for food, beverages and tobacco, for wood, paper, printing and publishing, which they explained partly by national preferences. Weaker border effects were found in machinery and electrical equipment as well as textiles. These findings - though somewhat vague due to the shortness of the observation period - correspond broadly to those of other studies such as *Head & Mayer (2000).*[46]

Szanyi (2005) looked at the electrical and optical equipment sector in Hungary from 1993 to 2004. Many former state-owned firms in that sector went bankrupt during 1993 to 1995. Up to the year 2000, FDI flows were characterized almost exclusively by inward investment flows. The largest foreign investors in the industry were companies like Siemens, IBM, Ericson and Nokia. After 1998 to 2000, re-locations started to play a role, such as re-location cases from Hungary to China or to Ukraine. Most relocations from Hungary were labour intensive activities in light industries or screwdriver-type activities in electronics. Still, far

---

45 *Hantke* is the maiden name of *Cordula Wandel.*

46 See summary on the magnitude of trade costs in section 2.2.3, in the latter part.

more expansions and new establishments were carried out than relocations, measured both by the number of cases and by the potential impact on employment. Not only were existing activities expanded, but in many cases new activities were picked up, or other types of corporate functions including R&D were moved to Hungary.

Finally, in its first evaluation of the economic effects of Eastern enlargement, the *European Commission (2006a)* compared expectations towards the enlargement with first data after its realisation. That paper gave a policy-sided view on the economic geography of Europe which emerged since the EU accession of Hungary and 9 other countries. Chapter 7 will discuss more in detail potential policy relevant inferences from the results of the current research. The enlargement on 1 May 2004 has increased the GDP by 5% of EU-25 GDP, or 9% in terms of purchasing power, yet population increased by 20%. The economic fields covered by that evaluation included macroeconomic growth, the labour and financial markets, trade integration, FDI, migration, and agriculture.[47]

That analysis of economic effects of Eastern enlargement *(European Commission 2006a)* further stated that the CEECs were net beneficiaries of the EU budget. Migratory flows from the new member states (CEECs) into the EU-15 countries remained small in general, even towards those member states which have allowed unrestricted movement of workers. Previous fears of re-location were not justified, according to the data on which the authors based their evaluation. Whilst agricultural markets in the EU-25 were quite heterogeneous, increased trade integration, an inflow of FDI and direct income payments by the EU had contributed to a modernisation of agriculture by 2006. Ample room still remains for further rationalisation and increases in productivity in the agricultural sector of the new member states. The study concluded that the economic changes induced by the Eastern enlargement have been absorbed quite smoothly overall, and that there was no evidence of disruptive impacts on the product or labour markets. While they saw optimism in order, they warned not to underestimate the remaining challenges such as the ageing population and related budgetary strains, the wide gap in living standards and per-capita income, and the steps to take towards a growth-oriented knowledge based society.

What can be concluded from this overview of previous empirical research in section 2.2? The few existing studies on industry agglomeration or regional specialization in Eastern Europe have three main shortcomings: (i) That the time period was too short, mostly from 1995 until 2000, or 1992 until 1999. The

---

47 That paper was more policy-driven than empirically motivated, however, as a view to the group of authors shows: the "Bureau for European Policy Advisers" and the "Directorate General Economic and Financial Affairs", both services of the European Commission.

present research will more than double that time span by the data base used here, namely from 1992 until 2008, spanning even the first five years since the EU accession of Hungary. (ii) Where the degree of concentration of industries was analysed regarding Eastern Europe, this has been done so at the country level, or with insufficient details about the regional level. This is the second speciality of this work in this respect, that it will analyse manufacturing agglomeration in Hungary based on data of the regional level. (iii) Finally, the subject of regional specialization in CEECs has hardly been dealt with in literature. This will be done in chapter 5 for the 20 regions of Hungary, an internationally open country, in the context of increasing European integration.

This concludes section 2.2 of this chapter which reviewed previous empirical research relevant for the topic dealt with in this research.

2.3 The Europe agreement with Hungary

This section deals with the institution of the Europe agreement[48] which provided the legal framework governing the economic integration of Hungary with the EU during the pre-accession period. The aim is to set out the parameters which could have been relevant for shaping the integration process and which will be taken up in the regression models in chapter 6. As the Europe agreement was in force approximately for 12 years of the time span for which data were available, namely from March 1992[49] [50] up to the end of April 2004, this context for industry agglomeration and specialization of regions in Hungary cannot be ignored.

Apart from the Europe agreement, the importance of the so-called Copenhagen conditions of 1993 being fulfilled by Hungary as a prerequisite for EU accession shall be mentioned. The European Council formulated them as being a functioning market economy, a state governed by the rule of law, and a pluralistic democracy, as well as having transposed most of the Acquis Communautaire[51] into national law. *Eger (2003)* pointed out the role which such conditionality can play for the ability of the government of an accession country to impose a "hard

48 *Official Journal of the European Communities (1994)*: Europe agreement Establishing an Association Between the European Communities and their Member States, on the one part, and the Republic of Hungary, of the other part, No. L/25, 29 January 1994, Brussels.

49 This was the date of entering into force of the Interim Trade Agreement which enabled the trade provisions to be applied in advance of the double ratification in all EU institutions and all EU member states and Hungary, which took 2 years longer.

50 *Official Journal of the European Communities (1992)*: Interim Europe agreement between the EU and Hungary, OJ No. L 116/92, No. L 195/93, and No. 200/93, Corrigendum to the Interim Europe agreement, OJ No. L 13/93 of 21 January 1993.

51 This refers to the legislation passed by and in force in the current EU.

budget constraint" on the enterprise sector. The results of an empirical test of the relation between declining employment and output for 21 transformation countries - among them 10 accession countries including Hungary - have verified the proposition that the perspective of full EU membership can bring about this more efficient outcome.

This section now deals with the main contents of the Europe agreement, more concretely with its economic and trade provisions of the institutional arrangement in force in parallel to Hungary's request and negotiations of full membership, the request for which had been deposited in 1994. When in 1990 and 1991, the European Commission negotiated a new type of association agreements with Hungary, Poland and Czechoslovakia in parallel, they were both a response to fundamental changes in the political situations as well as to serious economic problems in the wake of the fall of the Berlin wall, the break-down of trade relations within the Council for Mutual Economic Assistance (CMEA) and the strive to make a transition to a market economy and a pluralist democracy governed by the rule of law. The preamble reflected this large political step, stating that the contracting parties intend to *"establish close and lasting relations of a new quality"*.

The Europe agreement contained three broad types of provisions:

(i) Provisions regarding the free movement of goods, thus trade provisions;

(ii) Provisions setting up a level playing field with the EU, including such on competition policy, state aid rules, movement of workers, establishment of firms, and supply of services;[52] and

(iii) Political provisions, providing for an institutionalised political dialogue on economic matters, financial cooperation, and cultural cooperation.

The trade provisions shall be described here. For the remainder of this research, it can be assumed as given that the free transfer of capital in convertible currency - an important condition for FDI - and other preconditions of a free market economy such as private property, legal forms of enterprises, a taxation regime similar to those of the EU countries, a modern banking system, and a functioning court system governed by the rule of law were existing in Hungary during the period of this research.

52 Such rules are included in the European Treaties to govern economic relations in the European Single Market when the jurisdictions of several member states are concerned; they were included in the Europe agreement in an appropriate form to guarantee a level playing field, and probably in preparation for a future full membership of Hungary in the EU.

The creation of a *free-trade area* between the EU and Hungary within the time span of approximately 10 years[53] was the principal objective of the Europe agreement. Trade liberalisation was done by the EU first, which eliminated tariffs and quantitative restrictions on industrial products on the date of entry into force of the agreement, while Hungary opened up its markets more gradually. The trade-weighted average tariff (MFN) was to fall from 7.5% in 1992 to 1.9% in 1994, 1.2% in 1995 and 0.0% in 1997 onwards, according to the *European Commission (1994)*.

This trade liberalisation under the Europe agreement encompassed mainly trade in *manufactured goods*. According to the European *Commission (1994)*, 49.5% of Hungary's total exports entered into the EU duty-free in 1992, and some 75% of industrial exports from Hungary would enter the EU free of tariffs and quantitative restrictions by the end of 1994. A later publication of the EU *Commission (2006)* stated that this free-trade zone covered 85% of bilateral trade. As a matter of fact, mainly the agricultural goods and processed products thereof remained outside the scope of the Europe agreement, or - as in the case of certain industrial goods considered sensitive by EU member states - were allowed free trade much later than the general provisions foresaw.

What can be taken as given, however, is that the Europe agreement did liberalise most trade in manufactured goods. As the analysis of industry agglomeration and specialization undertaken by this research is based on data for manufacturing industries in Hungary, the Europe agreement and post-accession process can be considered as relevant frameworks under which the European integration of Hungary unfolded its economic effects.

2.4 The hypotheses

The theoretical models of the NEG - which have been chosen as the theoretical framework for this research - make general predictions about the location of industry and regional specialization in the course of economic integration. Proceeding economic integration is modelled through falling trade costs. While these are falling between countries due to the measures implied by a customs union and technological progress in the transport industry, they are also falling between regions within a country, not only due to the latter, but also due to infrastructure improvements such as those implied for beneficiaries of the European regional policy and the respective pre-accession instruments[54]. At

53 This period was later accelerated for most sectors, except for certain ones considered sensitive.

54 In the case of Hungary and the other CEECs, this was called ISPA.

initially relatively high trade costs, dispersion of industry will prevail (symmetry in two region models), firms will locate close to consumers; at medium-level trade costs, centripetal forces will reinforce agglomeration, centre-periphery structures will prevail, regional specialization will be highest; at relatively low trade costs, firms and workers will disperse again, a lower degree of regional specialization will be entailed.

The models by *Ludema & Wooton (1997)* - assuming inter-regional but not full migration of workers - and the model by *Puga (1999)* assuming no inter-regional migration could be used as theoretical framework. Which of these seems appropriate depends on the actual levels of inter-regional migration in Hungary (high or low).[55] The models by *Krugman & Venables (1996)* and by *Livas-Elizondo & Krugman (1996)* are also suitable for the international context involving regional implications in a country with more than one region.

Table 4: Formulation of the hypotheses

- Integration with the EU under the Europe agreement reinforced industry agglomeration in the manufacturing sector.
- This integration also led to an increase in regional specialization of the 20 regions at an inter-mediate stage.
- With proceeding integration, dispersion tendencies set in and regional specialization decreased.
- This turning point was reached prior to full EU-membership of Hungary.
- Integration with the EU determined to a certain extent where in space the concentration of manufacturing industries took place.

Source: Own formulation.

Questions which are posed by this empirical research are: Which influences did European integration have on regional development in Hungary? The location of industry and changes in the degree of industry agglomerations, were they shaped by the influence of European integration, or by domestic economic policies, or by other factors such as local labour markets, other locational advantages, or the role of history? Which development did agglomeration of manufacturing industries undergo during increasing integration with the EU? Did integration and trade reinforce industry agglomeration in the manufacturing sector? Did agglomeration

55 The inter-regional migration in Hungary is analysed in detail in chapter 3, sections 3.5.1, 3.5.2, and 3.5.3.

decrease? Were there perhaps phases of both? How did this affect the specialization of regions in Hungary? And where in space did the concentration of manufacturing industries take place? Was there perhaps a direct influence of the trade provisions of the Europe agreement on manufacturing concentration or regional specialization in Hungary? In light of these questions, the hypotheses shown in **Table 4** are formulated.

Most previous empirical research on industry agglomeration in CEECs only remained at the country level, such as *Hildebrandt & Wörz (2004)*, or - where it went to the regional level - such as that by *Traistaru et al. (2003)* - used data series which were too short or even contradictory. Hence, there is a need for in depth empirical research on the industry and regional level for individual countries in Central and Eastern Europe such as Hungary. The relatively long time period from 1992 to 2008 will be one of the advantages of the research results of this research.

A unique contribution of this research in measuring industry agglomeration in Hungary is that it applies six different concentration indices to the same set of data, thus allowing for a comparison of them. All of these indices were applied to Hungarian employment data by manufacturing subsector by region. The relatively long time series is the longest available and reliable at the time of writing using the Hungarian regional sectoral employment data series of the HCSO, namely 1992 to 2008. Regional specialization is measured also by means of calculating appropriate index figures.

The hypothesis of this research will be approached as follows by the remaining chapters of this research: Chapter 3 will evaluate the hypothesis by means of empirical descriptive analysis of main economic and regional indicators for Hungary. Chapter 4 will analyse industry concentration in Hungary by means of empirical calculations of 6 different concentration indices. Chapter 5 will present empirical results on the development of regional specialization in Hungary over the period. Chapter 6 will proceed with regression analysis on industry concentration and regional specialization. Finally, chapter 7 concludes this research with a view to policy recommendations regarding European regional policy and a perspective on future developments. Before proceeding with the remainder of this research, an overview of the data used as a basis shall be given in section 2.5.

2.5 Data used for this research

For the purpose of analysing industry agglomeration and regional development in Hungary in the context of European integration, I have chosen to use *Hungarian data* provided by the Hungarian Central Statistical Office (HCSO). This was decided in order to obtain data on the longest possible time period for my research, and also the most recent ones at the end.[56] This time period was 1992 to 2008 for the most important data series.[57] According to the opinion of Hungarian researchers which I interviewed on this subject, data from 1992 onwards are largely trustworthy by international standards. Therefore, that year has been chosen as a starting point. The main series used were the "Regional Statistical Yearbook of Hungary", the "Statistical Yearbook of Hungary", and the "Yearbook of External Trade".[58] The data for the years 1992 until 1998 had to be typed into the computer manually from the printed format, as electronic versions started to be available only from 1999 onwards. For 2006 until 2008, the data were available from a special database of the HCSO. As the methodology had changed slightly, the data for the latter three years were adapted for consistency.[59]

As this research deals with Hungary at the regional and industry level on the one hand and the EU on the other hand, there was no need to use data from Eurostat which would make several countries internationally comparable. More importantly, data on foreign trade provided by the HCSO also include exports from the so-called „customs-free zones" while Eurostat data do not. „Customs-free zones" were an important economic factor for Hungarian industry during the research period, as they contributed a share of 43% of Hungarian exports in 1999.[60]

With regards to the industry level, the manufacturing sectors have been chosen as the level of detail, as the Europe agreement, the institutional framework of pre-accession integration and trade, covered mostly manufacturing products. For the entire period 1992 to 2008, the HCSO provides data for 8 sectors (more sectors would have been available only from 1999 on). These are shown in **Table 5**.

---

56 Harmonisation and verification of national data by Eurostat typically takes around two years at least before Eurostat publishes them.

57 The data for 2008 for that series have been released on the HCSO website on 20th of February 2009.

58 Where different sources are used in this research, such as Eurostat, the European Commission, or some by the Hungarian government, this is explicitly mentioned.

59 The difference was that from the electronic platform, only data for the manufacturing subsectors per region for enterprises with more than 4 employees and also institutions of central and local government, social security and non-profit institutions were included. This makes a difference mainly for the capital of Budapest. Hungary is a rather centralised country by its administrative tradition. To abstract from the latter three categories for the data of Budapest, the difference of the employment for the overlapping years of the two data series (2003, 2004, 2005) was taken as a %, and then this divergence was averaged and used as a corrector on the raw figures for Budapest for the years 2006 to 2008.

60 For more details on these customs-free zones, see the summary of the article by *Vadász (2000)* in section 3.2.4.

Table 5: The 8 manufacturing sectors used in this research

food, beverages, and tobacco DA* 15,16**	**textiles**, wearing apparel, leather and fur products DB, DC 17-19	wood, **paper** and printing, publishing DD, DE 20-22	**chemicals** and chemical products DF, DG, DH 23-25
other non-metallic **mineral** products DI 26	basic **metals** and fabricated metal products DJ 27-28	**machinery and equipment** (n.e.c., electrical and optical equipment; transport equipment) DK-DM, 29-35	**other** manufacturing industries, **recycling** DN 36-37

Notes: *DA-DN: Hungarian TEÁOR-classification
** 15-37: Corresponding NACE 2-digit classification.
Sources of data: HCSO: Statistical Yearbook of Hungary, Regional Statistical Yearbook of Hungary, Statistical Yearbook of External Trade, Statistical Yearbook of Industry and Construction, subsequent years from 1992 to 2005 for each; database economy on HCSO website for 2006 to 2008, Budapest.

Where data on external trade are used, these were published according to the SITC classification. These also had to be entered manually into the computer for the years 1992 to 1998. In order to make these categories compatible, which by far exceeded the 8 sector classification in **Table 5**, and also suitable for common empirical and regression analysis, I have converted the SITC data into the 8 manufacturing industries used in my research according to the official product category descriptions of both classifications.

As one of the main new elements of this research is that it looks at the regional level when analysing industry concentration and specialization, the regional level of detail shall be explained here. It was chosen to use the 20 Nuts-3 regions in Hungary as the relevant level. Hungary consists only of 7 Nuts-2 regions; using those would have made the data base too small. Further, the Nuts-2 regions in Hungary are merely "planning-statistical regions" with no political structure behind, whereas the Nuts-3 regions correspond broadly to municipal district administrations. These 20 regions will be presented in their geography and main economic characteristics in chapter 3, section 3.3.

Furthermore, for the purpose of deepening the analysis with respect to border regions and the importance of closeness to EU markets, the 20 Nuts-3 regions were categorized into four groups of regions according to the actual length of their dominating border:[61] 7 internal regions (INT), and among the 13 border regions 2 regions bordering the EU-15 (BEU), 6 regions bordering CEECs (BCE), and 5 regions bordering external countries (BEX).

For the purpose of analysing industry concentration and regional specialization, I have used data on manufacturing employment per region in the 8 sectors. To give an illustration, this produced a data sheet for each region, say Budapest, with the 8 industries as rows and the 17 years 1992 to 2008 in the columns, with 20 such data sheets for the 20 Nuts-2 regions as a data base for the empirical calculations. My idea to use output/production data in addition to these employment data proved to be unrealisable, as production data are not published at the regional level for the 8 subsectors by the HCSO.[62]

At this point, it shall be pointed out that one of the specialities of my research is that it is based on regional sectoral manufacturing employment data as a basis for calculating industry concentration in Hungary, and not at sectoral country-wide data for a group of countries such as EU-15 or a set of CEECs, as most previous empirical studies in the field.

Data on the actual level of tariffs and quotas which prevailed during the period, for which the Europe agreement between Hungary and the EU was in force, are not publicly available. Even authors working within the European Commission, but in DGs other than the Customs DG or DG Trade, could not get access to such data (not even aggregates from the detailed customs code level). The data which I have found have been summarized in section 2.3. Those, however, are not suitable in any way for a chronological analysis over the entire period covered by this research.

I would have liked to also include into my analysis data on NTBs, as in my view this multitude of potential obstacles to trade in the norms, standards, packaging and safety rules areas are at least as important in the economic reality of internationally trading firms as tariffs and quotas. In a series of reports on the effects of the Single market done for the *European Commission (1998)*, the importance of NTBs and other regulations on different manufacturing sectors such as the pharmaceuticals industry, the motor vehicles sector, food, drink and tobacco, and telecommunications equipment are examined in a descriptive way and data based on firm level inquiries for selected years. Whilst some researchers

61 The km length of the 20 regional borders with neighbouring countries was provided by the Hungarian expert for Schengen implementation in Hungary, Prof. Dr. habil Janos Sallai, Colonel, Budapest. His information is gratefully acknowledged.

62 This was verified by using the series "Yearbook of Industry and Construction", and by a correspondence with a competent data official from HCSO.

also make reference to NTBs[63], there exists no set of consistent data on NTBs, however, for each year of the time period of this research. NTBs could not be used, therefore, as a variable in the regression analysis of chapter 6. In the theoretical framework of NEG models, they are assumed to be included in "transport costs" which comprise transport and other trade costs.

This concludes the overview of the relevant theoretical framework given in chapter 2, as well as of previous empirical work in the field, of the provisions of the Europe agreement, the formulation of the hypotheses, and of the data used for this research. Chapter 3 will now approach the subject "industry agglomerations and regional development in Hungary" by means of descriptive empirical analysis of economic data for the manufacturing industries and the regions in Hungary.

---

63 For example *European Commission (1994), Brülhart & Torstensson (1998),* as summarized in section 2.2.3., *Buigues & Ilzkovitz (1988)*, and *Sapir (1996).*

3. Main Characteristics of Hungary's Regions and Industries

This chapter approaches the hypothesis with respect to industry agglomerations and regional development in Hungary during European integration by means of descriptive empirical analysis. Economic developments in Hungary's regions and manufacturing sectors shall be taken into consideration as well as indicators of growing regional integration with the EU such as the development of foreign trade and foreign direct investment (FDI).

Chapter 3 is organised as follows: section 3.1 introduces Hungary and its geographic location, section 3.2 points out current macroeconomic developments and main government policies during the research period 1992 to 2008 which could have had an influence on the research subject. Section 3.3 introduces the 20 Hungarian Nuts-3 regions which shall be the general level of detail in this research. Section 3.4 presents main economic indicators of Hungary's regions, including GDP and employment. Section 3.5 analyses internal net migration at regional level over 1992 to 2008 and puts it into context with the development of manufacturing wages as well as with the housing market. Section 3.6 analyses the manufacturing industry sectors which will be the subject of further analysis of agglomeration in chapters 4 and 6. The final sections 3.7 and 3.8 analyse the integration indicators foreign trade with the EU as well as FDI. Section 3.9 draws first conclusions with respect to regional development in Hungary during the pre- and post-accession phase and summarises indications with respect to the hypotheses regarding agglomeration and regional specialization.

3.1 Introduction to Hungary and its geographic location

Hungary had a population of 10.1 million in 2005[64]. The average population density is 108.6 persons per km² in 2004, population growth was at -0.2 (average annual percentage change from 1995 to 2004). GDP per capita in PPS was at 64.0% of the EU-27 average in 2004. Annual GDP growth was 4.9% on average from 1995 to 2004. As to the structure of the economy, overall employment in industry accounted for 32.5% of total employment, agriculture for 4.9% of total employment in 2005, and the services sector for 62.7%. R&D expenditure was 0.4% as a percentage of GDP in 2004 *(European Commission 2007)*.

64 This was the most recent census date by the time of writing, May 2009.

Hungary is located in the Central and Eastern part of Europe and is as such included in the abbreviation of CEECs - Central and East European economies. The map in **Figure 4** presents the geographic location of Hungary.

Figure 4: Geographic location of Hungary among neighbouring countries

Source: Own map based on regiograph as tool.

Hungary has 7 neighbouring countries. Starting in the North-West and going counter clock-wise, these are Austria, Slovenia, Croatia, Serbia & Montenegro, Romania, Ukraine and Slovakia. The map also shows the Danube river, a main economic and transport axis passing from the North through the capital of Budapest to the South where it flows - after passing further countries - into the Black Sea. It also shows Lake Balaton, a recreation and tourism area, as well as the second main river, Tisza.

The Hungarian territory was settled around 900 A.D. King St. Stephen (1000-1038) converted himself to Christianity and was the first Hungarian king crowned by the Pope. Since that time, Hungary is divided into more or less the same regional structure prevailing up to this date (today, these are called Nuts-3 regions). Later on, Hungary became part of the Austro-Hungarian empire reigned by the Habsburgs from 1437 until the end of World War I. The Trianon peace treaty of 1920 placed one third of all Hungarians outside the new borders, causing a legacy of Hungarian minorities abroad up to today. The one-party system of the Stalinist type prevailed since 1949, which was challenged by the Hungarian people's insurrection led by Imre Nagy in 1956.

Economic reforms started in 1968, combining elements of a market economy with the existing planned economy. This was followed up in the 1970s and 1980s - including then reforms in the housing market leaning to private ownership - and developed into a special form called "goulash communism". The Hungarian people's voice became louder and louder in demanding a pluralist democracy in 1989 such that the break-down of the communist party became unavoidable. The opening of the Hungarian borders to Austria in the summer became instrumental to the fall of the Berlin Wall in November 1989 and to the reshaping of regimes over the whole Eastern part of the continent *(Hantke 1995[65])*.

Hungary was declared a parliamentary Republic on 23rd of October 1989. At the same time, the transition from a socialist-planned economy to a functioning market economy got a new impetus. A successful transformation process from a state-owned to a functioning market economy based on private enterprises, which the CEECs were undergoing each in a different way, had to include 3 common elements: (i) the privatisation of the state-owned enterprise sector; (ii) the liberalisation of prices, foreign trade, and of market entry for new companies; and (iii) the stabilisation of prices. The latter alludes to the upward correction in prices upon their liberalisation, which in Hungary was of the order of +35%, diminishing the large monetary savings which in former socialist countries were much larger than the supply of goods offered. The size of the correction was much less in Hungary than in Poland (+585%) for example, which was due to the fact that in Hungary, prices had been liberalised stepwise since 1975 and a large part was free by 1989 already *(Eger 2000)*.

The political events in 1989, both in the EU and at the national level, opened the way for Hungary's increasing integration with the EU. The institution of the Europe agreement entered into force in February 1992[66], opening up trade for the bulk of manufacturing goods, and Hungary applied for full membership in 1994 and became an EU member state in 2004.

65 Hantke is the maiden name of the author Cordula Wandel; Hantke (1995) pp. 48-51.

66 The trade provisions entered into force at this date, which are the essential for this study's economic analysis; the institutional provisions required ratification in all EU member states and followed two years later.

Hungary has a three year system of professional schooling and training on the job for blue collar workers[67] and professional and university education for white collar workers. The previous is perhaps one of the strengths of the Hungarian manufacturing industry - which is in the centre of this study's analysis of agglomeration developments - which gave Hungary a competitive advantage over most other CEECs and which resulted in the massive FDI-inflows in the later 1990s and early years of this decade, resulting in the largest FDI stock among CEECs.

3.2 Macroeconomic developments in Hungary

In order to be able to put the analysis of agglomeration in the manufacturing sector in Hungary - which shall be analysed in detail in Chapter 4 - into the right context, this section seeks to present Hungary as a country from the macroeconomic sight. Section 3.2.1 gives an overview of selected macroeconomic data of Hungary in recent years, while section 3.2.2 provides an international comparison to enable an evaluation in context with other Central and East European economies.

3.2.1 Overview of macroeconomic characteristics

An overview of selected macroeconomic data of Hungary is given in this section for the years 2006 to 2009. The figures result from the spring economic forecast of the *European Commission (2009a)*, values for 2009 and 2010 are forecasts. Real GDP growth in Hungary had declined from 3.9% in 2006 – when this was above the EU-25 average - to very low levels by 2008, with a severe contraction of -6.3% expected due to the world economic crisis for 2009.

Inflation in terms of the harmonised consumer price index was relatively high in Hungary. Between 2004 and 2008, it had been around 6% on average. The unemployment rate was 6.0% in 2008, slightly lower than the average for the EU-27. The activity rate in Hungary is around 60.8%, rather high in the EU comparison. This signals a high participation rate of women in the labour force.

Continuing with the main indicators of **Table 6**, the general government deficit had been an extraordinary -9.2% in 2006. Government gross debt amounted to 65.8% of GDP in 2007, but rising rather fast to an alarming 80.8% forecast for 2009, due to expansionary fiscal policies and declining tax revenues during the severe economic recession. With respect to Hungary's relations to the rest of the

67 System of "duale Berufsausbildung" stemming from the times of the Austro-Hungarian empire.

world, Hungary showed a current account deficit of -8.4% in terms of GDP in 2008. Exports to the world grew by 15.9% in 2008, yet for 2009 a decline of -11.9% is forecast compared to previous year levels. With respect to the attractiveness of Hungary for international economic investments, a look at real unit

Table 6: Overview of selected macroeconomic data for Hungary 2007 to 2010

HUNGARY	2007	2008	2009*	2010*
real GDP growth (annual percentage change at previous year prices)	1.1	0.5	-6.3	-0.3
inflation (harmonised Consumer Price Index)	7.9%	6.0%	4.4%	4.1%
unemployment rate (Eurostat def.)	7.4%	7.8%	9.5%	11.2%
general government deficit (as% of GDP)	-4.9%	-3.4%	-3.4%	-3.9
General government gross debt (as% of GDP)	65.8%	73.0%	80.8%	82.3%
current account balance (as a% of GDP)	-6.2%	-8.4%	-5.0%	-4.8
exports to world (goods and services), annual percentage change	15.9%	4.6%	-11.9%	0.8
real unit labour costs	-0.8%	2.3%	0.4%	0.7%
long-term interest rate	6.7%	8.2%	n.a.	n.a.

* forecast

Source: *European Commission (2009a)*: Economic forecast spring 2009, 4th of May 2009.

labour costs shows a decline or moderate growth from 2007 to 2009. Long-term interest rates in Hungary are higher than in the Euro area, with 8.2% p.a. in 2008. Hungary's real effective exchange rate, of the Hungarian Forint (HUF), has suffered a severe depreciation in international terms by half its value up to 2008 (year 2000 value set = 100), which presents a disadvantage for Hungary's economy, affecting firms and private persons severely.

The so-called *Balassa-Samuelson effect*[68] taken from neo-classical theory may explain part of what happened during European integration of Hungary and other

68 The Balassa-Samuelson effect model was developed in 1964 by both Béla Balssa and Paul Samuelson, working independently, and submitting their work simultaneously to

CEECs (*KfW 2004)*. The adjustment process taking place in the CEECs during economic catch-up and trade integration with the EU-15 brought about this effect due to different productivity development in the sector of tradable and non-tradable goods in the accession countries[69]. The European Central Bank estimates the order of magnitude of that effect in the 1 to 2 percentage points range even for countries undergoing very rapid traded-goods productivity growth *(Deutsche Bundesbank 2001)*. The effects of rising price levels coupled with a slowdown in productivity growth and a loss of competitiveness of exports to EU markets have indeed been observed in Hungary and other CEECs in the early years of this millennium.[70]

3.2.2 GDP growth in Hungary and other CEECs

This section puts Hungary's GDP growth performance into an international perspective. For Hungary, annual GDP growth rates ranged from 4.1% in 2005 in real terms to only 0.5% in 2008, with a severe decline of -6.3% forecast for 2009, worse than its neighbours. Table 7 shall put these developments in context with other CEECs.

Table 7 presents real GDP growth rates for the CEECs which became member of the EU in 2004 for the years 2005 up to 2009. As the comparison shows, Hungary is a country only ranging in the middle to low rates field with respect to real GDP growth during this period.

---

different journals. It is sometimes referred to as the Balassa-Samuelson "hypothesis" instead of the "effect".

69 It is assumed that the productivity level in the sector of tradable goods in the accession countries is below the productivity level in the EU-15 countries. During the catching-up process, productivity in the sector of tradable goods in the accession countries will rise and approach the level in the EU-15 countries. The better profit expectations in that sector will generate demands for higher wages. Consequently, demands for higher wages in the sector of non-tradable goods will also arise, as those workers will orient themselves at the development of wages in the sector of tradable goods. As productivity in the sector of non-tradable goods does not increase in the same way as in the tradable goods sector, however, prices will rise. At the end of this process, prices and wages will have risen in the whole economy. At the same time, the price level in the accession countries rises faster than in the EU-15 countries, which do not form part of the catching-up process. Due to the price increases, the currency of the accession country will be subject to a real appreciation, i.e. the goods of the accession countries will become more expensive relative to those produced by the EU-15 countries. At the same time, a shift will happen within the accession countries towards a relatively greater importance of the services sector (non-tradable goods sector) and a relatively lesser importance of the industrial sector (tradable goods sector). This shift in the importance of each sector even reinforces the *Balassa-Samuelson* effect.

70 As reported in numerous journal and newspaper articles.

Table 7: GDP Growth rates in large CEECs of the EU-27 for 2005 to 2009 (percentage change over previous year).

Region	2005	2006	2007	2008*	2009*
Hungary	4.1	3.9	1.3	0.5	-6.3
Bulgaria	6.2	6.3	6.2	6.0	-1.6
Czech Republic	6.4	6.4	6.0	3.2	-2.7
Poland	3.6	6.2	6.6	4.8	-1.4
Romania	4.2	7.9	6.2	7.1	-4.0
Slovakia	6.6	8.5	10.4	6.4	-2.6

* values for 2008 provisional, for 2009: forecast.
Source of data: European Commission (2009a), Economic forecast spring 2009, 4th of May 2009.

From 2005 to 2008, real GDP growth rates in Bulgaria, the Czech Republic and Slovakia reached the levels in the catch-up scenarios of the early 1990s such as that by *Hamilton & Winters (1992)*. These scenarios for a future membership of CEECs in the EU, born out of their political desire for stability and economic wealth, set out as target real GDP growth rates of between 6 to 7% annually. In this case, it would take the CEECs between 15 and 20 years to catch up with welfare levels in the EU of those times (then of only 12 member states). In the case of lower real average growth rates in CEECs, between 3 and 4% annually, it would take these countries 30 to 35 years to achieve the same.[71] According to the current economic data presented in **Table 7**, Hungary and to a certain extent Poland were rather in the latter range with respect to real GDP growth rates for the period 2005 to 2008.

A more recent study on cohesion with the EU average by *Hallet (2002)* was based on country-level GDP growth for the period 1995 to 2001. This study found that the overall speed of convergence was rather slow. A differentiation was made between the poorer CEECs which tended to grow faster and the richer CEECs which tended to grow slower. Among possible explanations for the speed, factors such as the rate of productivity growth, macroeconomic stabilisation, the design of the national transition process and the geographic location in Europe played a role.

71 The other side of Eastern enlargement concerns the economic effects on the current EU member states. Various studies have been made on these effects, the figures given by the European Commission seemed rather optimistic with hindsight. Straubhaar (2004) also warned about too optimistic expectations, while pointing out the opportunities to be ceased.

3.2.3 Main government policies with economic or regional implications

In this section, main or special government policies of Hungary shall be taken into consideration in order to identify any influences which could have worked on agglomeration and regional specialization in the sense of the hypotheses. Hungary was the first Central and East European economy to start economic reforms for a transition towards a market economy. Hungary introduced a two-tier banking system already in January 1987 and has recapitalised banks during reform of the banking system in the 1990s, ending a period of credit-crunch and high real interest rates for the economy. Hungary introduced a value added tax in 1989 to replace the old system of cumulative turn-over taxes, and further simplified the system in 1994. The personal income tax is progressive with 6 zones. The corporate income tax system foresees various exemptions and tax benefits for foreign investors. The law describing all forms for economic enterprises was initiated in 1988 and sparked a wave of new enterprise start-ups from 1989 onwards *(Hantke 1995*[72]*)*. The legislation protecting foreign investors (FDI) is at international standards, including tax benefits, free capital transfer in foreign currency and repatriation of profits and investments. The Hungarian policy towards privatisation is dealt with in section 3.7 in context with foreign direct investment.

Hungary is regarded as a functioning market economy since the 1997 Regular Report of the European Commission. In 2001, the privatisation process was viewed as almost completed. An extraordinary export performance in the late 1990s provided the proof for a high level of international competitiveness. In order to widen the economy's growth base and to address social problems, the Szenchenyi plan focused on structural reforms for the period 2001 to 2006. The territorial focus was to open up the economically less developed Eastern part of the country, including motorway development, home construction, tourism, R&D and employment policies *(European Commission 2001)*. More precisely, the Széchenyi plan - which was elaborated mainly during the year 2000 - started a ten-year industrial parks programme. The number of industrial parks grew to 146 after the end of the first year in 2001, on track towards the goal of 250 industrial parks by the end of the decade *(The Hungarian Economy 1/2002)*. The aims of this programme are also supported by the EU's structural funds in the pre- and post-accession phase.

A specific Hungarian policy which had great success is that of the customs-free zones. Industrial customs-free zones contributed to a rising share of Hungarian

---

72 *Hantke (1995)*, pp. 57-58.

exports, from 18.1% in 1996 to 43% by the end of 1999. For manufacturing exports, those from customs-free zones even exceeded those from the rest of the country in that year. Hungary's top ten exporters operated in eight industrial customs-free zones and produced 35% of Hungary's total exports in 1999; the 43% of total exports quoted above were produced by 101 companies operating in customs-free zones. According to a contemporary map, the majority of these industrial customs-free zones is located in the Western part of the country, some in the central part surrounding the capital Budapest, and some are located in Northern Hungary and the East near the border to Ukraine, almost none are in the Great Plains area *(Vadász 2000)*.

The policies of customs-free zones as well as the industrial parks programme under the Széchenyi plan are both liable to have had an influence on the location of manufacturing industry in Hungary. As such, they might have influenced the degree of agglomeration or dispersion of individual sectors, especially those with high economies of scale and those with a strong export orientation (see Figure 19 in section 3.6, and section 3.7). The two policies might also have contributed to the observed development regarding regional specialization (see Chapter 5). Finally, the importance of exports from customs-free zones played a role in the choice of Hungarian data over other data sources as a basis of this research (see section 2.5).

3.3 Hungary's regional set-up

This section shall introduce the territorial set-up of Hungary. A description of the regional set-up will be given, and particularities of the regions will be described. These shall be examined with a view to finding any influences which could have worked on agglomeration or regional specialization as in the hypotheses. Main economic indicators of the regions will be presented in the following section 3.4.

Hungary used to be divided into three large regions: Transdanubia in the West, the lands dominated by the presence of the river Danube, Central and Northern Hungary in the middle, and the agricultural Great Plain region to the South. Since the territorial reforms during the process of increasing integration with the EU, Hungary is organised in 7 Nuts-2 regions and 20 Nuts-3 regions. It shall be pointed out that these are merely planning-statistical regions, i.e. no regional government structure is behind them (unlike the German Länder and Landkreise, for example). **Figure 5** shows a map of the Hungarian Nuts-2 and Nuts-3 regions.

In this research, the focus will be on the 20 Nuts-3 regions in order to take account of a sufficient level of detail and broadness of data base for the calculations later on in chapters 4, 5 and 6.

Figure 5: Hungary's 20 Nuts-3 regions and 7 Nuts-2 regions.

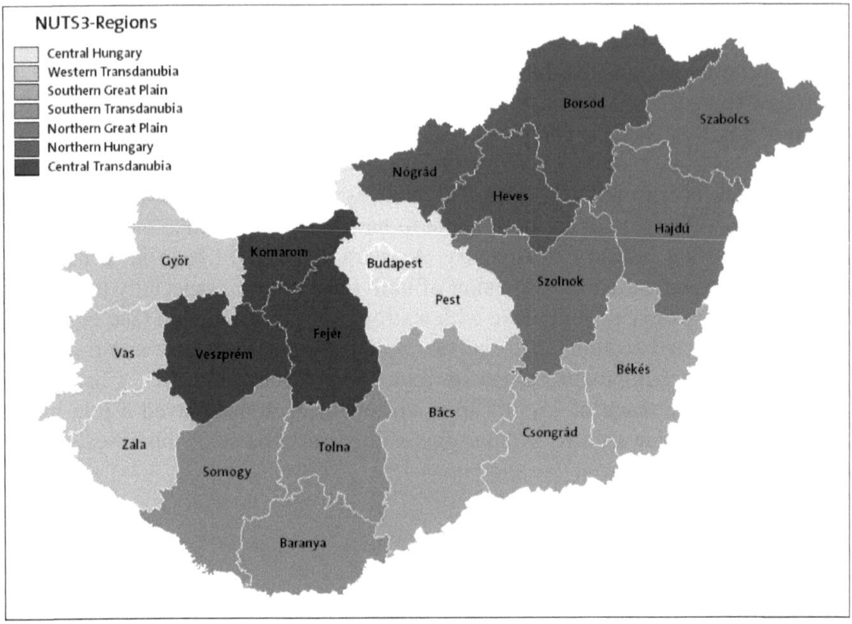

Source: Own map based on regiograph tool.

In the following paragraphs, selected characteristics judged of economic importance will be pointed out for each of the 20 Nuts-3 regions (the information is drawn from *Eurostat 2008*[73] unless indicated otherwise):

Budapest is the capital of Hungary, occupying 0.6% of the country's territory yet holding a population of 1.7 million in 2005 or 16.8% of the country's total. The international airport, several railway stations and the crossing of main motorways make it also an important hub for national and international transport. The central government and administration as well as many company head quarters are located here. **Pest** region is surrounding Budapest, forming together with the capital **CENTRAL HUNGARY**. Pest has a relatively low unemployment rate due to

73 Eurostat (2008): Portrait of the Regions, drawn from the Eurostat Website on 09.09.2008. While the text in that portrait was finalised in March 2004, most economic data such as employment and wages dated apparently from 2001 or 2002.

the proximity of Budapest. The region is characterised by an economy capable of development, but with inadequate basic services (according to *Eurostat 2008*). This perhaps can explain the much lower GDP at PPS than in Budapest (see also Figure 8 in section 3.4).

Passing towards the Western part of the country, to **CENTRAL TRANSDANUBIA**, **Fejér** was settled in Roman times and became the coronation and burial site of the Hungarian kings in the Middle Ages. Three important factors played the most important role in placing Fejér among the fastest economically developing regions: its favourable geographical location, the qualified labour force, and an infrastructure which helped to attract investments. **Komárom-Esztergom** was the birthplace of King St. Stephen, the first king of the Hungarians (see section 3.1). Almost half of Hungary's exploitable brown coal deposits are found in this region, yet the mining sector is in decline due to geological conditions of the reserves. The presence of the Danube encouraged the establishment of industrial activities requiring large quantities of water. The region's economic structure is decidedly industrial. Its metallurgy, food processing, machine and chemical industries are particularly advanced. The influx of international capital has been remarkable, with 550 companies with foreign interests operating there, including Japanese Suzuki automobile. **Veszprém**'s rich mineral deposits make it Hungary's most important supplier of many basic raw materials, most importantly bauxite. Unemployment was lower than nationally, and industry is diversified and export-oriented (in 2002, 84% of sales of the machinery and equipment industry went abroad).

Passing to **WESTERN TRANSDANUBIA**, the region **Györ-Moson-Sopron** shows a good economic performance thanks to its considerable foreign economic connections and a highly qualified labour force. The region's border situation with Austria and Slovakia is more of an advantage than a hindrance. The principal branches are engineering, food-processing and light industries. The country's largest exporter, AUDI Hungaria, is also located here. **Vas** is a region with economic variety and world class engineering. Wages and salaries are relatively low compared to the national average (4,289 Euro per month in 2001 as compared to 4,832 for Hungary as a whole). **Zala** borders on Croatia and Slovenia and is in a good geographical situation, including that it holds a part of Lake Balaton, yet with infrastructural problems, namely a dense road network but no motor ways. R&D requires more funds in this region, as only 0.3% of the total Hungarian personnel of the 19 regions (except for Budapest) were working there.

In **SOUTHERN TRANSDANUBIA**, the region **Baranya** is under a submediterranean climatic influence which is unique in Hungary. The settlement structure is characterised by small villages. The region's capital Pécs is a university city with

160,000 inhabitants and is set to become European Capital of Culture in 2010. The unfavourable transportation links to Baranya region were obstacles to economic development in the past; the government has promised, however, to complete the M6 motorway to the city by 2008 *(The Hungarian Economy IV/ 2005)*. **Somogy** is a forested region between Lake Balaton and the river Dráva. Significant oil fields have recently been discovered and there are plans to commence production. The services sector is the biggest employer there. Job losses during the transition to a market economy affected the region's most important economic branches, with the highest number of dismissals in agriculture with the closing of the large agricultural and food processing enterprises, but engineering was also hard hit. **Tolna** is characterised by a low population density, the presence of Hungary's only nuclear power plant, and a good agricultural base. More than 40% of manufacturing employment is concentrated in the production of textiles, leather and apparel products.[74] Tolna is lacking both foreign and domestic capital, making economic development extremely difficult. Waste water treatment and nuclear waste storage are environmental problems of the region.

NORTHERN HUNGARY is the mountainous Northern part of the country. Northern Hungary was the centre of Hungary's heavy industry under the former CMEA system. The caves of the Aggtelek karst have been declared a World Heritage Site by UNESCO. Since the start of restructuring in 1989, unemployment is consistently high. There are about 25 industrial parks located there (BOSCH is one of the large employers). Infrastructure is a key issue, with the M3 and M30 motorway connections needing further construction *(The Hungarian Economy IV/2004)*. **Borsod-Abaúj-Zemplén** is the second largest region by its territory. It was mining, the concentration of iron and steel, and the machine industry that determined the direction of economic development in the past. An economic crisis in this region began in the 1980s and peaked in 1993. The region's Northern strip adjoining Slovakia is a backward agricultural region with very little industry, undeveloped infrastructure, and a small entrepreneurial sector. South Borsod - which includes the volcanic Zemplén hills with the Tokaj wine region - is a more advantaged agro-industrial area. The level of FDI is less than would be expected given the region's area and population size. In **Heves,** heavy industry was established in the 1950s and 1960s. Today, the region has a qualified workforce but not enough jobs such that high unemployment affects the middle aged the most. Among the largest companies many are foreign owned. **Nógrád** is a mountainous region with industrial traditions, but a shortage of both domestic and foreign capital. Metallurgy and metal processing are the most prominent branches today.

74 The 40% figure was taken from Mafioli (2003), all the rest is from Eurostat (2008) again.

Passing to the South-Eastern part of Hungary, the **NORTHERN GREAT PLAIN, and Szabolcs-Szatmár-Bereg** is situated in Hungary's East, bordering Ukraine, Slovakia and Romania. It is a region with economic problems, no motorway connection, a low standard of living and high unemployment. The population is relatively young, with 35% below the age of 25 in 2003; the activity rate was 9.4 percentage points below the national average, and youth unemployment with 15.2% is one of the highest in Hungary. Radical reforms in agriculture began in 1990 with a drop in livestock, yields and labour force. **Hajdú-Bihar** is characterised by a flat landscape and a low population density. Unemployment is high as labour supply exceeds demand particularly in agriculture and in construction and steel production as well as in administrative-type jobs. The average wheat yield has decreased in the past decade due to natural and social reasons. **Jász-Nagykun-Szolnok** is located in the heart of the Great Plain and has the most continental climate in Hungary, which means the hottest summers, coldest winters and highest temperature fluctuations, low precipitation and common droughts. The settlement structure is typical of the Great Plain, with settlements sprawling, far from each other, and tending to be quite populous. The region is full of contradictions, bearing at the same time the marks of economic crisis and of prosperity, and it is still searching for the way towards development *(Eurostat 2008)*.

In the **SOUTHERN GREAT PLAIN**, the region **Békés** is predominantly agricultural with 70% of the area being arable land. The region lost its advantageous position held previously during the Austro-Hungarian empire due to the failure to switch to intensive agriculture caused by a lack of capital two or three decades ago. Throughout history, the region has been destroyed and depopulated several times. Industries present today are those which require large quantities of cheap, unskilled labour (textiles and shoe making, building materials). The region has a low purchasing power, wages are 78% of the national average, and 30% of the unemployed are under the age of 25. **Bács-Kiskun** is the region with the largest territory in Hungary. The flexible structure of its economy has been able to cope with the challenges of the transition period and has attracted considerable foreign capital. The region has an important place in Hungary's food industry exports. One of the biggest problems, however, is that of the water supply on the sand tableland where desertification threatens the region's traditional agriculture. Finally, the region **Csongrád** can most accurately be described as an industrial-agrarian region. While the soils are predominantly agricultural, the region provides three quarters of the national crude oil and two-thirds of the national natural gas production. Manufacturing is by far the most important industry branch of the region. The region's R & D outlays represented 9% of the national total and 75% of the 19 regions (without Budapest). Although well disposed by its infrastructure to serve as a multi-function logistic centre, a disadvantage for Csongrád has been the wage level which is comparatively higher than in neighbouring Romania and Serbia.

3.4 Main economic indicators of Hungary's regions

The intention of this section presenting the main economic indicators of Hungary's 20 regions is to identify influences which could have worked on the development of industrial agglomeration or regional specialization in the course of European integration.

Table 8 gives an overview over the area, population and population density of the 20 regions at Nuts-3 level and for Hungary as a whole. While the Great Plain regions are large in territory, Central Hungary and especially Budapest host the largest population. The capital region of Budapest, although the most populated with 16.85% of Hungary's total population in 2005, was the smallest in territory and the most populated, with 3,233 inhabitants per km² - a figure almost 30 times the national average. Most other regions except for Pest, Komárom-Esztergom and Györ-Moson-Sopron have a lower population density than the national average. Particularly low in this respect are Southern Transdanubia and the Great Plain regions in general, while Somogy is the region with the lowest population density in Hungary overall.

With respect to the area of the 20 Nuts-3 regions, there have been several territorial rearrangements in the period 1992 to 2005.[75] The regions Pest, Vas and Tolna were recut in 1995 by the third decimal of a km²; in 1996, Baranya and Bács-Kiskun were resized by 0.047 km². In 1999, the territory of Vas and of Hungary as a whole declined by one third decimal of a km². In 2001, a large set of regions was resized, perhaps due to political considerations in expectation of benefits from the European regional policy. The regions concerned were Pest, again, Fejér, Komárom-Esztergom, Veszprém, Györ-Moson-Sopron, Jász-Nagykun-Solnok, Szabolcs-Szatmar-Bereg, and Bacs-Kiskun, again. In 2003, the regions Pest and Nógrád were resized by 0.002 km². And finally, Baranya was resized in 2005 by one third decimal point of a km². For the purpose of simplicity, the territory recorded in 2005 will be the basis of further calculations in this research.

75 Source: Eurostat: http://epp.eurostat.ec.europa.eu.

Table 8: Area and population by region at Nuts-3 level

Region	Area		Population		Population density, persons per km²
	km² in 2005	% of national total	persons	% of national total	
Budapest	525	0.6	1,698,106	16.9	3,233.9
Pest	6,393	6.9	1,157,564	11.5	181.1
Fejér	4,358	4.7	428,332	4.3	98.3
Komárom-Esztergom	2,265	2.4	314,783	3.1	139.0
Veszprém	4,493	4.8	365,009	3.6	81.2
Győr-Moson-Sopron	4,208	4.5	441,606	4.4	104.9
Vas	3,336	3.6	264,361	2.6	79.2
Zala	3,784	4.1	294,175	2.9	77.7
Baranya	4,429	4.8	398,355	4.0	89.9
Somogy	6,036	6.5	329,399	3.3	54.6
Tolna	3,703	4.0	242,946	2.4	65.6
Borsod-Abaúj-Zemplén	7,247	7.8	725,779	7.2	100.1
Heves	3,637	3.9	320,886	3.2	88.2
Nógrád	2,546	2.7	214,824	2.1	84.4
Hajdú-Bihar	6,211	6.7	547,357	5.4	88.1
Jász-Nagykun-Szolnok	5,582	6.0	407,232	4.0	73.0
Szabolcs-Szatmár-Bereg	5,937	6.4	578,573	5.7	97.5
Bács-Kiskun	8,445	9.1	537,862	5.3	63.7
Békés	5,630	6.1	385,847	3.8	68.5
Csongrád	4,263	4.6	423,585	4.2	99.4
Total	**93,028**	**100.0**	**10,076,581**	**100.0**	**108.3**

Source of data: *HCSO (2006)*: Regional Statistical Yearbook of Hungary 2005, Budapest.

3.4.1 GDP

With a view to regional development in Hungary, the next series of figures and tables will focus on income of the regions compared to the national GDP or EU average, whichever is appropriate.

Figure 6: Share of Nuts-2 regions in national GDP, based on current prices in Euro (2005)

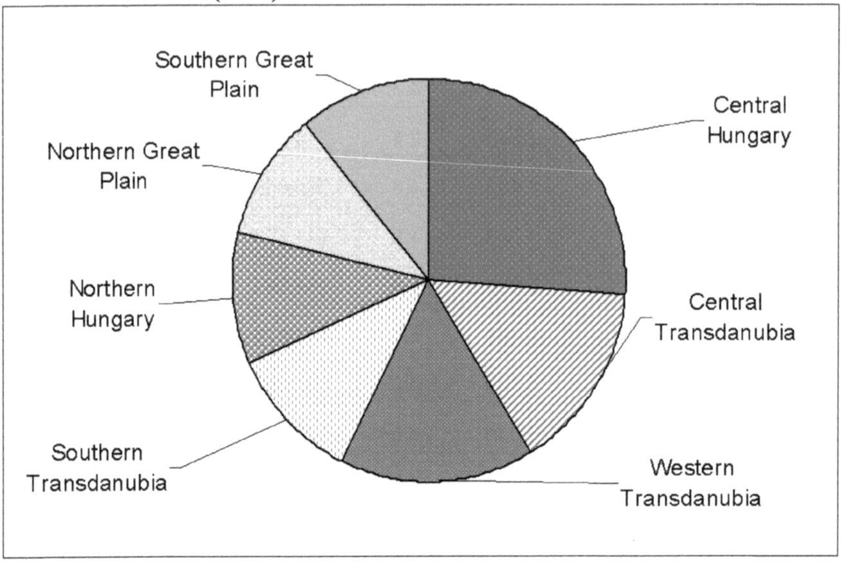

Source of data: *Eurostat* Website, regional database, 7th of October 2008.

Figure 6 shows the contribution of the seven Nuts-2 regions to national GDP (Nuts-3 level is not available). This provides a first indication as to the economic strength of the regions and to centres of industrial agglomeration. The lion share, namely 46%, is contributed to national GDP by Central Hungary, consisting of the capital Budapest and Pest region. Western Transdanubia, Central Transdanubia and Southern Transdanubia, the regions in the Western part near the EU-15, contribute together more than a quarter of national GDP. Northern Hungary, the former centre of heavy industry, contributed a mere 8% in 2005.

Table 9 shows real GDP growth rates for Hungary and for the 7 Nuts-2 regions for the years 2000 to 2005 as well as the average over the period.[76] The national

76 The figures are based on Eurostat's experts, as the HCSO does not publish these. 2005 were the most recent data available at the time of writing.

growth rates were well above the 3% soil required for net job creation according to the EU economic experts.[77] There are great variations in real growth rates at the Nuts-2 level from year to year. Therefore, the average growth rates will be evaluated here for that period. This can give an indication towards growth poles or overall declining regions in Hungary.

Table 9: Real GDP growth per Nuts-2 region 2000 -2005*

	2000	2001	2002	2003	2004	2005	Average rate
Hungary	**5.2**	**4.1**	**4.4**	**4.2**	**4.8**	**4.1**	**4.5**
Central Hungary	6.0	5.5	8.0	2.1	4.0	8.2	5.6
Central Transdanubia	9.1	2.1	-1.9	9.5	7.1	3.0	4.8
Western Transdanubia	5.6	-2.8	3.2	9.4	0.9	-1.1	2.5
Southern Transdanubia	1.1	4.3	2.2	1.8	4.7	1.1	2.5
Northern Hungary	2.8	5.0	2.7	4.7	8.3	1.7	4.2
Northern Great Plain	5.2	8.5	1.4	5.8	5.0	0.3	4.4
Southern Great Plain	2.6	2.5	2.3	2.4	7.7	1.0	3.1

* based on GDP at current prices, change in % of previous year

Notes: All figures are estimates by Eurostat; data at Nuts-3 level are not published; data for 2006 and 2007 were not available.

Source of average rate: Own calculations.

Source of data: *Eurostat* website, regional database, 8th of Oct. 2008.

Central Hungary was well above the national average, an important contribution given the economic size of the region (see Figure 6). Central Transdanubia's real growth was also higher than the national average over the period. Western Transdanubia - contrary to what would be expected - contributed below average, which was due to two years of economic decline or stagnation, while the years 2000, 2003 and 2005 showed much higher growth rates than the national rate. The Southern Great Plain can be called a declining region, as real growth there was below the national rate in all but one year.

77 See for example *European Commission (1995)*: White Paper on Competitiveness and Growth, Brussels.

3.4.2 Regional disparities in Hungary and other CEECs

A further analysis and evaluation of regional disparities at the level of the 20 Nuts-3 regions is presented in this section in order to obtain a true picture of economic disparities in Hungary, including an international comparison with other CEECs.

Figure 7: GDP per capita at Nuts-3 level at current prices (2005, in Euro)

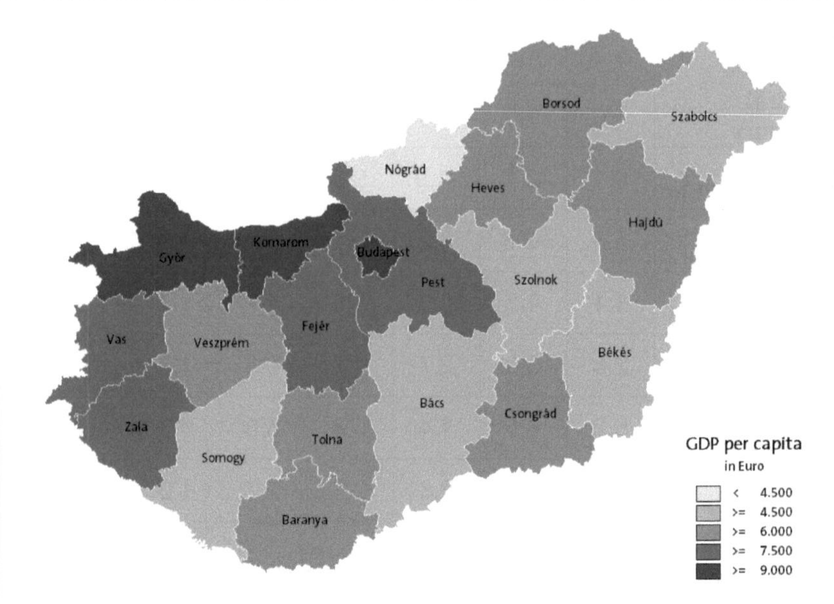

Source of data: *Eurostat* website, regional database, 7th of Oct. 2008.

Figure 7 shows a map of the regional per capita GDP in Euro in 2005.[78] While the capital Budapest has an exceptionally high income, the richest regions are located in the Centre and the Western part of the country. The poorest regions are located in the Northern part and in the Great Plain to the South-East of the country. The difference between Budapest with 18,807 Euro per capita and the poorest region Nógrád with 4,451 Euro per capita is more than 4-fold; when comparing with the next non-capital region, Komárom-Esztergom with 10,069 Euro per capita, this is more than the double.

78 The data for 2005 were the most recent available at the time of writing.

The next part will focus on GDP of the regions measured in Purchasing Power Standards (PPS) for groups of regions, according to their location in the country.

Figure 8: Comparison of GDP per capita in PPS for the 11 Western and Central regions, 1995 and 2005, as % of national average

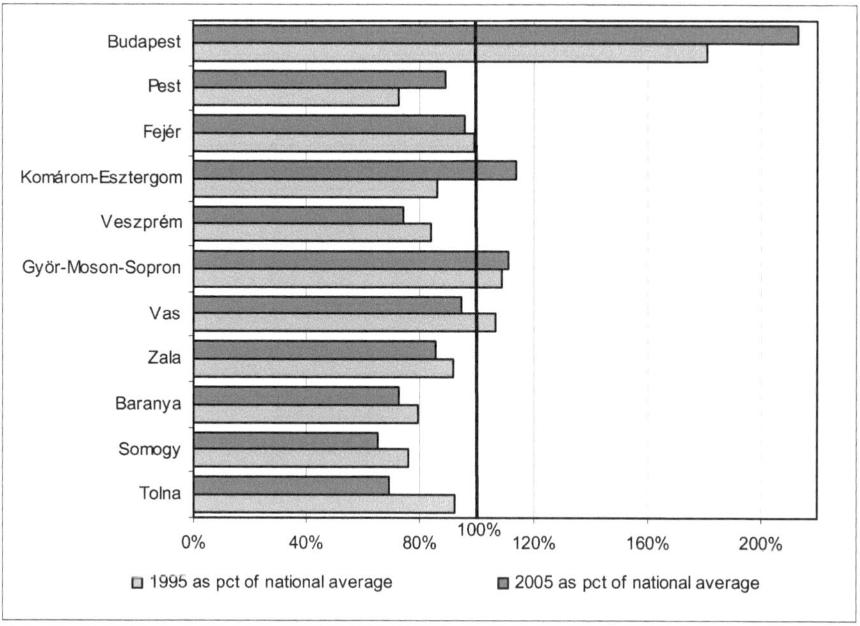

Source: Own calculations.
Source of data: *Eurostat* website, regional database, 7th Oct. 2008.

The graph in **Figure 8** shows the relative position of 11 Western and Central Nuts-3 regions with respect to per capita income in PPS measured relative to the national average (=100) in the years 1995 and 2005. This graph includes the regions with above average income, mainly Budapest with 213% in 2005, Komarom-Esztergom with 114% in 2005 and Györ-Moson-Sopron with 111% in 2005. Comparing 1995 and 2005, only four regions (even out of the 20 total regions) improved their position with respect to the national average, namely Budapest, Pest, Komárom-Esztergom and Györ-Moson-Sopron. **Figure 9** shows the development for the remaining regions located in Northern Hungary and the Great Plain regions.

Figure 9: Comparison of GDP per capita in PPS for 9 Northern, Eastern and Southern regions, 1995 and 2005, as % of national average

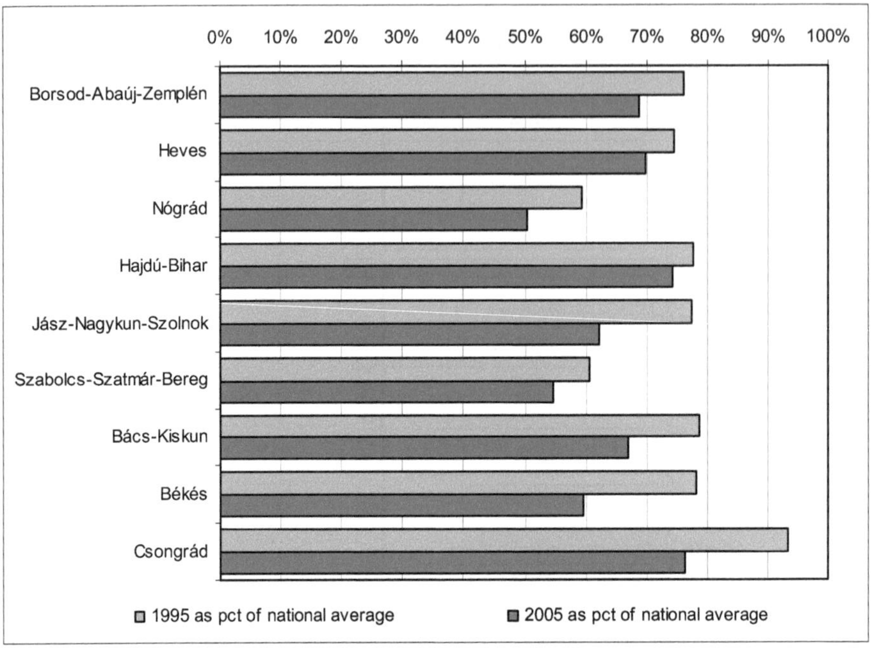

Source: Own calculations.
Source of data: *Eurostat* website, regional database, 7th Oct. 2008.

Figure 9 shows the development of per capita income in PPS relative to the national average for the remaining 9 Nuts-3 regions in 1995 and 2005[79]. All of these Northern and Great Plain regions suffered deteriorations with respect to their per-capita income relative to the national average over the period. The poorest regions in Hungary are also among this group. The average of this group declined from 75.1% of the national average in 1995 to 64.8% in 2005, whereas the average of the 11 Central and Western regions in Figure 8 remained almost constant at 98.1 and 98.7% respectively.

This gives a first indication as to the development shed in Hungary between relatively prosperous Central and Western regions and the relatively poorer Northern and Great Plain regions. It will be interesting to follow this up in chapters 4 and 5 when examining whether the agglomeration of industry and regional specialization patterns have contributed to this trend.

79 Please note the different scales in Figures 7 and 8 due to technical reasons.

Table 10: Regional disparities at Nuts-3 level based on GDP in PPS per inhabitant, as % of EU average, large CEECs (selected years)

	Hungary	Czech Republic	Slovakia	Bulgaria	Romania
1995	31.4%	15.4%	28.3%	24.4%**	12.8%
2000	37.6%	21.3%	27.8%	27.1%	28.7%
2005	40.0%	23.3%	33.8%	32.5%	31.9%

* Data for 1999 (2000 not available for Hungary).
** Data for 1996 (1995 not available for Bulgaria).
Note: Data for Poland at Nuts-3 level were not published at the time of writing.
Source of data: *Eurostat* website, regional database, 8th Oct. 2008.

Table 10 shows the development of regional disparities in Hungary and the large CEECs over the period 1995 to 2005, as measured for GDP per inhabitant in PPS as % of the EU average. The large CEECs consisting of many Nuts-3 regions were selected for this comparison (no data were available for Poland). Hungary had the greatest regional disparities among these CEECs, namely 40.0% in 2005. Regional disparities increased in all these CEECs over the period. The largest increase was observed in Romania with a rise of +19.1 percentage points, while regional disparities in Hungary increased by +8.6 percentage points over the period.

The figures in Table 10 clearly indicate that processes of divergence were going on in all of the CEECs, to a different extent. The general widening of regional disparities during the process of economic growth - which happened during the transition to a market economy and the early phases of the catching-up processes - points to new challenges for European regional and cohesion policy after Eastern enlargement of the EU. These will be discussed more in detail in chapter 7, section 7.2.

3.4.3 Employment and active enterprises at regional level

With respect to employment, the major difference after Hungary's transition to a market economy is that full employment has ceased to exist, and unemployment has become a mass phenomenon. The economically inactive share of the society has increased. Nearly 1.3 million people lost their employment between 1989 and 1993. Employment levels for Hungary reached its lowest point in 1996 with a workforce of 3.9 million, a number 30% lower than that registered at the end of the nineteen eighties.[80] In the following graphs, unemployment per region as well as the workforce and industrial employment per region shall be analysed more in detail.

Figure 10: Regional unemployment rates at the Nuts-3 level in %, 2005

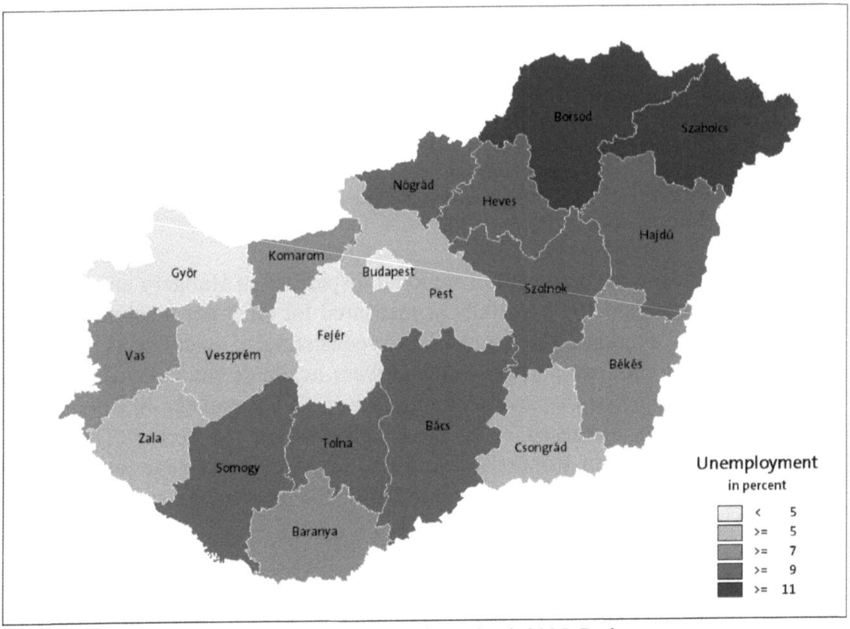

Source of data: *HCSO (2006),* Regional Statistical Yearbook 2005, Budapest.

The map in **Figure 10** shows the regional unemployment rates for Nuts-3 regions in the year 2005.[81] The highest unemployment was found in Szabolcs-Szatmár-Bereg, the Eastern-most region bordering Ukraine, followed by the three regions of Northern Hungary, Borsod-Abaúj-Zemplén, Nógrád and Heves. The Western part of Hungary and the Centre near Budapest are characterised by low unemployment. Unemployment in the Eastern part tended to be higher than in the Western part of the country. That points to a general decline and weaker economic base in regions bordering to the former Eastern bloc countries (CMEA), and a better economic base in regions bordering or situated near the large EU market.

80 HCSO (2005): "Change of course – Hungary 1990 – 2004", Budapest, 2005, pp. 60-61.

81 The data for 2005 were also the most recent available at the Eurostat Website at the time of writing (8.5.2009).

Table 11 shows the distribution of the labour force over the 20 regions and 7 Nuts-2 regions. Column 3 indicates the activity rates of the population. They are highest in Budapest and the Western regions and tend to be very low in Northern Hungary - where high unemployment prevails - and the Great Plain area.

Table 11: Economic activity of population aged 15–74 per region at Nuts-2 level, 2004

Region	Employed (in 1,000 persons)	% of national total	Activity rate,%	Unemployment rate,%
Central Hungary	1,226.3	31.4%	59.0	4.5
Central Transdanubia	455.3	11.7%	56.9	5.6
Western Transdanubia	424.6	10.9%	57.2	4.6
Southern Transdanubia	350.9	9.0%	50.1	7.3
Northern Hungary	431.1	11.1%	49.3	9.7
Northern Great Plain	523.5	13.4%	48.5	7.2
Southern Great Plain	488.7	12.5%	50.5	6.3
Total	3,900.4	100%	53.8	6.1

Source of data: *HCSO (2005)*, Regional Statistical Yearbook of Hungary 2004, Budapest.

When looking at the number of registered and unincorporated enterprises per 1000 inhabitants at the level of the 168 subregional entities, a map at the Nuts-4 subregional level would show that entrepreneurial activity is sparse in the North-Eastern part of the country. The Western and Central part, on the contrary, has multiple patches with higher entrepreneurial activity. These centres often span across county borders, and also across Nuts-2 regional planning borders. Two things shall be retained here: Firstly, this indicates clusters of economic activity, thus in the sense of agglomeration. Secondly, these areas of intense economic activity are not identical with the administrative entities and borders.

The final statistic in this section is the development of exports in industry for selected regions and for Hungary as a whole over the period 1992 to 2005. The data show the percentage of production which is exported, i.e. between 12 and 40% in 1993, and between 57% and 82% in 2005. **Figure 11** shows the dynamic growth of the share of production exported in five Western regions of Hungary. All of them were also regions with a large share of employment and output in industry, except for Somogy. Thus, it can be concluded that their industry is not only concentrated and efficient, but it is also internationally competitive, as its strong export orientation proves.

Figure 11: Development of exports per region: export share (to world) in industry production for five Western regions and Hungary as a whole, 1992-2005

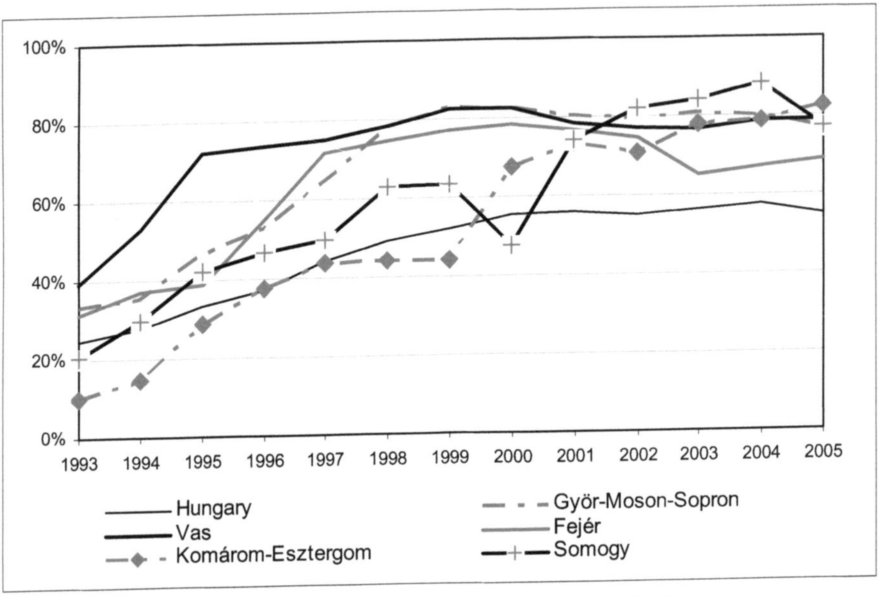

Source of data: *HCSO*, Regional Statistical Yearbook, subsequent years, Budapest.

3.5 Influences on internal net migration per region

In the theories of the NEG, workers migrate between regions due to regional differences in wage levels and living conditions. For this reason, section 3.5.1 examines internal net migration between the 20 Hungarian regions in the period 1992 to 2008. Section 3.5.2 looks at manufacturing wages per region and analyses whether there is a correlation between high wages and positive internal migration, or low wages and negative internal migration. With respect to living conditions, section 3.5.3 examines the housing market which can act either as an incentive for improving living conditions or as a restraint to attracting migrants where housing is scarce.

3.5.1 Internal net migration per region

This section analyses internal net migration between the 20 Hungarian regions during the period 1992 to 2008. This is done with the research question of this study in mind, namely whether there are any indications for influences which could be linked to processes of industry agglomeration or regional specialization during this period. It is taken as granted that the data shown for internal net migration in this section comprise only the voluntary changes in residence in the sense of the definition of migration by *Fischer & Straubhaar (1994)*.[82]

Figure 12: Internal net migration in the 20 Hungarian regions, balance over 1992 to 2008, number of persons

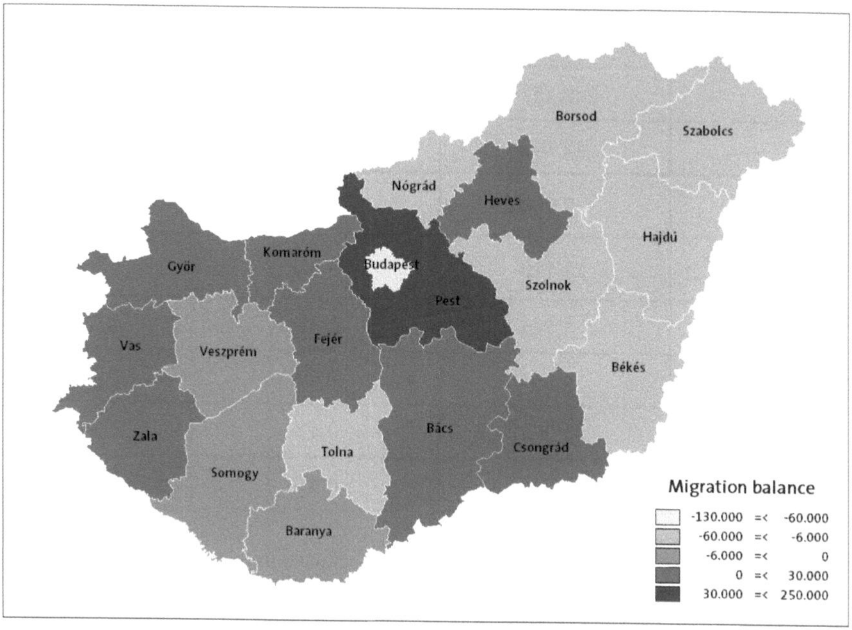

Notes: 2007 and 2008: provisional figures.
Source of figures for balance 1992 to 2008: own calculations.
Source of data: *HCSO*, Regional statistical yearbook, subsequent years, Budapest.

82 Migration is "voluntary" in the sense that political refugees would be excluded *Fischer & Straubhaar (1994)*. Political refugees fortunately do not exist at the inter-regional level within a country in the EU.

The map in **Figure 12** shows the overall picture for the 20 Nuts-3 regions with respect to internal net migration between Nuts-3 regions, number of persons, for the period 1992 to 2008.[83] As the map shows, the regions with positive balances are located either in the Centre of the country or in the Western part. The regions with clear negative balances, apart from the capital, are located in Northern Hungary, in the Eastern part of the country, and in the Great Plain area.

These migratory balances of the Hungarian Nuts-3 regions can be evaluated as follows: centres of agglomeration, such as those in the Western part of Hungary, show a higher economic attractiveness for industry and workers. On the other

Table 12: Nuts-3 regions with positive internal net migration balances from 1992 to 2008, number of persons

	Cumulative balance 1992 to 2008 (number of persons)	As % of the region's population in 2005*	As % of total positive net migration
Pest	248,157	21.4%	84.0%
Fejér	12,749	3.0%	4.3%
Komárom-Esztergom	7,000	2.2%	2.4%
Györ-Moson-Sopron	21,119	4.8%	7.2%
Vas	1,126	0.4%	0.5%
Heves	1,355	0.4%	0.7%
Bács-Kiskun	1,922	0.4%	0.7%
Csongrád	1,849	0.4%	0.6%

Source: Own calculations.

Notes: 2005 was the most recent figure for population per region available at the time of writing, HCSO Website, 8th May 2009; migration figures 2007, 2008 based on provisional data.

Source of data: HCSO, Regional Statistical Yearbook of Hungary, subsequent years, Budapest, and HCSO database on website.

83 The data by the HCSO for the internal net migration at Nuts-3 level are apparently a sum of permanent internal migration and temporary internal migration, as could be deducted in some years. No data were available, however, for the balances of just the permanent internal net migration at Nuts-3 level for all years from 1992 to 2008, although this would have been preferable and also in line with the above definition by Fischer & Straubhaar (1994).

hand, positive net migration contributes to creating a favourable environment for the location of further industry. Whether internal net migration between Nuts-3 regions and the degree of industry concentration were correlated in Hungary in this period will be analysed in Chapter 6 (regression 1 about agglomeration).

The data on internal net migration show that 8 of the 20 Nuts-3 regions had a positive balance during the period 1992 to 2008. These are shown in **Table 12**. By far the highest positive internal net migration was registered in Pest, with a total near 248,000 persons, or 84% of the total positive net migration of all regions. Second by numbers was Györ-Moson-Sopron, a region bordering EU-15, with 6.74% of the total. Third place was Fejér, a region bordering Pest in the West, with 4.5% of the total. The first 5 regions listed in the table are located in the Western part of Hungary and show a clear positive migratory trend. The 3 other regions located in the North and the Southern Great Plain not only had a small positive balance, but also varied between negative and positive data for net migration from year to year. These data illustrate the agglomeration processes going on among the population in Hungary. Industry agglomeration is analysed more in detail in chapter 4.

Figure 13 shows the overall development of positive internal net migration. The year with the highest balance in these 8 population attracting regions was the year 2000. In this year, 23,831 persons migrated to these 8 regions from within Hungary. This amounts to 0.23% of the total population of Hungary in that year. This is rather interesting. The year 2000 was the year with the largest FDI-inflow in Hungary over the period. Further, the year 1999 was found to be a turning point for the development of industry agglomeration (see Chapter 4) and for the degree of regional specialization (see Chapter 5).

The total positive internal net migration of these 8 regions amounts to 295,277 when summed up over the period. This amounts to 2.93% in relation to the total population of Hungary in 2005. These internal net migration figures seem to point to the *Ludema & Wooton (1997)* model - which is based on inter-regional partial migration of workers - as the appropriate framework for analysing agglomeration and regional specialization in Hungary.

The results of Table 12 and Figure 13 are interesting with respect to the questions posed by this research. Western regions have been attracting positive internal net migration flows over the period 1992 to 2008. They have also had the highest ratio of employees in industry over population as well as the highest industry output per inhabitant. The activity rates of the population were among the highest in the country (see Table 11), and the export share in industry output was higher than for Hungary as a whole.

Figure 13: Sum of internal net migration increases of the 8 regions with positive migratory balances, number of persons, 1992 to 2008

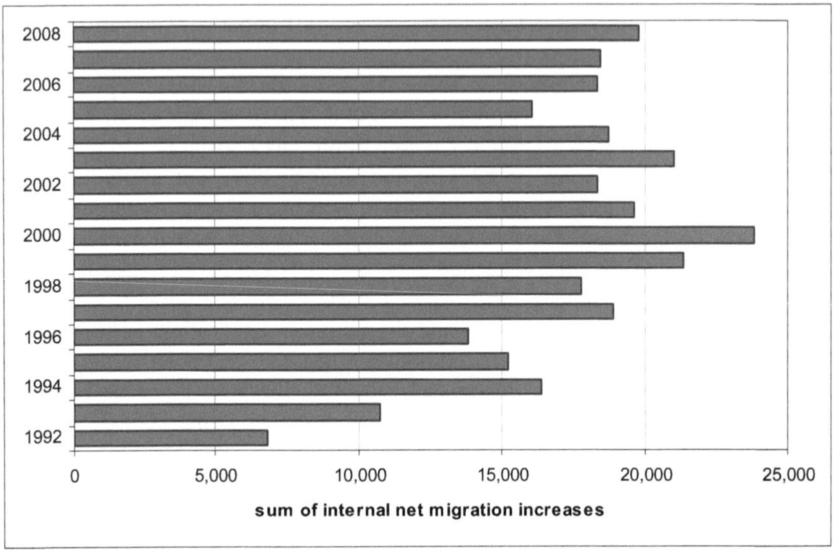

Source: Own calculations.

Notes: Internal net migration for 2007 and 2008 based on provisional data.

Source of data: *HCSO*, Regional Statistical Yearbook of Hungary, and database economy on website of HCSO.

These facts taken together can be seen as an indication for a higher degree of industry agglomeration in these regions. Section 3.5.2 will look at whether somewhat higher wage levels prevailed there.

The data for the 12 regions with negative balances of internal net migration are shown in **Table 13**. The highest loss of migrants was registered in Budapest, -125,000 or less than half of the total of these 12 regions. The number was less, however, than the inflow of positive internal net migration in the neighbouring region Pest (which had +248,000),[84] such that an urban sprawl belt phenomenon, which is typically going on around European capitals due to problems of congestion and high real estate prices, was - where it may have occurred - at least limited in extent here.

84 It is acknowledged that these data do not allow drawing direct conclusions on the destination of the internal migrants.

Table 13: Nuts-3 regions with a negative internal net migration balance from 1992 to 2008, number of persons

Region	Cumulative balance 1992 to 2008 (number of persons)	As% of region's population in 2005*	As% of total of negative internal net migration
Budapest	-125,538	7.4%	43.8%
Veszprém	-2.519	0.7%	0.9%
Zala	-1,808	0,6%	0.6%
Baranya	-2,903	0.7%	1.0%
Somogy	-4.814	1.5%	1.7%
Tolna	-8.685	3.6%	3.0%
Borsod-Abaúj-Zemplén	-53,216	7.3%	18.6%
Nógrád	-6,212	2.9%	2.2%
Hajdú-Bihar	-13.284	2.4%	4.6%
Jász-Nagykun-Szolnok	-16,397	4.0%	5.7%
Szabolcs-Szatmár-Bereg	-34.677	6.0%	12.1%
Békés	-16,708	4.3%	5.8%

Source: Own calculations.
Notes: 2005 was the most recent figure for population per region available at the time of writing, HCSO Website, 8.5.2009; migration figures for 2007 and 2008 based on provisional data.
Source of data: *HCSO*, Regional Statistical Yearbook of Hungary, subsequent years, Budapest, and HCSO database on website.

The second largest negative balance of internal net migration was registered in Borsod-Abaúj-Zemplén, a region of Northern Hungary, with -53,000 persons or 18.6% of the total. In third place was Szabolcs-Szatmár-Bereg, the Eastern-most region bordering Ukraine and the region with the second lowest per capita income in Hungary, with -35,000 or 12.1% of the total.

3.5.2 Internal net migration and manufacturing wages

In NEG theory, internal net migration between regions is linked to the development of real wages in the manufacturing sector. NEG theories state that workers migrate from regions with lower real wages to regions with higher real wages, causing an intensification of industrial agglomeration, as in *Krugman (1991a)* and *Ludema & Wooton (1997)*. In their theoretical overview of factors causing migration, *Fischer & Straubhaar (1994)* point out that differences in wage levels have a strong positive influence on the migration decision taken by individuals.[85] In this section, data on manufacturing wages per region shall be analysed in context with internal net migration in Hungary.

Figure 14: Monthly gross wages in manufacturing per region as % of national average for 2005 and 1992

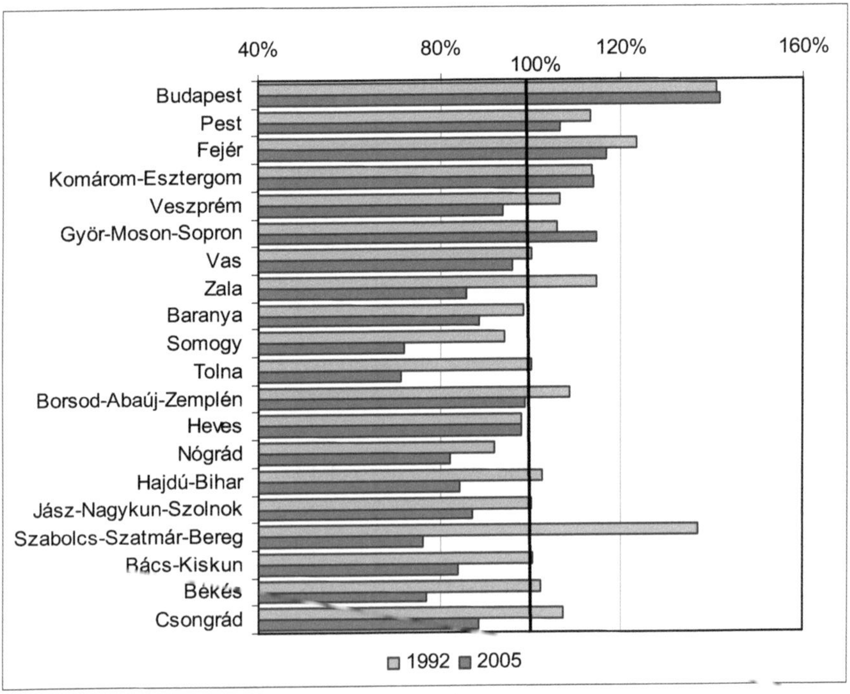

Source: Own calculations; own graphical illustration.
Source of data: *HCSO,* Regional Statistical Yearbook of Hungary, Budapest.

85 *Fischer & Straubhaar (1994),* p. 100.

In an analysis of real earnings during the 1990s, the *HCSO (2005)* stated that real income per inhabitant reached its level before 1989 by the year 2000. In fact, real income decline from year to year by an average of -5% between 1990 and 1996, in the worst year, 1995, even by -12%, in comparison to 1989. Real income started to recover from 1997 onwards. From 2000 until 2003, real earnings rose by 7%, 14% and 9%, in 2004 they declined slightly by half a percentage point.[86] The severe decline in real earnings points at the constraints in overall living standards which the Hungarian population had to endure during the transition to a market economy and during increasing integration with the EU aiming at full membership from 2004 onwards. As this research analyses industry agglomeration and regional developments, the following analysis points out regional differences in manufacturing wages for 2005 and 1992 in comparison.

The graph in Figure 14 shows the wage level for the manufacturing industry for the 20 regions in 2005 and 1992.[87] For the year 2005, apart from Budapest with the highest wage level, regions with above average wages in manufacturing were Pest, Fejér, Komárom-Esztergom, and Györ-Moson-Sopron. These 4 regions also had positive balances of internal net migration during the period 1992 to 2005 (see Table 12). Comparing wage levels in 2005 with those in 1992, the 5 regions with above-average wages in 2005 had an increase over the period, while 13 other regions suffered a decline in relative wages over the period. The most dramatic decline in manufacturing wages was registered in Szabolcs-Szatmár-Bereg, the Eastern-most region. This region also registered the third strongest negative migration balance over the period (Table 13) and had the second lowest per-capita income nationally. The data of Figure 14 seem to confirm that higher wage levels acted as a pull-factor in Hungary, attracting migrants to these regions or agglomeration centres, and lower or declining wage levels were an incentive for individuals to rather leave these regions. Figure 15 analyses the relationship of the two in more detail.

The bar diagrams in **Figure 15** and **Figure 16** show the net change in gross manufacturing wages per region and the balance of internal net migration wages over the period 1992 to 2005.[88] Figure 15 shows 10 Hungarian regions for which

---

86 HCSO (2005): Change of course - Hungary 1990 - 2004, pp. 64-65.

87 A disadvantage is that the data of Figure 14 is that they abstract from the sectoral composition, regional specialization and industry-specific characteristics, i.e. not taking into account that some sectors like the manufacturing of chemicals and chemical products tend to be rather high-wage while other sectors like textile and clothing tend to be rather low wage.

88 More in detail, the bar diagrams of Figure 15 and Figure 16 show net migration per region (persons) which was summed up over the period 1992 to 2005, then expressed as % of a region's population in 2005 (in %), on the one hand; and the change in monthly gross

Figure 15: Cumulative changes in internal net migration and gross manufacturing wages for 1992 to 2005 (%), 10 regions with both values exceeding 1 %

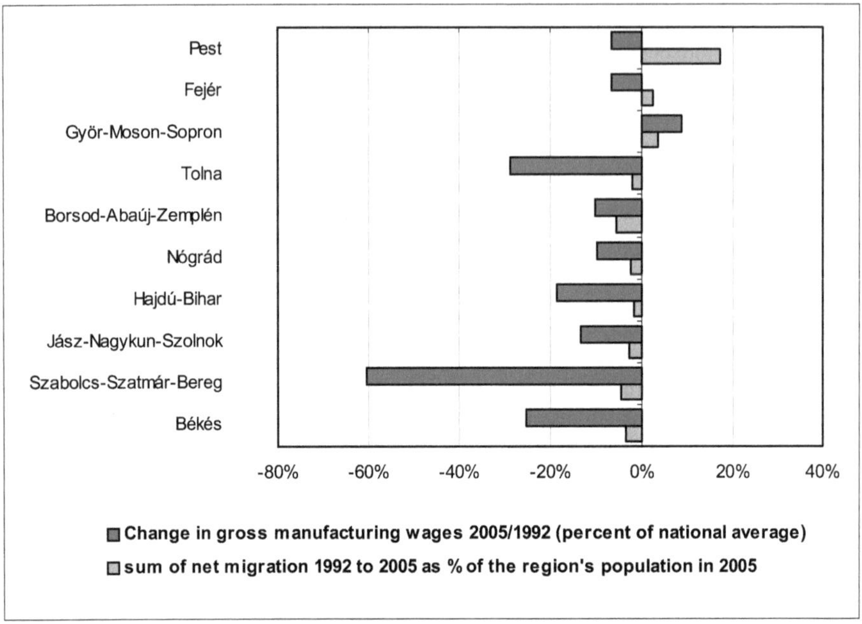

Source: Own calculations; own graphical illustration.
Source of data: *HCSO,* Regional Statistical Yearbook of Hungary, Budapest.

both values exceed 1%, while Figure 16 shows the remaining 10 regions for which either value or both are smaller 1%. For the first group of regions in Figure 15, the two bars for the wage development and internal net migration point in the same direction for all regions except for just two. For the second group of regions in Figure 16, the bars for internal net migration and the development of gross wages point in the same direction for 5 regions. Of those where this is not the case, for one region even both values are smaller than 1%. Taken together, the two are correlated for 13 out of 20 values.

This is striking evidence for a positive correlation between the two factors, the manufacturing wage level and internal net migration, although this analysis does not indicate the direction of causation, i.e. falling wage levels and living standards

wages per region, (in HUF) as % of national average, for the year 2005 and the year 1992 (in %).

Figure 16: Cumulative changes in internal net migration and gross manufacturing wages for 1992 to 2005 (%); remaining 10 regions where either value is less than 1%

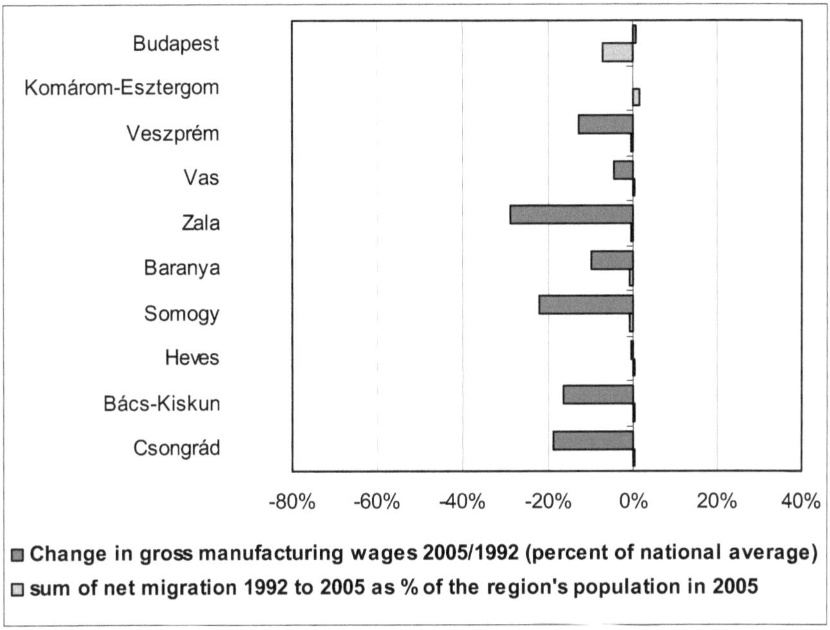

Source: Own calculations; own graphical illustration.
Source of data: *HCSO,* Regional Statistical Yearbook of Hungary, subsequent years, Budapest.

are entailing negative net migration. It also confirms the theories of NEG at the basis of this research, namely by *Krugman (1991a, Ludema & Wooton (1997), Krugman & Venables (1995) and Livas-Elizondo & Krugman (1996).* This is also more or less in line with empirical findings of *Cseres-Gergely (2003)* for the 1990s only based on mobility and migration on a settlements - not inter-regional - level. He found that the flow of people followed wage and unemployment differences during 1990 to 1999. He also pointed out that mobility in Hungary was among the least frequent in Europe, while migration was more comparable to that of other European countries.

3.5.3 Internal net migration and the housing market

With respect to living conditions, the section will also look at the housing market which can act either as an incentive for improving living conditions or as a restraint to attracting migrants where housing is scarce. Housing privatisation in

Hungary started already in the late 1980s, even prior to the fall of the Berlin Wall. Hungarians were first introduced to the concept of private ownership by the housing privatisation scheme. Under this scheme, 622,000 tenement dwellings were sold by the year 2004. The share of tenement dwellings owned by local governments diminished below 5% of the total dwelling stock by the end of 2004 *(HCSO 2005)*.[89] The regional development of the housing market was quite differentiated, however.

Figure 17: Internal net migration and change in dwelling stock, Nuts-3 regions, 1992 to 2005

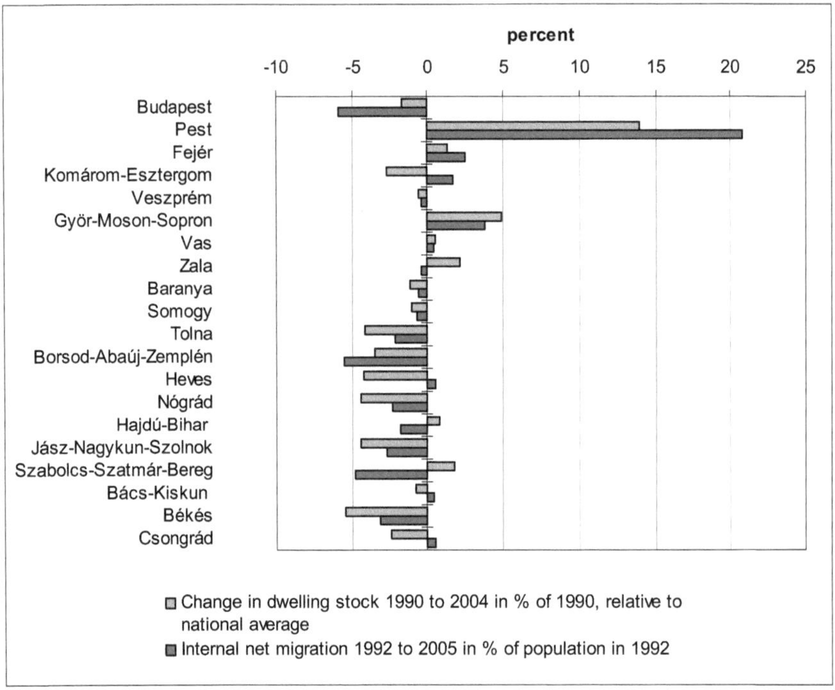

Source: Own calculations; own illustration.

Notes: the data for dwelling stock were not available for 1992 to 2005, so the closest date which was 1990 was chosen.

Source of data: *HCSO*, Regional Statistical Yearbook, Budapest.

The analysis in **Figure 17** shows the development of internal net migration in the 20 Hungarian regions and of the regional housing market in context. The first bar for each region shows the change of the dwelling stock from 1990 to 2004 in %,

89 *HCSO (2005)*: Change of course – Hungary 1990 – 2004, pp. 6-7.

relative to the national average. This gives an indication as to whether living conditions in the region developed better or worse than the national standard.[90] The second bar shows the internal net migration in % of the population in 1992 for the period 1992 to 2005.[91] Calculations for net migration have also been tried in % of the population in 2005. As the differences with the shown values are only marginal, it has been decided to stick with the start year of the period for consistency with the dwelling stock.

The graph in **Figure 17** shows that for the majority of regions (13 out of 20), internal net migration and the net change in dwelling stock developed in the same direction. Among these regions, for 9 regions the development of the dwelling stock was better than the development of net internal migration. This seems to indicate that better housing conditions acted as an incentive for or did at least not hinder internal net migration. For 4 regions, the development of the housing stock lagged behind internal net migration. The latter can be seen best for Pest, the region with the strongest positive internal net migration. Pest region also fell back by 12 positions in the national ranking of regions with respect to per capita income during the period 1995 to 2005.

This analysis of the regional housing market in context with internal net migration in Hungary seems to confirm the aspect of the NEG theories that workers migrate between regions in order to improve their living conditions with respect to housing. Stronger positive net migration than housing improvement also seem to indicate that the situation on the housing market did not act as a constraint on internal net migration in Hungary during the period 1990 to 2005.

3.6 The sectors of the manufacturing industry

This section analyses developments in the different manufacturing sectors in Hungary during the period 1992 to 2008 with a view to getting useful indications with respect to the hypotheses. As other CEECs, Hungary also suffered a severe decline in industry output at the start of the transformation period to a market economy. In 1992, the level of industrial output (IPAR[92]) was equal to merely two

90 For example, the stock of dwellings in Pest improved by 21.21% over 1990; this was better by 13.93% than the national improvement of 7.28%.

91 The periods differ slightly due to the limited availability of data.

92 The Hungarian IPAR (industry) comprises industry sectors C+D+E, C=Mining and Quarrying, D=Manufacturing, E=Electricity, gas and water supply. IPAR is used in this research where no data for manufacturing alone are available. It is a good approximation, however, as the manufacturing sector amounts to over 80% of Industry output or value added.

thirds of the output of 1989. It took almost 10 years for the level of output to reach and exceed that of 1989, which happened in 1998. In 2004, it was 65% higher than 15 years before. Value added of industry rose more moderately, by 35% in 2004 compared to 1989.

Figure 18: Sectors' shares in total manufacturing output, percent, 1992 to 2008, based on the value of production in million HUF

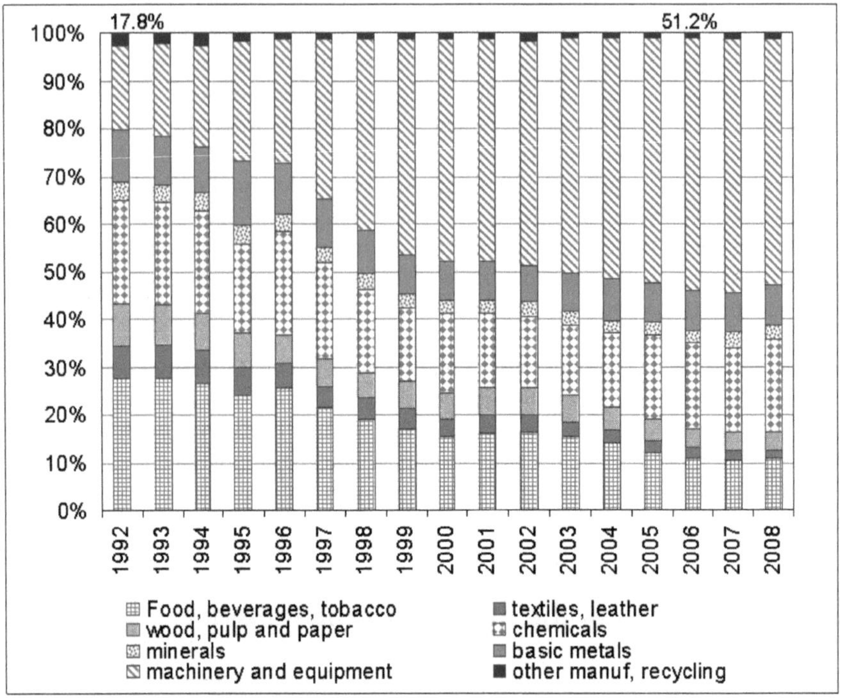

Source: Own graphical illustration.
Source of Data: *HCSO,* Statistical Yearbook of Hungary, subsequent years, Budapest.

The bar diagram in **Figure 18** shows the sectoral composition of manufacturing output in percent of each year's total output for the period 1992 to 2008. The largest increase was achieved by the machinery and equipment sector, from 17.8% in 1992 to 51.5% in 2008. The share of food, beverages and tobacco declined from 27.4% to 10.8% over the period. The textiles, leather and clothing sector also realised a decline from 7.2% in 1992 to 1.7% in 2008. The shares of the other sectors remained more or less unchanged. The above figures exhibit a strong specialization pattern in Hungary at the aggregate level which emerged over the period.

Figure 19: Export ratio (to world) as % of sales per manufacturing sector in 2004, based on figures in million HUF.

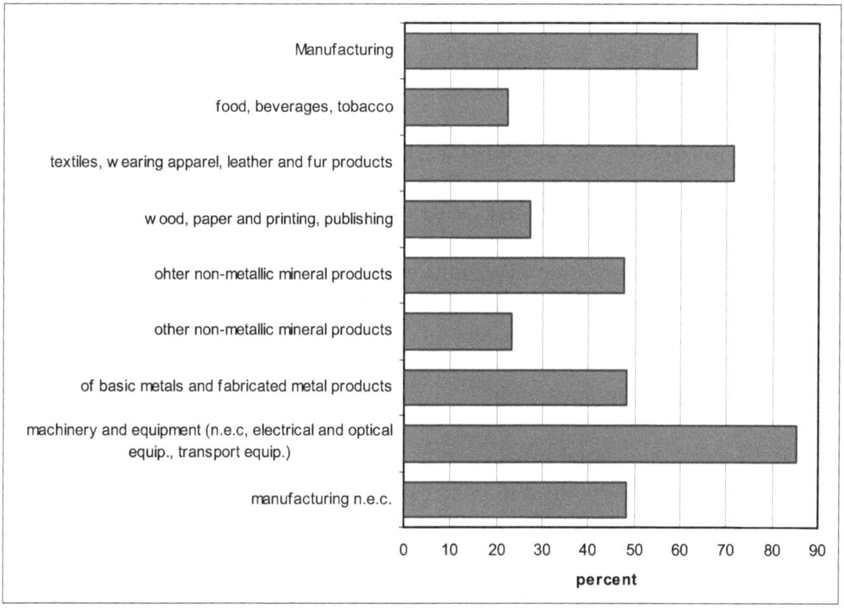

Source: Own graphical illustration.
Source of data: *HCSO,* Statistical Yearbook of Hungary, subsequent years, Budapest.

The bar diagram in **Figure 19** shows the degree of export orientation of each manufacturing sector based on the share of exports (to world) in sales for the year 2004. The export ratio for manufacturing as a whole was 63.3% in that year. This is confirmation for Hungary as a country being a "small open economy", i.e. a country with a relatively small domestic market due to its population (10 million in Hungary) and a large dependence on export markets, manifested in a large share of sales or production being exported.[93]

The machinery and equipment sector achieved the highest export ratio among the sectors with 85.4%. Textiles and clothing was also above average with 71.3%. The lowest export orientation prevailed in the food, beverages and tobacco sector where only 22.3% of sales were destined for export.

93 The contrary example, i.e. not a "small open economy", would be the U.S.A. with its population of about 296 million, which exports only about 10% of its production internationally.

The extraordinarily high export ratio of the machinery and equipment sector points to the fact that production of this sector is internationally competitive. The rising share in manufacturing resulting from Figure 18 shows the rising importance for the manufacturing industry in Hungary. The two facts taken together will be kept in mind for further analysis of manufacturing agglomerations in Hungary in the sense of the hypotheses.

3.6.1 Regional set-up of manufacturing in Hungary

This section analyses the regional set-up of manufacturing in Hungary. The aim is to find indications for larger manufacturing industry agglomerations in the regions. Further, the location of regions with a higher proportion of industry shall be determined which could have influenced their regional development in turn. This touches on the second aspect of the research question of this research, namely industry agglomerations and regional development in Hungary seen in context with European integration.

Table 14 shows industrial production as a share of total industrial production in Hungary in the first column, and industry output per inhabitant as a percentage of national average in the second column.[94] Budapest and the Western regions Pest, Fejér, Komárom-Esztergom as well as Györ-Moson-Sopron each contribute a share of around 10% to national industry output, followed by Borsod-Abaúj-Zemplén in Northern Hungary with 6.4%. Industrial production per inhabitant was highest in Komárom-Esztergom with almost 4-fold the national average. Four other Western regions, namely Fejér, Györ-Moson-Sopron, Féjer, Zala and Vas, were also well above the national average with between 210% to 141% respectively. These data indicate the importance of industry for these regions. It could also mean that industrial production in these regions is particularly efficient, perhaps due to above average presence of foreign direct investment (see section 3.8). Finally, the high per-capita production in industry is a hint towards the specialization of these regions in this field, a topic which shall be analysed further in chapter 5.

94 Industry based on the Hungarian IPAR = C+D+E, where C is Mining and quarrying, D is manufacturing, and E is electricity, gas and water supply; Data only for manufacturing production per region are not published. For Hungary as a whole, D has the lion share in IPAR with around 80% of output.

Table 14: Production of industry per region in 2004, based on million HUF

Region	Industrial Production (IPAR)* in 2004 % of national total	Industrial production per inhabitant 2004 % of national average (=100)
Budapest	15.5%	92.2%
Pest	8.8%	78.3%
Fejér	8.9%	210.7%
Komárom-Esztergom	12.2%	388.9%
Veszprém	3.0%	81.5%
Győr-Moson-Sopron	10.2%	233.4%
Vas	3.7%	141.6%
Zala	4.6%	155.5%
Baranya	1.7%	42.0%
Somogy	3.0%	91.5%
Tolna	1.3%	54.7%
Borsod-Abaúj-Zemplén	6.4%	87.7%
Heves	2.7%	85.0%
Nógrád	1.1%	51.3%
Hajdú-Bihar	3.3%	60.9%
Jász-Nagykun-Szolnok	3.4%	84.1%
Szabolcs-Szatmár-Bereg	2.8%	48.2%
Bács-Kiskun	3.1%	57.5%
Békés	1.9%	48.9%
Csongrád	2.4%	57.4%

* IPAR = C+D+E, where C is Mining and quarrying, D is manufacturing, and E is electricity, gas and water supply.

Source of data: *HCSO (2005),* Regional Statistical Yearbook of Hungary 2004, Budapest.

Table 15: Development of manufacturing employment per Nuts-3 region, 1992 to 2008

Region	% of national manufacturing employment 1992	% of national manufacturing employment 2008	change 2008/ 1992 in percentage points
Budapest	20.9%	19.9%	-1.0
Pest	6.9%	9.8%	+2.9
Fejér	4.7%	7.0%	+2.6
Komárom-Esztergom	3.3%	7.3%	+4.0
Veszprém	4.0%	3.8%	-0.2
Györ-Moson-Sopron	5.3%	6.8%	+1.5
Vas	3.7%	4.3%	+0.6
Zala	3.6%	2.1%	-1.5
Baranya	3.3%	2.6%	-0.7
Somogy	2.3%	3.2%	+0.9
Tolna	2.2%	1.7%	-0.5
Borsod-Abaúj-Zemplén	8.1%	5.3%	-2.8
Heves	2.9%	2.9%	0
Nógrád	2.4%	1.6%	-0.8
Hajdú-Bihar	4.8%	3.9%	-0.9
Jász-Nagykun-Szolnok	4.2%	3.9%	-0.3
Szabolcs-Szatmár-Bereg	4.0%	3.3%	-0.7
Bács-Kiskun	5.0%	5.0%	0
Békés	4.1%	2.5%	-1.6
Csongrád	4.4%	3.0%	-1.4

Source: Own calculations.
Source of data: *HCSO*, Regional Statistical Yearbook of Hungary, and HCSO database on website.

Overall manufacturing employment in Hungary declined from 857,000 in 1992 to 648,000 in the year 2008, or by -24.2% over the period. **Table 15** shows manufacturing employment per region as a share of national manufacturing employment for the years 1992 and 2008. The last column shows the change in 2008 over 1992. The greatest decline was suffered by Budapest, followed by Borsod-Abaúj-Zemplén, a Northern region with heavy industry. The regions of the Great Plain area also suffered a decline in their manufacturing employment shares. A rise in manufacturing employment share was strongest in Komárom-Esztergom, followed by Pest, Fejér and Györ-Moson-Sopron.

These figures provide indications as to certain developments in the manufacturing sector in Hungary during the observation period 1992 to 2008. In particular, they hint at agglomeration tendencies towards the Western part of the country, and a relative decline of manufacturing in the Eastern part and the North of Hungary. Looking at individual Nuts-3 regions, however, the relative importance of a region as a location for industry has changed only moderately in the national context over the period. These results will be kept in mind as a first reply contrib.-uting to analyse the hypotheses, namely of actual manufacturing agglomerations in Hungary in the pre- and post-accession period.

3.7 Foreign trade developments

This section analyses Hungary's foreign trade with thc EU in order to find indications for factors which could have had a direct influence on manufacturing industry agglomerations and regional development in Hungary in the research period. For the purpose of this study, foreign trade data published by Eurostat are not suitable.[95] Foremost, the EU data for exports from Hungary into the EU-15 do not include the goods from the so-called customs-free zones, which are an important economic factor for Hungary. A majority of enterprises with FDI and export orientation are located in such customs-free zones. The exports from these made up over 40 % of of exports from Hungary to the EU in 1999. Therefore, these exports should not be ignored (see section 3.2.3). For these reasons, I have decided to base my analysis for this section and for the later analysis in Chapter 6 on the Hungarian foreign trade data.

Historically, the geographic distribution of Hungary's exports - especially those to the EU countries - underwent significant changes *(Hantke 1995[96])*. Main

95 On the Eurostat Website, data for the EU-15 (SITC nomenclature) with the CEEC group as a whole are published since 1989, thus not for Hungary bilaterally with EU-15; date of Website consultation 08.10.2008.

96 *Hantke (1995)*, p. 69.

influences were certainly the overall political conditions as well as the trade regimes prevailing, notable the Council of Mutual Economic Assistance (CMEA) and its internationally planned division of labour, as well as economic conditions after the break-down of communism and of the former Soviet Union in 1989.

Figure 20: Share of Hungary's exports and imports to the EU in total exports and imports, 1993 to 2008, based on figures in Euro

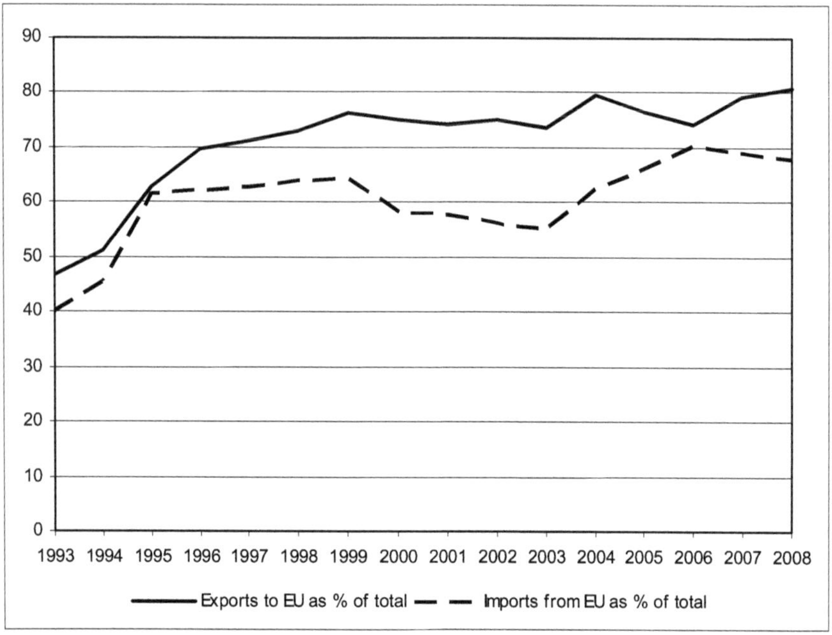

Notes: Based on data of imports and exports at current prices in Euro; exports and imports with the EU: data declared by Hungarian importers at cif basis, exports on fob basis; trade according to the combined customs nomenclature.

Sources of data: European Commission (1998, 2003): Monitoring reports on Hungary; *HCSO*: Statistical Yearbook of External Trade (2004, 2005); more recent years: HCSO website, database economy.

After the break-down of the CMEA, three effects prevailed: (1) a terms of trade effect; (ii) a market loss effect; and (iii) a removal of exchange rate subsidies effect[97]. The share of exports directed to the EC was 49.7% in 1938, and 10.3% to European CMEA countries (including the former Soviet Union). In 1978, the respective shares were 27.8% to the EC and 45.9% to the European CMEA countries (30.5 percentage points to the former Soviet Union). In 1988, just before

97 Trade effects according to *Rodrik (1992)*.

the breaking-down of the Iron Curtain, the EC had a share of 22.6% and the CMEA of 39.3%, while in 1992, the EC had risen to a share of 49.8%, whereas the former CMEA had declined to a mere 19.3% *(Gács 1993)*. Trade liberalisation with the EU under the Europe agreement - whose trade provisions entered into force in February 1992 - has certainly contributed to the speed of redirection of Hungary's external trade flows towards the EU.

It should be kept in mind that the trade provisions of the Europe agreement covered about 80% of Hungary's prior trade with the EU countries, according to the *European Commission (2006a)*. **Figure 20** shows the rapid increase in the share of exports to the EU in total Hungarian exports from 46.5% in 1993 to over 80% in 2008. The development in imports was similar, from a share of 40.1% in 1993 to 68.0% in 2008.

Figure 21: Composition of Hungary's manufacturing exports to the EU-27, in % for 2008, based on data in HUF

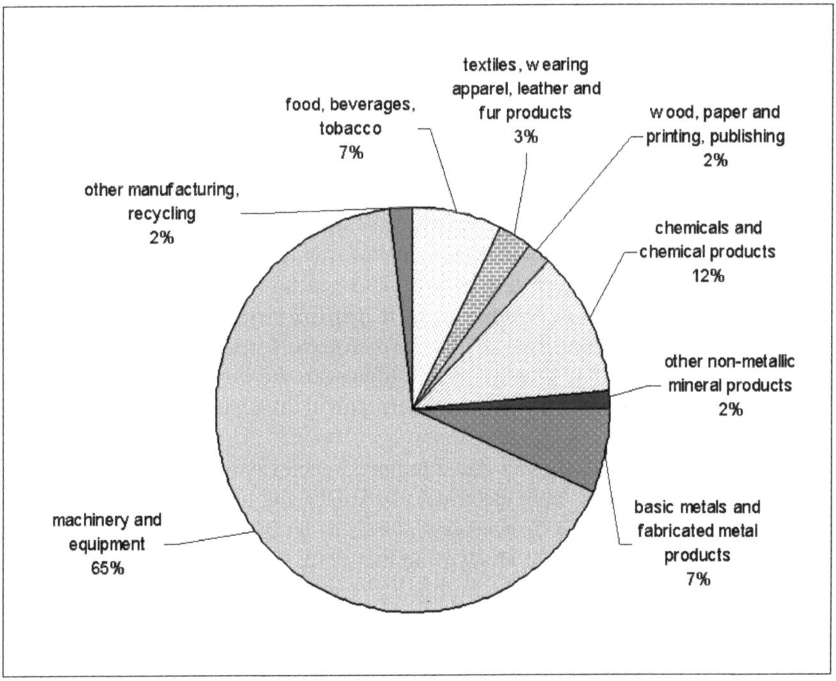

Source: Own conversion from SITC into the Hungarian TEÁOR industry classification which is generally used in this research.
Source of data: *HCSO,* database economy on website, 27th of April 2009.

Figure 21 shows the composition of Hungary's exports to the EU for the year 2008 in terms of the 8 manufacturing sectors which are the focus of this study. The overwhelming majority, 65%, was contributed by the machinery and equipment sector (machinery, electrical and optical equipment, transport equipment, machinery n.e.c.). The second largest sector in terms of export share were chemicals and chemical products with 12%, followed by basic metals with 7% and food, beverages and tobacco with 7%. This is quite different from the times prior to the Europe agreement. In 1988, food and agricultural products had a share of 28.5% in Hungary's exports to the EU and of 23.8% still in 1990, while textiles and clothing made up for 15.8% in 1988 and 15.5% in 1990 respectively *(Hantke 1995*[98]*)*. Therefore, as the data show, a profound transformation of the export oriented production structures of the Hungarian economy has taken place in these two decades, namely from rather basic towards higher valued and more sophisticated products.

Looking at this in perspective, the share of Hungarian exports of manufactured goods, machinery and transport equipment made up 74.6% of total exports to EU countries in 1992, rising up to 87.4% in 2008 (EU-27). The equivalent share of manufactured goods imports from the EU remained more or less at the same level over the period, with 87.7% both in 1992 and 2008.

Figure 22 shows the development of Hungary's manufacturing exports per sector to the EU (in million HUF). In order to correct for inflationary effects of the base currency, the exports were converted to constant prices of 1992 by means of the producer price index.[99] In these terms, overall manufacturing exports to the EU had increased 5.5-fold over the period. The machinery and equipment sector contributed most to this development, as it had the largest share in every single year since 1994. The contribution of the other sectors remained more or less the same over the period. The graphic clearly illustrates the fast pace of integration of the goods markets in Hungary into the international division of labour in Europe.

The expansion of the machinery and equipment sector could be explained by two reasons: on the one hand, light electrical machinery and household equipment was identified by the *European Commission (1994)* as an area of potential growth due to a comparative advantage of Hungary in this field. On the other hand, this sector was liberalised early on under the Europe agreement's trade provision, opening up

98 *Hantke (1995)*, p. 71.

99 The export statistic of the HCSO is published at current prices; it was corrected by a producer price index for each sector in prices of 1992. I constructed this index based on the HCSO producer price index per sector, which is published annually as an index with previous year =100. To give an example, the producer price index for manufacturing as a whole had increased from 1992=100 to a value of 352.7 in 2008.

the access to the EU market for these products. A slightly later analysis of revealed comparative advantage (RCA) by *Baldone & Sdogati (1997)* found that Hungary showed a traditional RCA in relatively advanced sectors such as chemicals, machinery and mechanical appliances, iron and steel products, and motor vehicles.[100]

Figure 22: Hungary's exports to the EU 1992 - 2008 (million HUF), 8 manufacturing sectors in constant producer prices of 1992

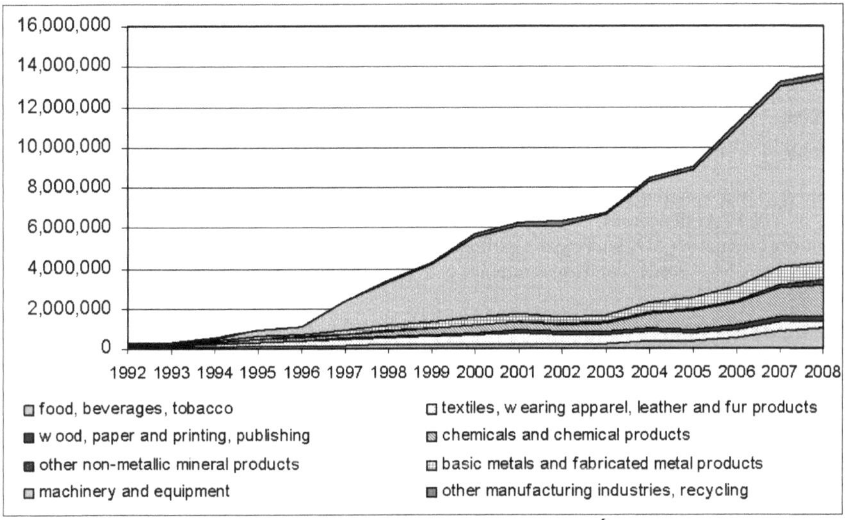

Source: Own calculations; own conversion from SITC to the 8 TEÁOR sectors.
Source of data: *HCSO,* Statistical Yearbook of External Trade; subsequent years, and Statistical Yearbook of Industry and Construction (for the producer price index), subsequent years.

These figures underline the importance of the trade liberalisation under the Europe agreement which encompassed almost exclusively these sectors, notably leaving out unprocessed agricultural goods of which Hungary was a potential supplier to the EU market. This also justifies the focus of my analysis on trade of the manufacturing goods. Further, the extent to which regional development was influenced by the change in agglomeration of the manufacturing industry in Hungary will be analysed in context with economic integration with the EU from 1992 to 2008.

100 Own calculations for RCA based on the formula by Balassa (1985) were not feasible with the data base used in this study; and the procurement of data from other sources just for this purpose was judged too expensive in comparison to the expected result, as the present analysis already speak a clear language with respect to Hungary's strength in international trade.

Table 16: Trade coverage ratios per manufacturing sector for Hungary's trade with the EU 1992 to 2008, selected years.

	food, bevel-rages, tobacco	textiles, wearing apparel, leather and fur products	wood, paper and print-ing, publi-shing	chemi-cals and chemical products	other non-metallic mineral products	basic metals and fabri-cated metal products	machi-nery and equip-ment	other manu-facturing industries, recycling
1992	5.2	1.7	1.1	0.8	1.5	0.9	0.7	N/A
1999	3.4	1.2	0.8	0.5	0.6	0.8	1.2	0.4
2004	1.2	1.0	0.6	0.6	0.5	0.6	1.3	0.5
2008	1.3	0.8	0.7	0.8	1.2	0.6	1.5	0.6

Source: Own calculations of trade coverage ratios, and own conversion from SITC to the 8 TEÁOR sectors.

Sources of data: *HCSO*, Statistical Yearbook of External Trade, 1992, 1999, 2004; data for 2008: *HCSO* website, database economy.

Hungary's imports from the EU in general grew less and not as consistently as exports to the EU did. Especially imports in the machinery and equipment sector declined between 2001 and 2004 in absolute terms and continued to increase only thereafter. Instead of showing the detailed development for Hungary's imports from the EU, the concept of "trade coverage" will be used here. For a given sector, the trade coverage index shows the ratio of Hungary's exports to the EU over Hungary's imports from the EU. This gives an indication about Hungary's relative strength in certain exports. It is also a notion for intra-industry trade between the two. The concept cannot give a picture, however, of whether Hungary perhaps imported relatively more in the sector from other parts of the world (as would be the case for textiles in recent years, for example). In fact, at the start of the period in 1992, Hungary imported 38.6% of chemical products from the former Soviet Union countries and another 19.7% from other CMEA countries, while the imports of this product from the EC amounted to only 16.1% *(Hantke 1995)*. The data presented in Table 16 should be interpreted in this light.

Table 16 shows the development of trade coverage ratios for the 8 manufacturing sectors.[101] In the food, beverages and tobacco sector, the initially high ratio of 5.2 still shows the previous orientation of Hungary; the ratio declined to 1.0 as a result of the Europe agreement and the price competitiveness effects. For the more traditional textiles sector, there was also a decline from 1.7 in 1992 to 0.9 in 2005,

101 Trade coverage ratio is the ratio of exports (X) to imports (M) of the sector, $TCR_i = X_i / M_i$. The concept is applied here to Hungary's trade with the European Union only.

as for the wood, paper and printing sector from 1.1 in 1992 to 0.6 in 2005, and for mineral products from 1.5 to 0.6. A marked increase could be noted for the machinery and equipment sector from 0.7 in 1992 and to 1.4 in 2008.

This analysis confirms Hungary's comparative advantage in the machinery and equipment sector. Moreover, it stresses the importance for Hungarian exports overall as for the development of the manufacturing sector and the linked employment and agglomeration effects in the national and regional context.

3.8 Foreign direct investment in Hungary

The final section of this chapter analyses foreign direct investment (FDI) in the manufacturing industry in Hungary during the research period. This is done with the following question in mind: Could the development of FDI have contributed to increase agglomeration of certain sectors? Or could FDI have enhanced the development of certain Hungarian regions over others?

The total stock of FDI in manufacturing amounted to 4,850 billion HUF in Hungary in the year 2008. The pie diagram in **Figure 23** shows how this stock of FDI was distributed over the 8 manufacturing sectors. More than half was invested in the machinery and equipment industry, followed by chemicals and chemical products with 21% of the total. Third place ranged the food, beverages and tobacco sector with a 10% share. The share of manufacturing FDI invested in the machinery and equipment industry corresponds almost exactly to the share of this sector in total manufacturing output in Hungary, 51% for FDI and 51.5% for output respectively (see Figure 18).

Privatisation has influenced FDI inflows in the CEECs to a large extent.[102] Hungary pursued a policy of early privatisation via the capital market. This attracted comparatively large FDI inflows into all sectors, which proved to be an advantage for the competitiveness of Hungarian industry, as compared to other countries such as Romania and Bulgaria which opted for a voucher privatisation scheme.

During the privatisation period 1990 - 2004, the Hungarian privatisation and state holding company received HUF 1.9 trillion (at current prices).[103] The greatest

---

102 *Kalotay & Hunya (2000)* have analysed the relation between FDI inflows and privatisation policies in CEECs to this effect.

103 The so-called Act on Pre-Privatisation, adopted in 1990, was the start phase encompassing the sale of shops of state-owned enterprises providing commercial, catering and other

Figure 23: FDI stock in manufacturing industry in Hungary 2008, shares of the 8 sectors (billion HUF)

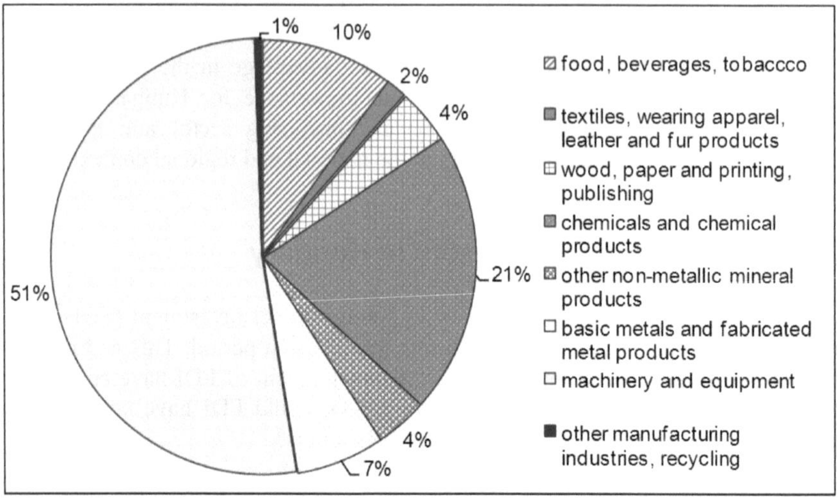

Source of data: *HCSO* website, database economy.

sum, one quarter of the receipts, was deposited in 1995 as the counter-value of a determined proportion of state-owned shares of strategic companies; the second largest sum was deposited in 1997. The sum deposited by foreigners (FDI) during these 15 years exceeded HUF 1.2 trillion. In a table indicating the origin of FDI for the period 1990 to 2004, the share of Germany is the largest single country share with 23.4%, second place ranges the USA with 13.3%, followed by the EU member states France and Austria. The total of EU member states came to a share as large as 49%.[104]

In an international comparison, the stock of inward FDI as a percentage of GDP reached 39.9% in Hungary in 1999. This was higher than in the Czech Republic with 33.0% and Poland with 17.2%. In the countries of the EU, Ireland stood out with the exceptionally high rate of 50.7%. The share of FDI in gross fixed capital formation was around 20% on average in Hungary over the period 1992 to 1999 *(Csengodi et al. 2003).*

---

consumer services. The purchase was targeted exclusively to resident private persons. This scheme was completed in 1994. In the remaining fields of the national economy, the transformation of state-owned enterprises into private economically operating firms started in 1990.

104 HCSO (2005): Change of course – Hungary 1990 – 2004, pp. 6-7. In that table on the foreign revenues in the Hungarian privatisation, the shares of individual countries add up to 66.6%, the remainder of 33.4% is shown to be the international placement of shares.

Table 17: FDI stock in the Hungarian manufacturing industry (in million Euro), selected years

Year	Manufacturing FDI (million Euro)	Index, 1992 =100
1992	2,135	100
2000	4,046	189
2004	17,118	802
2008	21,117*	989

Notes: * provisional data.
Source: Own conversion from HUF into Euro.
Sources of data: HCSO Statistical Yearbook of Hungary and Website Database Economy, Budapest; for annual average exchange rates HUF-EUR: HCSO for 1992-1998, ECB-Website for 1999-2008.

Table 17 shows the development of the FDI stock in the Hungarian manufacturing industry for selected years from 1992 to 2008 (in million Euro).[105] Hungary had been able to attract a stock of FDI of over 21 billion Euro over the period. Compared to 1992, the stock of FDI increased more than 9-fold by the year 2008.

The bar diagram in **Figure 24** shows the FDI intensities for the Hungarian manufacturing industry as a whole and for the 8 sectors in the year 2005.[106] The manufacturing industry had an average FDI intensity of 32%. FDI intensities of individual sectors varied. They were lowest for the textiles sector with 22% and for other manufacturing industries and recycling with 15%, and highest for other non-metallic mineral products with 46%. For the machinery and equipment sector, the FDI intensity was equal to the average of the manufacturing sector. A comparison with the FDI intensities calculated for the year 1992 resulted in the following: The average FDI intensity was 11% for manufacturing industry in 1992, i.e. much lower than the 32% average for the year 2005.

105 The FDI data were originally published in HUF. They have been converted into Euro, as they originated to about half from countries of the European Union. This was also done in order to filter out the inflationary effects of the HUF. Finally, the conversion to Euro makes sense as machines and equipment for new production sites in Hungary were probably purchased abroad to a large extent.

106 FDI intensity was calculated as the ratio of the FDI Stock of the sector (in million HUF) over output of the sector (in million HUF).

Figure 24: FDI intensities in the manufacturing industry sectors in Hungary in % for the year 2005, based on FDI and output in million HUF

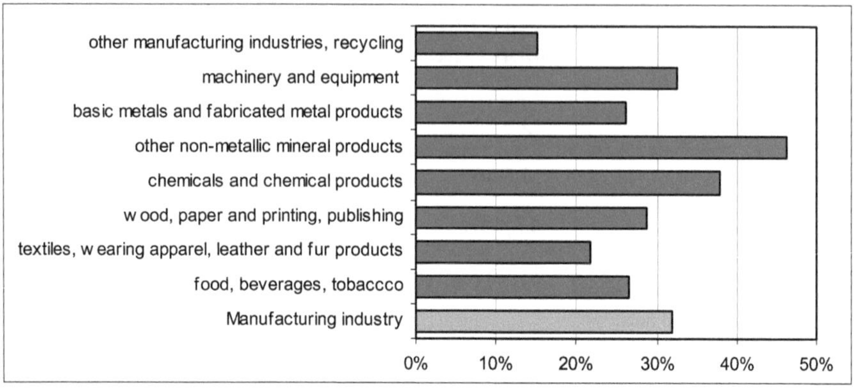

Source: Own calculations.
Source of data: *HCSO*, Statistical Yearbook of Hungary, Budapest.

An interesting question is whether higher FDI intensities in certain sectors promoted stronger agglomeration of these industries than in other sectors. This shall be analysed further with a view to the hypothesis in the regression analysis of Chapter 6.

The final analysis of this section focuses on the spread of FDI over the country. This is based on data for the share of FDI in enterprises with FDI per region (in billion HUF).[107] **Table 18** shows the results for two groups of regions, those in the Western part and those in the Eastern part of Hungary (division according to *László Faragó (1999)*. While FDI for Hungary as a whole has increased over the period, the relative shares of the Western and Eastern part of the country have changed only slightly. The 13 Western regions accounted for 91.3% of the total in 1992 and 87.3% of the total in 2008, while the 7 Eastern regions had only 8.7% in 1992 and 12.7% in 2008. Thus, the industrial parks policy of the Széchenyi plan seems to have yielded certain positive effects in this respect.

The facts regarding the high FDI stock can be taken as a hint at the extent to which the Europe agreement induced foreign direct investors from EU member states to locate in Hungary. The still unequal distribution of FDI over the country seems to be one of the factors which could have contributed to the strong economic development shed between a prospering Western part and a declining

107 This statistic is not available just for the manufacturing sector and per region.

Table 18: FDI stock in Western versus Eastern regions 1992 to 2008 (based on billion HUF), selected years

Year	Share of 13 Western regions in total	Share of 7 Eastern regions in total
1992	91.3%	8.7%
1999	88.3%	11.7%
2004	91.1%	8.9%
2008	87.3%	12.7%

Source: Own calculations.
Notes: Division in Western and Eastern part according to *László Faragó (1999)*.
Source of data: *HCSO,* Regional Statistical Yearbook of Hungary, subsequent years, Budapest.

Eastern part. The strong overall increase of the level of FDI in the Hungarian manufacturing industry can be taken as a strong indication for the proceeding degree of integration of Hungary's economy with that of the EU.

3.9 First conclusions with respect to the hypotheses

This chapter has analysed the economic situation in Hungary by means of descriptive empirical analysis with respect to regional development and the condition of the manufacturing industry during the period 1992 to 2008. Integration variables relevant for the development in the pre- and post-accession period, such as external trade and foreign direct investment, have been analysed at the country and regional level.[108] First influences have been identified with respect to the hypothesis regarding industry agglomeration and regional development over the almost two decades.

About one fifth of the total population of Hungary of around 10 million is concentrated in the capital Budapest, while the rest is spread over the 19 remaining Nuts-3 regions. The economic weight of Central Hungary in terms of its share in the national GDP is even higher than the concentration of population.[109] This was a first indication towards increased agglomeration in a central location. The spread in GDP-per-capita among the 20 Hungarian regions is great, ranging between 50% of the national average for Nógrád and 213% for Budapest in 2005.

108 Exports per region were available and have been presented in Figure 11.
109 46% share in GDP in 2005, whereas the population share was 28.3% in that year (see Figure 6 and Table 8).

GDP-per-capita increased for most Western regions from 1995 to 2005, while that of the regions of Northern Hungary and the Great Plain decreased to levels well below the national average.[110] Hungary had the highest level of regional disparities at the Nuts-3 level among the large CEECs[111] relative to the EU average; they increased from 31.4% to 40.0% over the period 1995 to 2005. This pointed to profound restructuring processes at the regional level.

Regional activity rates as well as unemployment rates tend to reflect regional differences in welfare. High unemployment coupled with low activity rates prevailed in the Eastern-most region and in Northern Hungary, lower unemployment and higher activity rates in Central Hungary and the Western regions in 2005.[112] More enterprises were concentrated in central locations and in the Western part of Hungary than in the Eastern part. Regions with a higher employment in industry tended to have a larger output of industry per inhabitant. The Western regions had a higher export share in industry production than the other regions. These data point to a specialization of Western regions in industry and increased agglomeration of export-oriented sectors in this part of the country. They also confirm a certain pull-factor of the EU market, attracting the location of industry agglomerations in the Western part of the country closest to the EU market.

The analysis of internal net migration among the 20 regions showed that 8 mostly Western and Central regions had a positive balance over the period 1992 to 2008 while the 12 other regions registered negative migration flows. The years of the strongest internal migration were 1999 and 2000, which is interesting when put in relation with industry agglomeration and regional specialization trends.[113] The regions which attracted positive migration flows also registered higher and rising wage levels in the manufacturing sector over the period 1992 to 2008.[114] The analysis of the regional housing market seemed to confirm the idea that people migrated between regions not only to earn higher wages, but also to improve their living conditions. Overall, the agglomeration pull-factor seemed to have been exerted by the Western regions and Pest in Central Hungary.

In the analysis of the manufacturing industry, the rising importance of the machinery and equipment sector in terms of output, employment and export orientation

---

110 See Figure 8 and Figure 9.

111 No data were available for Poland at the Nuts-3 level.

112 See Figure 10 and Table 11.

113 These years were a turning or peak point in the development of agglomeration and of regional specialization, as the results of Chapters 4 and 5 will show.

114 See sections 3.5.1, 3.5.2 and 3.5.3.

stood out.[115] The very high export ratio of the sector of 85% indicates international competitiveness. It also points to an enhanced role that the machinery and equipment sector may have played during increasing integration of Hungary with the EU. This seems to confirm that the focus of this research on manufacturing is a well-chosen basis for analysing developments in the pre- and post-accession period. The regional data on the development of manufacturing employment and output point to an increased concentration of this industry in certain Western regions, relatively little importance in the Great Plain, and a declining role in the regions of Northern Hungary. The results give another hint towards centres of regional agglomeration of manufacturing activities in the direction of the hypotheses.

The analysis of Hungary's foreign trade showed the rising importance of the EU as an export market, with the share in total exports rising from 46% in 1993 to 80% in 2008, and a similar development on the import side. The Europe agreement - whose trade liberalisation benefited about 80% of Hungary's prior trade with the EU countries - certainly contributed to this development. Among manufacturing exports to the EU, which rose 5.5-fold measured in constant prices of 1992,[116] the outstanding sector also was machinery and equipment, with a share of 65% in 2008. This sector also showed a high degree of intra-industry trade. The analysis confirmed Hungary's comparative advantage in the machinery and equipment, electrical appliances and transport equipment sector. It further stressed the importance to locate employment and agglomeration effects in the national and regional context.

The final analysis of the stock of foreign direct investment (FDI) in Hungary showed a 9-fold increase in manufacturing FDI during the period 1992 to 2008. The sector with the largest FDI stock was the machinery and equipment sector, followed by the chemicals and chemical products. The FDI intensity was 32% for the manufacturing industry as a whole. The regional distribution of the FDI stock was very uneven, with the Western part of the country holding 87.3% and the Eastern part a mere 12.7%. This seems to point to agglomeration trends and towards an enhanced influence of FDI on regional development in the Western part of Hungary.

In the next chapter, the development of agglomeration in the Hungarian manufacturing industry shall be analysed in detail with the help of empirical tools. This shall be based on the series of HCSO data of the 8 manufacturing sectors on the Nuts-3 regional level for the period 1992 to 2008.

---

115 See sections 3.6 and 3.6.1.

116 The producer price index with base year 1992. See footnote 99 for the methodology.

4. Manufacturing Industry Concentration in Hungary 1992 to 2008

This research analyses various questions regarding industry agglomeration. Which development did agglomeration in the manufacturing sectors in Hungary undergo during increasing integration with the EU, first under the Europe agreement and then in the post-accession phase: Did integration reinforce industry agglomeration in the manufacturing sector? Did agglomeration decrease? Were there perhaps phases of both? Was there a turning point, and if so, when was it reached?

Chapter 4 shall approach this part of the research topic by presenting results of empirical calculations. The data shall be treated in a way such that information shall be provided about the actual development of agglomeration in Hungary during the period 1992 to 2008. The results will be commented and put into context of the predictions made by NEG theories (chapter 2.1.2), by previous empirical studies, and, where applicable, by the descriptive empirical analysis of chapter 3.

4.1 Measuring industry agglomeration

Before embarking into the analytic part, the issue of concentration versus specialization shall be set out here clearly.

Concentration looks at the industry, a sector of manufacturing, at the degree of its agglomeration or dispersion in space.
Specialization looks at the region, at the structure of sectoral employment, whether only a few sectors are dominant, or whether a region is highly diversified.

While industry concentration is analysed in this chapter, the topic of regional specialization is reserved for the following Chapter 5.

With respect to concentration, this research looks at the research questions whether manufacturing industry concentration in Hungary has increased or declined in the course of European integration, or whether there were both trends and at which stages of the integration process. It also verifies whether there may have been a turning point in the development up to which there was an increase and after which there was a decline. Such a development would correspond to the predictions made by the selected NEG models (*Puga 1999, Ludema & Wooton*

1997, *Livas-Elizondo & Krugman 1996)*. The analysis shall also find out whether such a peak point was already reached prior to full EU-membership of Hungary.

Here again, the speciality of my research is that it is based on regional sectoral manufacturing employment data as a basis for calculating industry concentration for the country of Hungary, and not at sectoral country-wide data for a group of countries such as the EU-15 or a set of CEECs, as most previous empirical studies in the field.

The subject of industry agglomeration can best be measured using the tool of concentration indices. The unique contribution of this research is that it applies six different concentration measures to the same set of data, thus allowing for a comparison of them. The period under study is 1992 to 2008, which is the longest available and with reliable data at the time of writing using the Hungarian regional sectoral employment data series of the HCSO.

4.2 Overview of indices

Table 19 gives an overview of the six concentration measures used in this research. They were all calculated based on Hungarian regional employment data by manufacturing sectors. The detailed formula of each index will be given in the

Table 19 Concentration measures used for measuring agglomeration.

1)	**Krugman concentration index:** a relative measure of concentration of the industry in space;
2)	**CR3:** an absolute measure (usually used in competition policy); shows the concentration accounted for by the three largest regions in each sector's country-wide employment;
3)	**Herfindahl index:** measures absolute concentration of the sector; also referred to as HHI (Herfindahl-Hirschman index);
4)	**relative Herfindahl index** (modified form)**:** measures relative concentration of the sector compared to the benchmark of manufacturing employment;
5)	**Hoover-Balassa index:** measures the relative concentration of a specific industry in a region with respect to the average concentration in the country, Hungary;
6)	**Entropy:** measures the degree of dispersion of an industry in space as an absolute number (thus the inverse concept of concentration).

Source: Own selection and formulation.

respective subsections. Some of these indices are absolute measures of concentration, some are relative measures, i.e. in relation to some other benchmark value.

All of these indices were applied to employment data by manufacturing sector and for the 20 Hungarian regions. The idea to calculate values for these indices also based on output, production or value added data was not feasible due to the lack of such data at the regional level; they are not available from HCSO.

Some of the 6 indices were used in previous studies of agglomeration, some of them rather rarely though. These 6 are not the only existing concentration indices, however. Two other indices could not be applied here due to the unfitting set-up of the data. These are the Ellison-Glaeser index *(Ellison & Glaeser 1997* and *1999)* the calculation of which would require firm-level data; such were not publicly available for Hungary. Another index not applicable here is the so-called spatial separation index *(Midelfart-Knarvik et al. 2000)*; calculations for that index would require regional output data by subsector which are not available for Hungary either; from its conceptual definition, that index cannot be transformed to using employment data, so that this possibility had to be ruled out. Another recent paper by *Giacinto & Pagnini (2008)* proposed two modified indices measuring industry agglomeration in Italy. These include properties of the economic environment such as regional adjacency. As they also require plant level data, they are not feasible for my research.

The remainder of this chapter is structured as follows: first, industry agglomeration is analyzed by means of the 6 different concentration indices or measures. Each section first presents the index, then the results obtained by its calculation; where applicable, they are put into relation with the results of other empirical studies. A comparative section analyses all 6 concentration indices based on their results for the data set. The final section of this Chapter draws first conclusions with respect to industry concentration in Hungary under the Europe agreement.

4.3 The Krugman concentration index

As first index, the Krugman concentration index shall be presented here. As *Krugman* is one of the founding fathers of the theories of the New Economy Geography regarding the development of industry agglomeration in space *(Krugman 1991a)*, this index is presented first. The Krugman concentration index is a relative measure of the degree of an industry's agglomeration or dispersion in space. In this form, it was derived from the index proposed by *Krugman (1991b)*. The index shall be applied here to the 8 manufacturing subsectors and 20 Nuts-3 regions in Hungary based on HCSO employment data, i.e. regional employment by manufacturing subsector for the 20 Hungarian regions for the years 1992 to 2008.

4.3.1 Formula of the Krugman concentration index

The formula of the index is as follows:[117]

$$K_i = \sum_{j=1}^{N} \left(s_{ij} - x_{ij}\right)$$

K_i is the numerical value of the Krugman concentration index for industry sector i. In the term on the right hand side, s_{ij} is the share of industry i's employees working in region j and x_{ij} is the share of total manufacturing employment in region j; the Krugman index for industry i takes the absolute value of this term and sums it over all regions j=1 to N (N=20) to give the value of the index.

A specific industry i is considered to be concentrated, if a large part of production is carried out in a small number of regions. The higher is the value of the index, the larger is the degree of concentration of the industry.

4.3.2 Results of the Krugman concentration index

In this section, the results of the calculations of the Krugman concentration index for the 20 Hungarian Nuts-3 regions for the years 1993-2008 shall be presented.[118]

Figure 25 shows the values of the Krugman index for the four manufacturing sectors food, beverages, tobacco, chemicals and chemical products, other non-metallic mineral products, and basic metals and fabricated metal products. At the first glace, the results show strong differences between the degree of concentration of the industries in this sample. While the mineral products industry had values of 0.7416 at the start of the period, the food, beverages and tobacco industry industry showed much lower concentration levels of around 0.2940 only.

---

117 Formula according to *Traistaru et al. (2002)*. They applied this index to a (private) database collected under a Phare ACE project, on five Central and East European countries on manufacturing industry and total employment for the years 1990-1999 (even though the initial years 1990, 1991 and to some extent 1992 can be regarded as distorted by the end of communist regimes data collection). In my research, it will be targeted more precisely on manufacturing employment.

118 The data for 1992 were also calculated, but were left out here for clarity, as they seemed to be still under some influences from the strong restructuring recession.

Figure 25: Krugman concentration index for industry agglomeration based on manufacturing employment data per region, 1993-2008, 4 sectors

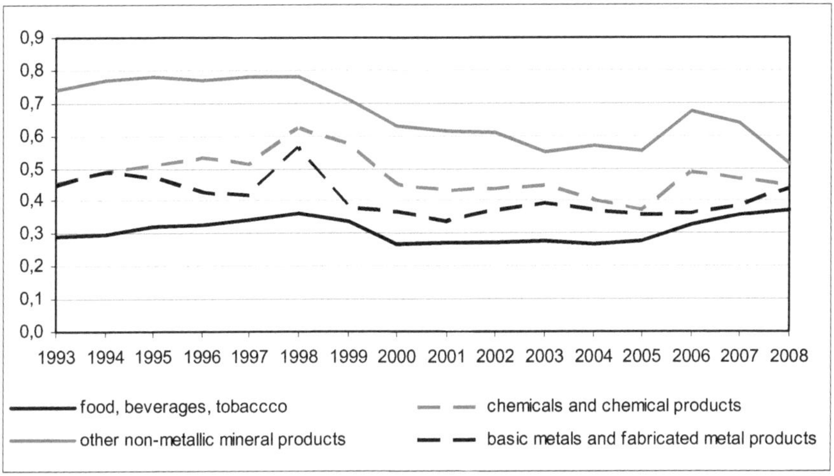

Source: Own calculations; own illustration.
Source of data: *HCSO,* Regional Statistical Yearbook of Hungary, subsequent years, Budapest.

The larger concentration of the former can be attributed to the fact that natural resources rich in minerals are located in only a small number of regions of the country as a location factor, whereas the food, beverages and tobacco industry has a broader resource base which is also easier transportable.

As to the development over the period, the graph shows a clear rise in overall industry concentration levels from 1993 up to a peak in the year 1999; from then onwards, concentration levels were falling; by the year 2004, the date of EU membership of Hungary, they were generally below the start level. For the remainder of the period up to 2008, they were rising again, for mineral products and chemicals a decline set in towards the end of the period.

Figure 26 illustrates industry concentration for the remaining 4 manufacturing industries for the same period, 1993-2008[119]. At the first glace, the results show noticeable differences between the degree of concentration of the industries in the second sample. The highest concentration at the start was found in the wood, paper and printing, and publishing industry, 0.5290. This is due to the resources

119 See footnote 121.

Figure 26: Krugman concentration index based on manufacturing employment data per region, 1993-2008, remaining 4 sectors

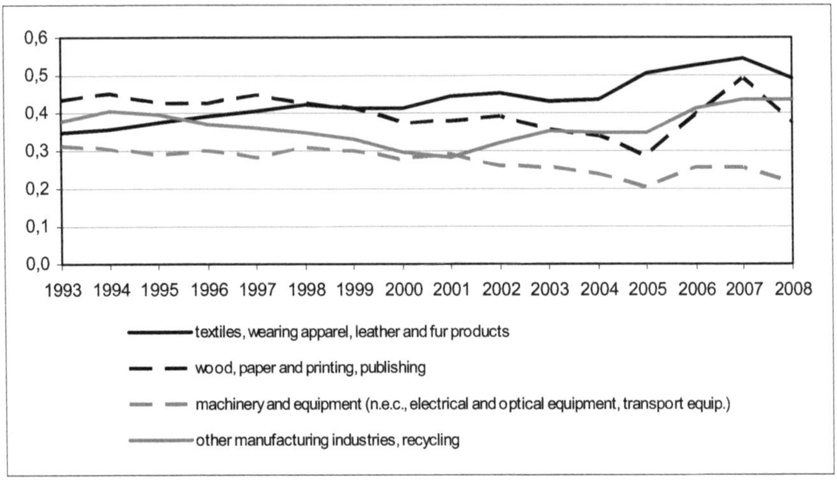

Source: Own calculations; own illustration.
Source of data: *HCSO,* Regional Statistical Yearbook of Hungary, subsequent years, Budapest.

for wood and paper manufacturing and to the concentration of the publishing activity in the Budapest agglomeration. The lowest concentration was found in the machinery and equipment sector at the start and at the end, with a decline over the period, namely 0.3117 in 1993 and 0.2176 in 2008.

As to the development, interestingly, these four industries all show a pronounced hub after 2004, i.e. since the EU membership of Hungary, with the decline setting in from 2007 onwards. The prior period, up to 2004, shows a rather shallow development for these four industries. The only clear line is the textiles industry with a rising concentration up to 2007.

4.3.3 Comparison of the empirical results with NEG

The model by *Livas-Elizondo & Krugman (1996)* for regional integration modelled in the context of international trade described that an (irreversible) agglomeration would form within the country consisting of more than one region. The model by *Puga (1999)* predicted an Ω-shaped relationship between agglomeration and trade costs with proceeding integration. The model by *Ludema & Wooton (1997)* predicted (less than complete) agglomeration to form at some intermediate level of trade costs, followed by dispersion as trade costs decline even further in the course of proceeding integration.

The empirical results based on calculations of the Krugman concentration index for the Hungarian manufacturing industry in the period 1992 to 2008 show the following: for a majority of manufacturing industries, concentration has generally increased up to a point around 1999; afterwards, decreasing concentration set in to lower levels than at the start. The highest value for concentration, i.e. the degree of agglomeration, was reached in 1999, thus prior to EU accession of Hungary. Since 2004 a second rise but to lesser levels than in 1999 set in, which was followed by a new decline by 2007.

With regards to the hypothesis, the empirical results provide an overall confirmation in the sense that agglomeration in the manufacturing industry in Hungary under the Europe agreements, i.e. up to 2004, first increased, before dispersion set in to lower degrees of agglomeration than at the start of the period. The highest concentration was indeed reached prior to EU membership of Hungary, namely in 1999.

It would be interesting to find out whether there were other influences at work than the mere decline in trade costs, especially which might have triggered the turning point in 1999. Trade costs – as important as they may have been – are one factor among various factors which influence an industry's concentration in space. The Hungarian privatisation regime underwent different phases throughout the period, new sectors and enterprises were opened up to foreign investors gradually, larger scale enterprises which were formerly state owned were put for sale in specific years, and there was also a tendency towards more green field investments rather than the take-over of existing plants or companies in the latter part of the period *(Csengodi et al. 2003)*. These developments could have contributed to the reaching of the turning point and the reversal of the concentration trend in 1999.

Moreover, there was a phase of privatisation and recapitalisation of the national banking system as part of the transition to a market economy, a policy which was also supported by the PHARE programme. Further, the availability of a more stable banking system all over the country rather than only in Budapest and other economic centres around towns could also have been a precondition enabling the spreading out of economic activity from 1999 onwards. Furthermore, the internal policy of the Széchenyi plan with its industrial parks scheme spread out on purpose in the Eastern and Western part of the country and in new sites could have contributed to the turning of the tendency of concentration (see chapter 3, section 3.2.4).

Finally, an external factor in 1999 which took place in Hungary's main export market, the EU, was that 1999 was the start year of the Euro in the majority of EU member states, which were Hungary's main trading partner already at that point. As the Euro brought with it more stability and better planning for foreign investors, these could have been incited to locate their investments more spread out over the country. Indeed, the following year 2000 saw the largest single FDI inflow over the almost two decades analysed in this study. Whether FDI had a significant influence on manufacturing industry concentration and on regional specialization will be analysed by econometric analysis in Chapter 6. To sum up, apart from falling trade costs and the predictions of the NEG models regarding a turning point of industry concentration during proceeding integration, various other factors were also potentially influencing the development of manufacturing concentration in Hungary around the turn of the millennium.

4.3.4 Comparison of concentration ranks

In this subsection, the values of the Krugman concentration index for the 8 industries shall be ranked according to their degree of agglomeration and be compared. **Table 20** compares ranks for the start and end years 1993 and 2008 respectively.

Table 20: Ranks of manufacturing industry concentration in Hungary, 1993 and 2008 in comparison; Krugman concentration index based on employment data

Manufacturing industry	Rank in 1993	Rank in 2008
food, beverages, tobacco	8	6
textiles, wearing apparel, leather and fur products	6	2
wood, paper and printing, publishing	4	7
chemicals and chemical products	2	3
other non-metallic mineral products	1	1
basic metals and fabricated metal products	3	4
machinery and equipment (n.e.c., electrical and optical equipment, transport equip.)	7	8
other manufacturing industries, recycling	5	5

Source: Own calculations; own presentation.
Source of data: *HCSO,* Regional Statistical Yearbook of Hungary, subsequent years, Budapest.

As **Table 20** with the comparison of concentration levels in 1993 and 2008 demonstrates, the highest concentration level prevailed in the mineral products industry. This high absolute concentration level of the industry is due to the natural resources in minerals being found in only a few regions over the country, and due to the difficulty to transport them, creating a strong reason for firms of the industry to locate near them. The chemicals industry was still highly agglomerated in 2008, ranking third instead of second. This industry is one in which economies of scale in production play an important role, according to the *OECD (1994)*. Industries with low concentration were machinery and equipment, as well as food, beverages and tobacco, with ranks 8 and 6 respectively. The most marked change in concentration ranks was undergone by the textiles industry, from rank 6 to second rank, a sign for the ongoing consolidationof that industry.

Figure 27: Employment in the textiles sector in Hungary, number of employees, 1993-2008

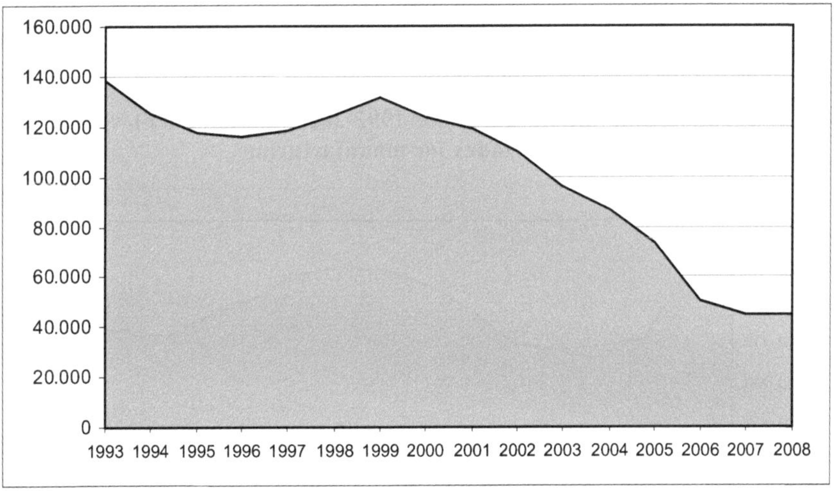

Source: Own illustration.
Source of data: *HCSO,* Statistical Yearbook of Hungary, subsequent years, Budapest.

For the various manufacturing sectors, very different conditions prevailed and played a role in shaping the developments of the industry and the degree of concentration. In the following, a closer look at the Hungarian textiles industry shall be taken, one of the specialities of Hungary during the CMEA division of production, which also played a specific role during the early phases of integration with the EU under the Europe agreement. The industry was in strong decline during the period 1992 to 2008 - as in most European countries in the 1990s and around the turn of the millennium - due to increased competition in a context of global trade liberalisation, producers in the Far Eastern countries, mainly India, Bangladesh, and China took increasing shares of the market. Thus, globalisation had its effects on the textiles industry in Hungary, too.

Figure 27 shows the development of employment in the textiles industry in Hungary from 1993 to 2008. The number of employees in the textiles sector in Hungary declined from 138,140 at the start of the period to 44,565 in 2008, thus only 32% of the start level. Looking at the graph, however, it can be seen that there was an initial slight decline until about the year 1995, then a rise to a peak in 1999, and the steep decline followed only after this 1999 peak. Thus, there must have been some other influence apart from globalisation and sticky firm restructuring explaining this shape.

While employment was in decline, the output of the textiles, wearing apparel, leather and fur products sector - corrected by the producer price index for manufacturing[120], remained more or less at the 1993 level until 2003, when the decline in output to 91,500 million HUF in 2008 set in. For the output development in the textiles industry, please see **Figure 28**.

Figure 28: Output in the textiles sector 1992-2008 (million HUF), corrected by producer price index for manufacturing

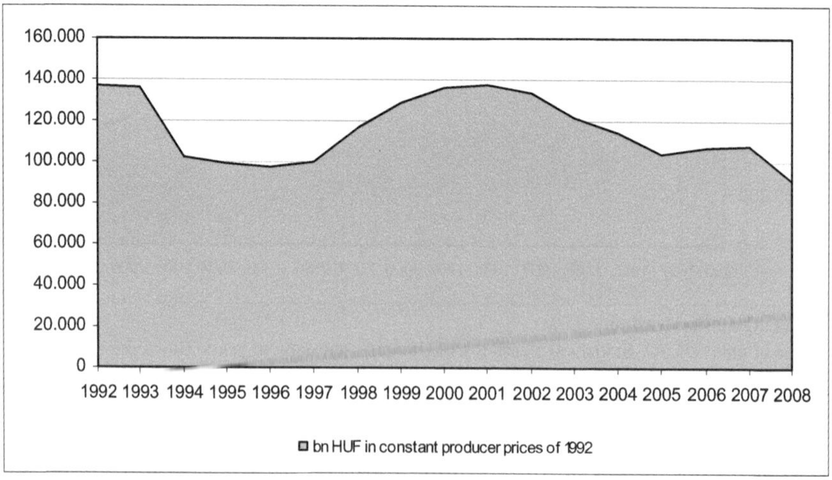

Source: Own calculations; own illustration.
Source of data: *HCSO,* Budapest.

120 As that index is published by HCSO with previous year =100, it was converted here to an index holding the prices of 1992 constant and =100.

Given that the number of employees in the sector declined to 32% of the 1992 workforce by 2008, these figures point to an increase in productivity per employee. Measured in HUF and using the output figures corrected by the producer price index, this increase was from 990,100 HUF per employee in 1993 to 2,0522,400 HUF per employee in 2008, i.e. more than the double.[121]

How can the hub in output of the sector around the years 2000 to 2003 and the preceding increase in employees of the sector in the years 1997 to 2000 be explained? Were there any special phenomena going on which could explain this development? *Sdogati et al. (2002)*[122] analysed the competitiveness of the textiles industry in two founding EU member states, Germany and Italy, in relation to eight CEECs, including Hungary, using customs data provided by textile and apparel firms for the years 1988 to 1997. Those data allowed for a distinction between final versus temporary imports and exports. That analysis revealed that German and Italian firms responded to the global cost pressure due to the competition from Far Eastern producers in the mid-1990s by means of outward processing trade (OPT) to the CEECs. That strategy enabled them to benefit from the lower labour costs in CEECs, yet selling the final product under the high-quality, high-prestige labels "made in Italy" or "made in Germany", as the majority of value added was still generated in those countries.

This international division of labour was made possible through provisions specially included in the Europe agreements with CEECs making the arrangements ruling over OPT even more favourable. The authors concluded by estimating the cost savings realized by German firms through OPT with CEECs in the order of 50% and for Italy in the order of 40% to 50% in the period analyzed.

As relative and real production costs in Hungary and other CEECs increased over the years though, especially in the late 1990s and early 2000s, Hungary and other CEECs gradually lost their cost advantage. The firms in the EU-15 responded by delocating their outward processing trade to Far Eastern production sites instead. This could explain the observed hub in employment in the Hungarian textiles industry in the late 1990s and the hub-shaped increase in output around the year 2000 as well as the steep drop in output from 2003 onwards, which only happened in the textiles sector and was not observed in any of the other 7 manufacturing sectors examined in this research.

---

121 Output corrected by the producer price index with base year 1992; see footnote 102 for the methodology.

122 Chapter 5 in *Sdogati et al. (2002)* entitled "Moving to Central-Eastern Europe: International Fragmentation of Production and Competitiveness of the European Textile and Apparel Industry".

4.3.5 Comparison of the results with previous studies and for other countries

Coming back to the results of my calculations of the Krugman concentration index based on employment for the 8 Hungarian manufacturing industries, this section shall put them into context with previous empirical research.

There is study on economic geography in five CEECs edited by *Traistaru et al. (2003)* which analysed several aspects of the general economic set-up in those countries for the years 1990 to 1999. Yet data for the first years of this period have certainly been under a distorting influence from thc communist era and from the severe restructuring recession. For Hungary, *Mafioli (2003)* calculated a concentration measure called the dissimilarity index for industry. The results obtained there have to be treated with caution, however, as they refer to total employment, whereas my study is to a great extent more focussed by using as a benchmark manufacturing employment only. Additionally, the categories of the industries have been agglomerated to fit the scheme of the overall five country study, leaving a certain element of error. Finally, the results are shown giving merely two digits after the decimal, which is not as accurate in the analysis of changes of agglomeration, as often there is no visible change this way from one year to the next. Thus, that study is only vaguely and in part comparable with the results of my calculations.

As a trial, the numerical values presented by *Mafioli (2003)* - based on total employment - and the results of my calculations - based on manufacturing employment - have been plotted in graphs together by industry.[123] The picture was such that the lines for the concentration found by *Mafioli* were generally above those obtained in my calculations; and further, they showed a different direction of development of concentration. Most importantly, they end at the point where my calculations become most interesting, i.e. with the year 1999, which is a great disadvantage of that study to my mind, as that peak became a turning point prior to the EU accession of Hungary.

In a comparative summary of five CEECs, *Traistaru et al. (2003)* showed average concentration for manufacturing as a whole (not individual industries) for 1990 to 1999, based on the data and method just described for *Mafioli (2003)*. In comparison with other countries, Hungary had a relatively low overall concentration in manufacturing, which kept rising until about 1997, then falling in 1999, the last year of that study, below the start level. Higher average concentration was observed in Bulgaria, Slovenia (a country with 2 million inhabitants and thus too

123 As this would methodologically not be accurate, it is not shown here.

small to conduct such a study in my view), and the highest in Romania. To give a range of values to put that into perspective, the average manufacturing concentration for Hungary was shown in the range of 0.45 to 0.48, falling to 0.43 in 1999; the average for Romania was in the range of 0.61 to 0.66, falling to 0.64 in 1999. Those results have to be taken with caution, as was explained before.

4.4 Concentration rate CR_3

After these first results on the actual development of industry agglomeration in Hungary as measured by the values provided by the Krugman concentration index, it is interesting to see which results the other measures will provide. In this section, the measure CR_3 shall be introduced. CR_3 stands for the market concentration share made up by the 3 largest entities. CR_3 is a concept used primarily in competition policy by the competition authorities to determine market power held by firms. It is applied here to the market share of an industry country wide contributed by regions instead of firms.

4.4.1 Formula of the CR_3 measure

The employment share of the 3 largest regions in total Hungary-wide employment of an industry sector i is denoted as follows:

$$CR_{3i} = \sum_{j=1}^{3} s_{ij}$$

where the index i refers to the manufacturing industry sector (8 manufacturing sectors), j to regions (20 Nuts-3 regions). The values of the three regions contrib.-uting the largest share of country-wide employment of the industry are summed up to give the value of CR_3 for industry i.[124]

This concentration index is perhaps the most intuitive measure of industry agglomeration. To interpret the values of this measure using an example from competition policy, $CR_3 = 0.60$ would mean that the sum of the market shares of the three largest firms is 60% of the total market. A disadvantage of the measure is that the relative market share of the 3 largest entities is not taken into consideration; i.e. a $CR_3 = 0.60$ could have been made up either of 3 entities with a

124 Formula according to *Aiginger & Pfaffermayr (2004)*; they apply this to 99 NACE 3-digit industries and 14 EU-countries, for 3 years 1985, 1992, 1998, in context of analyzing Single Market effects.

share of 0.20 each, or of one large entity with a share of 0.50 and two small ones with a share of 0.05.[125]

4.4.2 Results of the concentration rate CR_3 for Hungary

The results of the calculation of CR_3 for industry concentration are shown in Table 21 for the 20 regions in Hungary based on the HCSO employment data. Firstly, the results of CR_3 calculations in **Table 21** allow an identification of industries with an overall high, medium and low concentration. A comparatively high concentration, with a market share of over 40 to more than 50% in three regions, is prevailing in the chemicals, basic metals and the wood, paper and printing industries. Medium level concentration, below 40 to more than 30%, characterises the mineral products, machinery and equipment and other manufacturing sectors. Low concentration levels, with less than 30% market share, are found in the food, beverages and tobacco as well as the textiles sectors.

As for the development of industry concentration, the last column of Table 21 shows the overall trend prevailing over the entire period, 2008 compared to the start year 1992. Concentration had risen in 4 sectors, declined in 3 sectors, and remained more or less at the start level in one sector, that of chemical products. Comparing this with the share in manufacturing employment of each sector, 3 sectors with a low employment share had become more concentrated and only one with a high employment share did so, the food, beverages and tobacco industry.[126] Among those with a falling concentration was one with a high employment share, the machinery and equipment sector, the other had rather low shares. The more or less constant concentration industry, chemicals, had an intermediate employment share in overall manufacturing employment. Therefore, no generalisation about the trend in concentration and the employment share of the industry is possible from these data.

In the subperiods, however, the development of CR_3 concentration was different from the overall result. From 1992 compared to 1999, the value of CR_3 had risen for 6 out of the 8 sectors, when a peak was reached. These industries were food, beverages and tobacco, textiles, wood and paper, chemicals, machinery and equipment and other manufacturing industries. From 1999 to 2004, concentration has fallen for five of these industries (except for the food, beverages and tobacco sector). For the two remaining sectors, concentration has either remained more or less constant - for the mineral products sector, or it has kept falling until 2004:

125 *www.mikrooekonomie.de* on 20th Sept. 2007 „Messung der Anbieterkonzentration".

126 The textiles industry which had a high employment at the start and a low employment share at the end of the period, was classified here with its end of period employment.

Table 21: CR_3 concentration rate per industry based on regional manufacturing employment data, selected years

Manufacturing of	1992	1999	2004	2008	Direction of change 2008/1992
food, beverages, tobacco	0.2747	0.3089	0.3228	0.3715	↑
textiles, wearing apparel, leather and fur products	0.2999	0.3462	0.2572	0.3754	↑
wood, paper and printing, publishing	0.4494	0.5267	0.4333	0.4809	↑
chemicals and chemical products	0.5201	0.5978	0.4685	0.5099	≈
other non-metallic mineral products	0.3571	0.3529	0.3314	0.4480	↑
basic metals and fabricated metal products	0.5057	0.4353	0.3671	0.4105	↓
machinery and equipment (n.e.c., electrical and optical equipment, transport equip.)	0.4495	0.4573	0.3361	0.4104	↓
other manufacturing industries, recycling	0.3989	0.4067	0.3281	0.3795	↓

Source: Own calculations; own presentation.
Source of data: HCSO, Regional Statistical Yearbook of Hungary, subsequent years, Budapest.

This was the case for the metal products sector where a marked decrease took place, implying a fall in market share for the 3 largest regions from 50.6% to 36.7%. For the remainder of the period since the EU accession of Hungary, all industries showed an increase in CR_3 concentration levels, yet the end levels in 2008 were generally below the 1999 peak.

4.4.3 Regional composition of industry concentration CR_3

The concentration measure CR_3 allows for a detailed analysis of the regional set-up of industry agglomeration. More precisely, it is possible to see in which regions held the largest centres of each industry in employment terms. As the greatest shifts are expected over the longest period possible, the years 1992 and 2008 are compared in Table 22.

The comparison in **Table 22** shows that for two industries, namely the food, beverages and tobacco, and chemicals and chemical products, the agglomeration centres have not changed for 1992 and 2008 respectively, i.e. the main concentration was still located in the same three regions. For the remaining six industries, there was a change in the top three regarding one region - although for some of these industries, the position of the regions with respect to the start year changed.

Table 22: Regions making up the largest shares in Hungarian manufacturing employment per industry in 1992 and 2008, based on the CR_3 concentration rate

Manufacturing of	3 largest regions in 1992	3 largest regions in 2008
food, beverages, tobacco	Budapest, Bacs, Pest	Budapest, Pest, Bacs
textiles, wearing apparel, leather and fur products	Budapest, Györ, Vas	Budapest, Vas, Szolnok
wood, paper and printing, publishing	Budapest, Szabolcs, Bacs	Budapest, Pest, Szabolcs
chemicals and chemical products	Budapest, Borsod, Pest	Budapest, Borsod, Pest
other non-metallic mineral products	Borsod, Budapest, Veszprem	Budapest, Pest, Veszprem
basic metals and fabricated metal products	Budapest, Borsod, Fejer	Budapest, Pest, Fejer
machinery and equipment (n.e.c., electrical and optical equipment, transport equip.)	Budapest, Pest, Fejer	Budapest, Pest, Komarom
other manufacturing industries, recycling	Budapest, Zala, Csongrad	Budapest, Vas, Zala

Source: Own calculations; own presentation.
Source of data: HCSO, Regional Statistical Yearbook of Hungary, subsequent years, Budapest.

Budapest region was among the three regions contributing the largest shares in industry employment for all manufacturing sectors in the years 1992 and 2008. For the mineral products industry, however, Budapest was not the largest concentration area overall. The prominent position of Budapest is not unusual when taking into account that about one fifth of Hungary's workforce live in Budapest, namely 19.6% of manufacturing employment in 2008, and 20.9% for the year 1992 respectively.

Pest region advanced from being 3 times among the largest three production sites to being 6 times among the top 3. This shows an increasing economic importance of this region surrounding Budapest, located in Central Hungary. As the analysis of internal net migration in Chapter 3.5.1 showed, Pest region was also the region with the largest positive internal net migration of the period, with +248,000 persons over the period.

4.4.4 Comparison of the results with theory

The overall evolution of manufacturing industry concentration in Hungary as measured by the CR_3 concentration index is broadly comparable to the predictions made by NEG theory for agglomeration in the course of integration processes. The model by *Livas-Elizondo & Krugman (1996)* for regional integration modelled in the context of international trade described that an (irreversible) agglomeration would form within the country consisting of more than one region. More in particular, the model by *Puga (1999)* which predicts first a rise to a peak, then a fall in concentration levels, called Ω-shaped evolution, is confirmed by the data from my own calculations. The model by *Ludema & Wooton (1997)* predicted for some intermediate level of trade costs between regions of a country agglomeration (less than complete) to form, followed by industry dispersion as trade costs decline even further in the course of proceeding integration. There were such phases in the manufacturing sectors in Hungary during the observation period, even though the second rise of concentration after EU accession could not fully be explained. Trade costs would be presumed to have fallen more since 2004 due to Hungary being part of the Single Market and all regulations then in force; apparently, however, what could have happened is that international trade costs increased due to a surge in NTBs applied to a stronger degree or newly to products "made in Hungary" upon full EU membership.

4.4.5 Evaluation of the results by means of other empirical studies

The results of this research are not directly comparable to those of other empirical studies, as the industry scope and country coverage as well as data sources are different. One study working explicitly with the CR_3 concentration measure is the one by *Aiginger & Pfaffermayr (2004)*, which analysed concentration effects in 14 EU member states for selected years from 1985 to 1998 in order to identify concentration effects entailed by the European Single Market programme. The authors based their calculations on Eurostat data of value added for 99 3-digit industries. First of all, they found an overall increase of CR_3 concentration of the 3 largest of these 14 old EU countries from 64.6% to 65.0% (unweighted average) from 1985 to 1992, then a decrease by 2.1% to 63.7% in 1998. Overall, they observed a decrease in industry concentration measured by CR_3 by 1.5%

from 1998 - post Single Market - over the year 1985 - prior to the political decision for the Single Market programme. Compared with their results, the changes of industry concentration observed in Hungary by this research during the almost two decades were much stronger. They ranged between +13% and -19% of the initial CR_3 concentration levels for 2008 compared to the 1992 start level.

Calculation of such unweighted averages - equivalent to the method used in *Aiginger & Pfaffermayr (2004)* - on my results based on Hungarian manufacturing employment data for the years 1992, and 1999, as well as 2004 and 2008, gave the figures presented in **Table 23**.

Table 23: Unweighted averages in CR_3 concentration in Hungarian manufacturing industry based on employment, selected years, and percentage change

	1992	1999	2004	2008	%age change 99/92	%age change 2004/92	%age change 2008/92
CR3 level	0.4069	0.4290	0.3556	0.4233	+11.2%	-11.8%	+4.0%

Source: Own calculations.
Source of data: HCSO, Regional Statistical Yearbook of Hungary, subsequent years, Budapest.

The overall concentration level measured by CR_3 of the three largest regions in terms of manufacturing employment was 40.69% in 1992, rose to 42.90% in 1999, fell to 35.56% in 2004, and finally rose to 42.33% in 2008. Comparing the percentage change, this meant a rise of 11.2% in the first period, and a decline of -11.8% for the entire period of the Europe agreement, 2004 compared to 1992. Overall, concentration measured by CR_3 rose by +4.0% in 2008 relative to the 1992 start level.

This shape of the development of industry agglomeration goes broadly in line with the trend observed by *Aiginger & Pfaffermayr (2004)* in their EU-14 Single Market analysis, first a rise, then a fall offsetting the initial rise and making up for an overall fall when comparing the end to the start year of the analysis. This leaves the question whether perhaps similar processes might have set in among the Hungarian industry on the regional level under the Europe agreement as in the EU-14 under the influence of the Single Market Action plan.

A comparison of the level of CR_3 of *Aiginger & Pfaffermayr (2004)* and my data shows much lower figures for the Hungarian regions than for the country-based EU-14 study. While these average CR_3 concentration levels for the manufacturing industries in Hungary ranged around 40%, for the country level in the EU-14 they were shown to be around 60%. This could be due to the vast differences in the database of the two studies and also due to the much larger size of at least 5 of the countries of the EU-14.

4.5 The Herfindahl index

The development of agglomeration of the manufacturing industries in Hungary shall now be measured using the Herfindahl index, sometimes called Herfindahl-Hirschman index. In its original form, this index results in an absolute measure of industry concentration. In another context, when applied to export data of countries, the Herfindahl-Hirschman index can measure the degree of export concentration of a country's exports, as in *Guerson et al. (2007)* for Argentina. Back to the context of spatial industry concentration where it is used here, the Herfindahl index is sometimes called a comprehensive concept as it includes information about the whole distribution, unlike the CR_3 measure (see section 4.4.1). The comprehensiveness of the Herfindahl index also has a disadvantage to it, however, as the very largest shares tend to dominate the results. A modified form of the Herfindahl index, then resulting in a relative concentration measure, shall therefore be presented in section 4.6 of this chapter.

4.5.1 Formula of the Herfindahl index

The formula of the Herfindahl concentration index in its absolute form can be denoted as follows:

Herfindahl index (absolute)

$$H_i = \sum_{j=1}^{N} (s_{ij})^2$$

where the index i refers to the industry sector (8 manufacturing sectors), and j to the regions (20 Nuts-3 regions).[127] Thus the Herfindahl index for industry sector i takes the value of the sum of the squared regional employment shares of industry i for all 20 regions j. The result can take values between 0 and 1. The higher the value, the more concentrated is the industry.

127 Formula according to *Aiginger & Pfaffermayr (2004).*

4.5.2 Results of the Herfindahl index

The Herfindahl index has been calculated for the 8 manufacturing sectors based on regional employment data for selected years: 1992, 1995, 1999, 2004 and 2008. Figure 29 presents the results for the 4 sectors with the higher absolute concentration values, while Figure 30 will present the remaining sectors.

Figure 29: Absolute Herfindahl index based on employment data, 4 manufacturing sectors, selected years

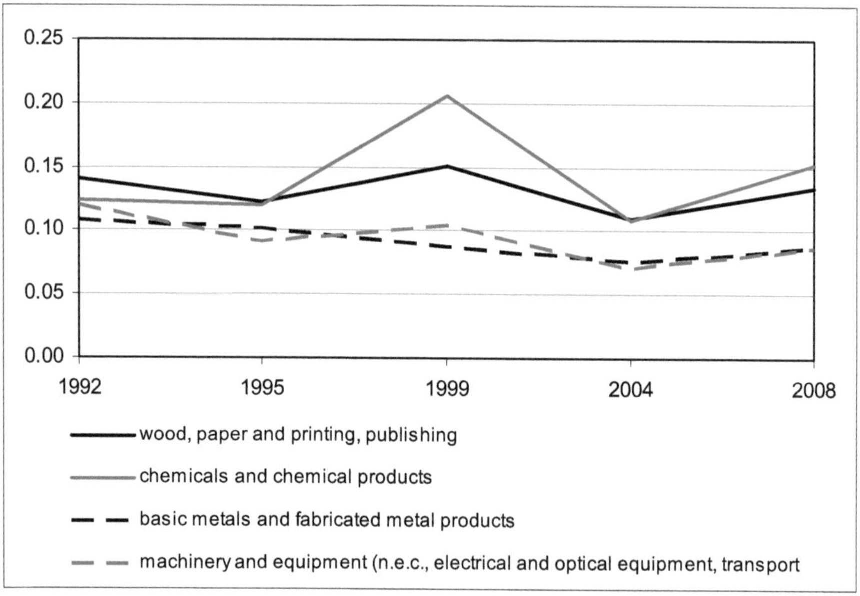

Source: Own calculations; own graphical illustration.
Source of data: HCSO, Regional Statistical Yearbook of Hungary, subsequent years, Budapest.

The chemicals sector shows the steepest rise in concentration levels of the four sectors in **Figure 29**, from the start in 1992 at 0.1236 to a high of over 0.2057 in 1999, whereafter it falls below the start level. This is a rise by more than 66%. The wood, paper and printing sector also shows a rise to a peak in 1999, then a fall below start levels. This corresponds to 22% beneath the start level. The recycling and other manufacturing industries also follow the trend with a peak in 1999, then fall below start levels. Finally, the machinery and equipment sector initially falls from the start in 1992 until 1995, then rises to an intermediary peak in 1999, then keeps on falling to an absolute level of 0.0714 in 2004. That concentration for the machinery and equipment sector is over 40% lower than the start level. Finally, for the post-accession period, a rise in concentration levels set in for all four industries, but to lesser levels than in 1999.

Figure 30: Absolute Herfindahl index based on employment data, remaining 4 manufacturing sectors, selected years

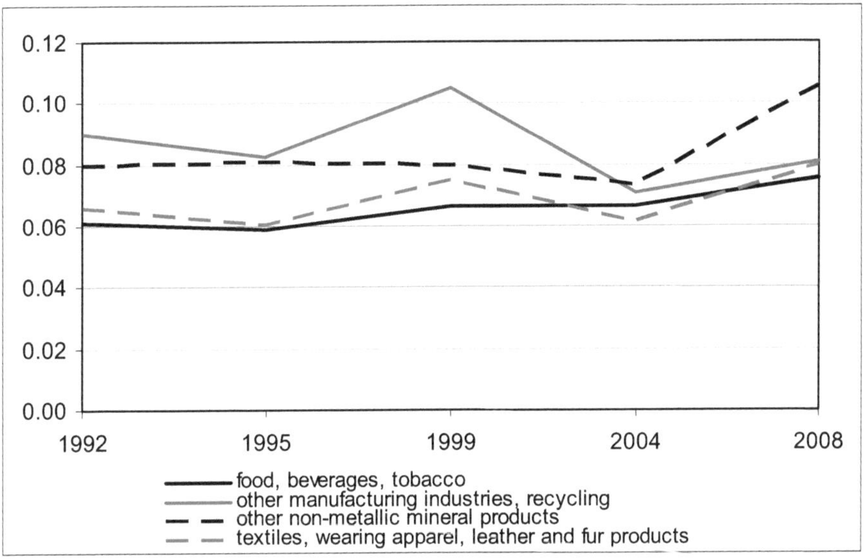

Source: Own calculations; own graphical illustration.
Source of data: HCSO, Regional Statistical Yearbook of Hungary, subsequent years, Budapest.

Figure 30 shows the results of the Herfindahl index calculated for the remaining sectors. These sectors tend to have lower concentration levels than those in Figure 29. The mineral products sector shows a fall in concentration from the start to the year 2004, the concentration level was 30% lower in 2004 than in 1992. Two sectors show a rise to a peak in 1999, the textiles sector as well as food, beverages and tobacco. All of these four sectors show a rise of concentration from 2004 to 2008, most pronounced for the mineral products sector.

4.5.3 Comparison of the results with theory

The development regarding agglomeration of the 8 manufacturing sectors in Hungary during the period 1992 to 2008 as measured by the Herfindahl concentration index is overall in line with models from NEG. The model by *Livas-Elizondo & Krugman (1996)* for regional integration modelled in the context of international trade described that an (irreversible) agglomeration would form within the country consisting of more than one region. More concretely, the predictions made for agglomeration in the course of integration processes of the model by *Puga (1999)* are verified by my results. They notably predicted first a rise in manufacturing industry concentration up to a peak, thereafter a fall in concentration levels - called Ω-shaped evolution; that shape is confirmed by the graphs and data of my calculations. The model by *Ludema & Wooton (1997)* predicted (less than complete) agglomeration to form at some intermediate level of trade costs, followed by dispersion as trade costs decline even further in the course of proceeding integration. For the period under the Europe agreement, this was also the case in Hungarian manufacturing industries.

There are few empirical papers using the Herfindahl index on EU data. One paper is that by *Giannetti (2002)* who, based on a modified new growth model, conducted an analysis based on income data for 10 EU countries from 1980-86, and from 1986-92 in which she used the Herfindahl index for country employment concentrated in one of the three macro-sectors of the economy as a control variable (that paper was interested in isolating the role of technological spill-overs for regional growth). This was done to control for the exceptionally good performance of regions which derive their wealth from being political centres of major importance, such as Paris and Brussels, and to account for other regions with higher levels of public sector employment, such as in Italy, and finally, to account for regions endowed with natural resources (such as Nordrhein-Westfalen in Germany) where performance is likely to depend on national endowments rather than on a mechanism of technological transmission.

4.6 The relative Herfindahl index

The next index to be presented in this effort to measure the development of manufacturing industries' agglomeration in Hungary in the course of European integration is the relative Herfindahl index, a modified form of the Herfindahl index. This index measures sectoral geographic concentration with respect to a benchmark, which is the overall geographic concentration of the manufacturing sector.

4.6.1 Formula of the relative Herfindahl index

The formula of the relative Herfindahl index is as follows:

$$Hr_i = \sum_{j=1}^{N} \left(s_{ij} - x_{ij}\right)^2$$

where s_{ij} is the share of industry i's employees working in region j and x_{ij} is the share of total manufacturing employment in region j. The index for industry i then takes the sum of these differences squared over all 20 Hungarian regions j.[128] The index can take values between 0 and 1. The higher the value, the more concentrated is the industry.

4.6.2 Results of the relative Herfindahl index for Hungary

The relative Herfindahl index has a different nature than the other indices presented so far due to the fact that it measures an industry's concentration relative to a benchmark. The benchmark chosen is total manufacturing employment in a given region as a share of country-wide manufacturing employment. It then puts the

Figure 31: Relative Herfindahl concentration index for 8 manufacturing sectors based on employment data, years 1992 and 2008 in comparison

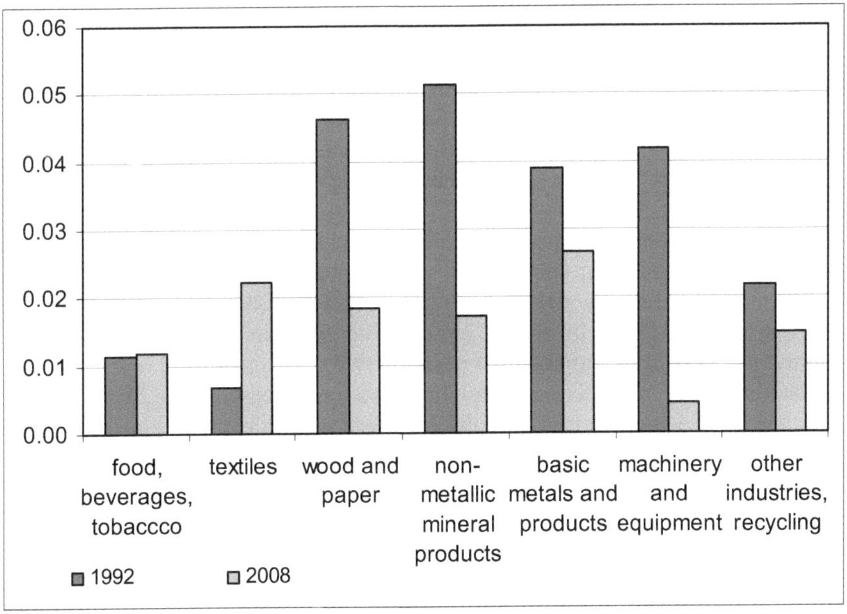

Source: Own calculations; own graphical illustration.
Source of data: HCSO, Regional Statistical Yearbook of Hungary, subsequent years, Budapest.

128 The Formula is spelt according to *Giacinto & Pagnini (2008)* and an earlier version of that paper. They used this index on Italian data from 103 industrial subsectors for the year 1996, census data from the Italian National Institute of Statistics.

industry i's agglomeration measured in employment terms in relation to overall manufacturing employment. The values of this relative Herfindahl index could be ranging from 0 to 2. The index would take on a value of zero when a specific sector's employment was distributed across regions in the same way as total manufacturing employment. The results of the calculations are shown in Figure 31.

Figure 31 presents the results of the relative Herfindahl concentration index for the 8 manufacturing sectors in Hungary for the years 1992 and 2008, the start and the end year of the observation period. For most sectors, concentration as measured by the relative Herfindahl index fell over the period. This decline was by more than half the initial concentration value for wood and paper, and mineral products, and by about a third for basic metals and other manufacturing industries. The strongest decline was observed in the machinery and equipment sector, to less than one fifth of the original concentration, thus a strong relative dispersion of this sector as measured by the relative Herfindahl index. Exceptions to this falling tendency were the (shrinking) textiles and wearing apparel sector (see section 4.3.5), and food, beverages and tobacco, which remained almost the same

A word of caution should be added when evaluating the results of the relative Herfindahl index: as the comparison of indices in section 4.9 demonstrates, the relative Herfindahl shows the rise and fall in concentration in the strongest way of the 6 concentration measures. Thus, also such extreme values as the result for the manufacturing and equipment sector should be viewed in this light.

To put these figures in perspective, a look should be taken at the development of Hungarian manufacturing employment in absolute terms. Overall manufacturing employment in Hungary decreased over the period from 854,913 in 1992 to 648,454 in 2008, that is by almost 25%.[129] The graph in **Figure 32** shows the 8 sectors' manufacturing employment in Hungary for the years 1992 until 2008. On the one hand, the machinery and equipment sector increased from 24% to 39.5% over the observation period. In absolute terms, employment increased from 148,000 in 1995 to 256,500 in 2008. This went along with the relative dispersion or strong fall in relative Herfindahl concentration just described for the results shown in Figure 31.

On the other hand, the food, beverages and tobacco sector went from a share in manufacturing employment of 21% in 1992 down to 14% in 2008. This corresponded to a decline in absolute employment figures, from 184,000 in 1992 to 91,800 in 2008.

129 Data source for these figures: HCSO, Regional Statistical Yearbook of Hungary series.

Figure 32: Development of Hungarian manufacturing employment in the 8 sectors, 1992 to 2008

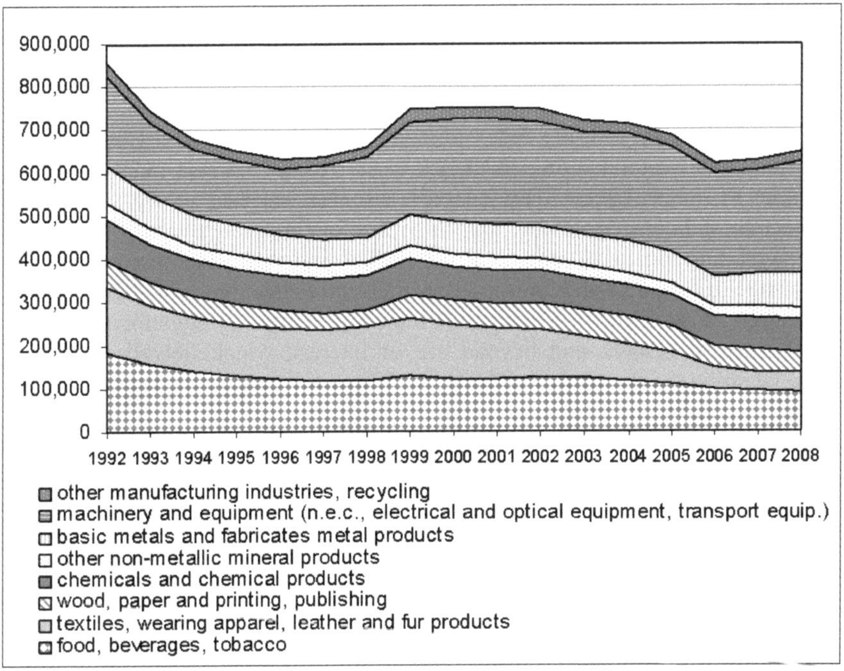

Source: Own graphical illustration.
Source of data: *HCSO,* Regional Statistical Yearbook of Hungary, subsequent years, Budapest.

This went along with relative dispersion also, as measured by the Herfindahl index (see Figure 31). Thus, while the absolute employment figures provide some information, they can by no means provide an indication about the direction of spatial concentration or dispersion tendencies in the manufacturing industry in Hungary. Only the calculation of concentration indices based on sectoral regional employment data can.

4.6.3 Results of other empirical studies

The specific form of a relative Herfindahl index has not been applied to Central and East European data so far. *Di Giacinto & Pagnini (2008)* conducted a plant location study for 103 industrial sectors and regions in Italy, for a single year based on Italian census data from Italian National Institute of Statistics, based on employment and for the year 1996 for 95 administrative provinces and 20 regions.

It is therefore judged not meaningful to compare those results here in any way with the calculations made for Hungary in this study.

4.7 The Hoover-Balassa index

The one before last measure to be presented in this analysis of agglomeration of the Hungarian manufacturing industries is the Hoover-Balassa index, a relative measure of concentration. This concept has been selected as Bela Balassa, a Hungarian, did breaking research in the context of European integration regarding the integration indicator trade, creating Balassa indices to measure comparative advantage of countries and intra-industry trade specialization. As for this research, the effects of integration on Hungarian regions and industry agglomeration under the Europe agreement and beyond are of interest, which liberalised trade in manufacturing goods, this researcher's contribution should not be left out.

The Hoover-Balassa index is a relative measure of concentration. It is applied here in a modified form in order to adjust for differences in regional sizes, in accordance with *Haaland et al. (1999)*.

4.7.1 Formula of the Hoover-Balassa index

The formula of the Hoover-Balassa index as used here is as follows:

$$CONC_i = \sqrt{\frac{1}{j}\sum_j \left[\frac{x_{ij}}{\sum_j x_{ij}} - \frac{\sum_i x_{ij}}{\sum_i \sum_j x_{ij}} \right]^2}$$

where the index i refers to the industry sector (8 manufacturing sectors), j to regions (20 Nuts-3 regions). The term in brackets is the share of industry i's employees in region j, minus region j's share in total manufacturing employment in Hungary, squared; summed over all regions, times 1/20 (0.05) for the 20 Nuts-3 regions in Hungary, taken the square root of, equals the Hoover-Balassa index for the industry sector i.[130]

The Hoover-Balassa index is a relative concentration indicator as it measures the difference of an industry's spread of employment to the average spread of

130 The Formula is given according to *Hildebrand & Wörz (2004)*. They applied this index to 10 countries in Central and Eastern Europe, to output and employment data for 11 industries from 1993 to 2000 (*wiiw* database).

employment. Thus, an industry is relatively concentrated if its employment is more concentrated than total manufacturing employment in Hungary is.

4.7.2 Results of the Hoover-Balassa index

The results of the calculation of the Hoover-Balassa concentration index based on regional sectoral employment data for Hungary are presented in form of a bar chart in Figure 33.

Figure 33 shows the percentage changes in industry concentration measured by the Hoover-Balassa index for the 8 manufacturing sectors. The first bar for each industry shows the percentage change in relative concentration in 1999 over the start year 1992, the second bar shows the percentage change in concentration in 2008 over the start year 1992. For the chemicals and chemical products industry, the rise in concentration to a peak in 1999 is most marked, a rise by 70%.

Figure 33: Hoover-Balassa concentration index based on employment data, percentage change per sector, 1999 and 2008 relative to 1992

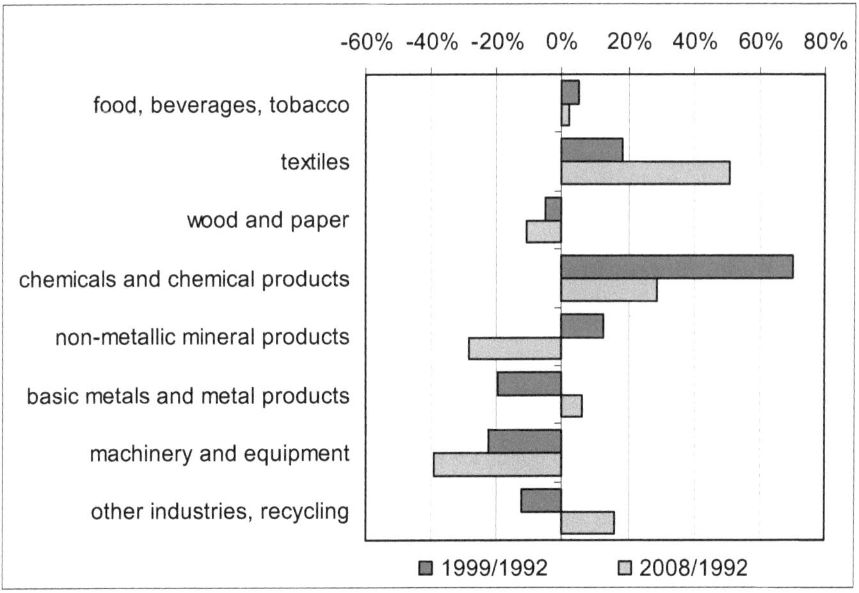

Source: Own calculations; own graphical illustration.
Source of data: *HCSO,* Regional Statistical Yearbook of Hungary, subsequent years, Budapest.

The textiles industry also shows a rise in 1999 over 1992, by 18%, mineral products by 12%, and the food, beverages and tobacco sector by 5%. For the other four sectors, relative concentration as measured by the Hoover-Balassa index fell in 1999 compared to 1992, by between 5% for the wood, paper and printing industry and 22% for machinery and equipment.

Looking at the end year 2008 compared to 1992, three industries show on overall decline in concentration. The strongest decline as measured by the Hoover-Balassa index was in the machinery and equipment industry, by almost 40%, followed by the mineral products industry. The other five industries showed a rise as compared to the start year, most pronounced for the textiles and second the chemicals industry. In general, the rise was less than for 1999 compared to 1992 - with the exception of the shrinking textiles industry.

4.7.3 Comparison of the results with theory

The Hoover-Balassa index does not show the hub-shaped development in such a clear way as other concentration indices calculated in previous sections of this research do, thus this index is only a relatively weak confirmation of the predictions by the *Puga (1999)* model. The weaker form of the hub-pattern for this index could be due to the formula and the smaller absolute values which the Hoover-Balassa index takes for each year and industry. The values range from 0.0147 for the machinery and equipment sector in 2008 to a high of 0.0482 for the chemicals industry in 1999, thus overall roughly one decimal smaller than for the four indices presented up to this point. The results of the Hoover-Balassa index for Hungary do confirm, however, the decrease in concentration overall, as NEG theory predicts in multi-country models in context with economic integration, such as *Livas-Elizondo & Krugman (1996)*.

4.7.4 Evaluation in the light of other empirical studies

The results obtained for relative manufacturing industry agglomeration in Hungary using the Hoover-Balassa index for the years 1992 to 2008 shall now be put in context with other empirical studies. In the study by *Hildebrandt & Wörz (2004),* the Hoover-Balassa index is applied to production data and employment data of 11 industries from 10 countries in Central and Eastern Europe for the years 1993 and 2000 using a database of their institute, the wiiw. Please note that the authors take as a whole the sum of these 10 countries and as components per-country data, whereas I take Hungary as a whole and the sectoral data for the 20 Hungarian Nuts-3 regions as components.

Hildebrandt & Wörz (2004) found that relative concentration had risen for 7 sectors in 2000 as compared to 1993 and fallen for 4 sectors. The chemicals sector - which had the strongest rise in 1999 over 1992 in my Hungarian calculations - remained almost constant in their data set. The machinery and equipment sector, which was split in two sectors, showed a rise in 2000 for electrical and optical equipment and a slight decline for machinery and equipment n.e.c.. The overall order of magnitude of the values taken by the Hoover-Balassa index is between 0.0124 and 0.0407 for the start year 1993 (*Hildebrandt & Wörz 2004)*. This corresponds more or less with that of the year 1992 Hungarian data of my calculations where values range from 0.0222 to 0.0409, as a plausibility verification of the results. As the scope of that study is very different from mine, though, the results cannot be compared in any detail.

In an analysis of Single Market effects in the EU-15, *Haaland et al. (1999)* used the Hoover-Balassa index in a simplified form for country-based data of 13 EU countries and 35 ISIC sectors of the OECD STAN data base. The results for the years 1985 and 1992 serve as input into a more complex econometric model. A table in the annex nevertheless presents these in a 3-digit precision such that several sectors come out equal or same rank. The industries are not directly comparable with the 8 Hungarian manufacturing sectors. The 3-digit presentation of that study is judged too raw for my analysis of Hungarian concentration based on regions, which is why 4-digit precision was chosen throughout this study.

4.8 Entropy

The final measure is the entropy, which shall now be applied to the Hungarian data in order to measure manufacturing industries agglomeration under the Europe agreement and beyond. Entropy is a concept stemming from physics where it is used to describe the difference between the start and the end extension of a gas in space. Entropy gives an absolute number for the degree of dispersion in space, thus this is the inverse idea of concentration in a way. As in this research, the main idea is to analyze agglomeration or dispersion tendencies in manufacturing industries in Hungary due to European integration, this concept is suitable for application in this analysis when transposed to the extension or dispersion of an industry in space.

4.8.1 Formula of the entropy

The formula for calculating the entropy is as follows:

$$E_i = \sum_{j=1}^{J} s_{ij} \times \ln s_{ij}$$

where the index i refers to the industry sector (8 manufacturing sectors), j to regions (20 Nuts-3 regions), and s_{ij} is the employment share of industry i in region j (expressed as %), times the logarithm of the share of industry i in region j (expressed as %), then summed up over all regions to give the entropy figure for industry i.[131]

To evaluate the results of entropy, it should be said that due to this formula, the effect of a dominance of large regions is mitigated by multiplying shares and log shares. Therefore, the entropy has the advantage that it gives the role of large regions a fair but not dominant share.

4.8.2 Results of the entropy for Hungary

The results of my calculations of the entropy applied to the sectoral regional employment data of HCSO are presented in the two following graphs, each for a set of 4 industry sectors.

Figure 34: Entropy based on employment data, 4 manufacturing sectors, selected years

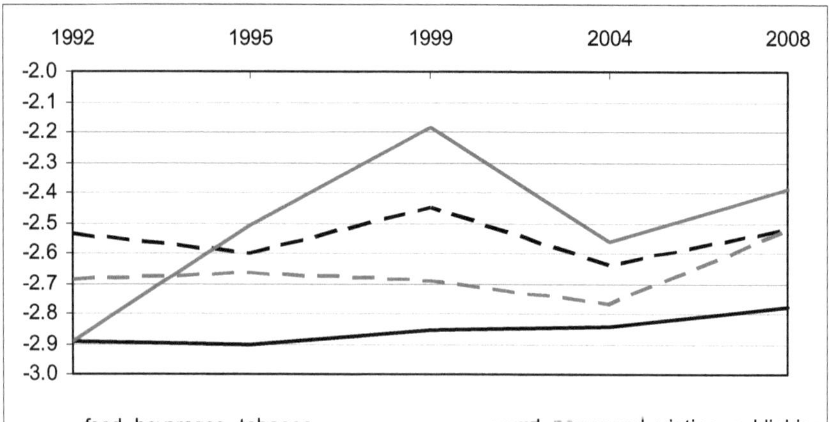

Source: Own calculations.
Source of data: *HCSO,* Regional Statistical Yearbook of Hungary, subsequent years, Budapest.

131 Formula according to *Aiginger & Pfaffermayr (2004).* They applied the entropy to 99 NACE 3-digit industries and 14 EU-countries, for 3 years 1985, 1992, 1998 in order to measure concentration tendencies due to the EU Single Market programme.

Figure 34 shows the results of my calculations of the entropy applied to the sectoral regional employment data for 4 of the 8 manufacturing industries in Hungary for the years 1992, 1995, 1999, 2004 and 2008. For the chemicals industry, the graph shows a steep rise from 1992 to 1999, even a rise from 1992 to 1995 already, with a peak in 1999; from 1999 to 2004, concentration falls to about the 1995-level. For the wood, paper and printing sector, there is a rise in entropy from 1992 with a peak in 1999, followed by a decline. For the food, beverages and tobacco sector, entropy also rises to 1999, thereafter remains at the new level. Only for the mineral products sector, entropy does not show a peak in 1999, but remains at about the start level, then falling slightly to 2004. For the post-accession period, entropy rises for the four sectors up to 2008.

Figure 35: Entropy based on employment data, remaining 4 sectors, selected years

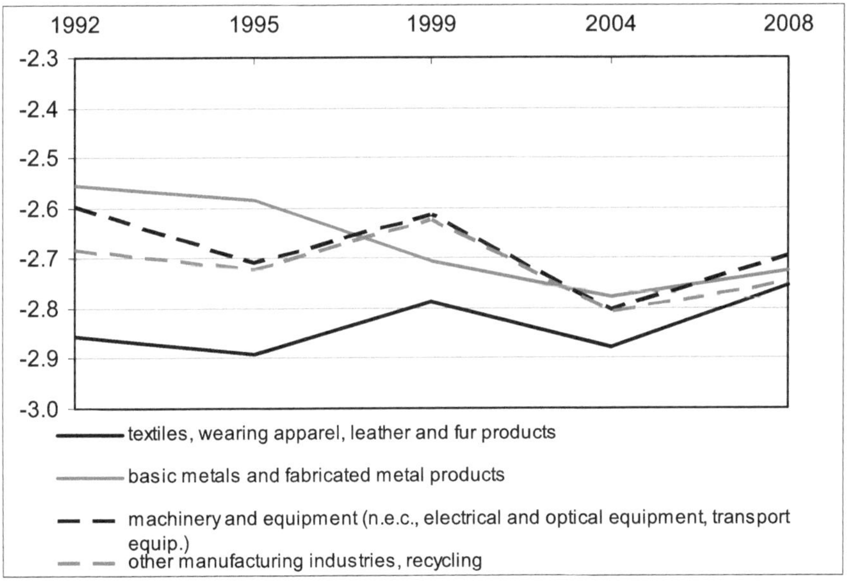

Source: Own calculations; own graphical illustration.
Source of data: *HCSO,* Regional Statistical Yearbook of Hungary, subsequent years, Budapest.

Figure 35 shows the results of the entropy calculations for the remaining 4 sectors. Three sectors of these show a rise to a peak in 1999, after an initial slight decline from 1992 to 1995; these are the machinery and equipment, textiles as well as the other manufacturing industries and recycling sectors. After this peak, concentration declines up to 2004, for all industries below the start level.

Finally, the measure shows a rise up to 2008 again for all the 4 sectors. Table 24 analyses in more detail the percentage changes in entropy for the peak year and the year 2004 compared to the start.

Table 24: Percentage changes in entropy for the 8 manufacturing sectors based on employment data, selected years

Manufacturing of	Percentage change 1999/92	Percentage change 2004/1992
food, beverages, tobacco	1.4%	1.7%
textiles, wearing apparel, leather and fur products	2.4%	-0.8%
wood, paper and printing, publishing	3.2%	-4.1%
chemicals and chemical products	24.6%	11.5%
other non-metallic mineral products	-0.1%	-3.1%
basic metals and fabricated metal products	-5.9%	-8.7%
machinery and equipment (n.e.c., electrical and optical equipment, transport equip.)	-0.7%	-7.9%
other manufacturing industries, recycling	2.2%	-4.7%

Source: Own calculations; own presentation.
Source of data: *HCSO,* Regional Statistical Yearbook of Hungary, subsequent years, Budapest.

Table 24 presents the percentage change in the entropy in the expected peak year, 1999, over the start year 1992, and 2004 over 1992. There is a strong increase in concentration by almost 25% in the chemicals and chemical products industry for 1999/1992. For 4 other industries, there is a moderate increase by between 1.4% and 3.2%.

As to the comparison of the year 2004 to 1992, for 6 industries the overall agglomeration measured by entropy is lower than in 1992. Only for the chemicals industry, concentration has increased by 11.5%, and for food, beverages and tobacco, it has slightly increased by 1.7%. This overall decline of concentration for most industries over the period of validity of the Europe agreement - 1992 to 2004 - is more or less in line with the results for the other concentration indices used in this analysis.

4.8.3 Comparison of the results with theory and other empirical studies

The overall development of manufacturing industry concentration in Hungary as measured by the entropy is comparable to the predictions made by NEG theory for agglomeration in the course of integration processes. The model by *Livas-Elizondo & Krugman (1996)* for regional integration modelled in the context of international trade described that an (irreversible) agglomeration would form within the country consisting of more than one region. More precisely, the model by *Puga (1999)* which predicts first a rise to a peak, then a fall in concentration levels, called Ω-shaped development, is confirmed by the data from my own calculations. The case 5 of the model by *Ludema & Wooton (1997),* agglomeration at intermediate levels of trade costs which disperses during even further integration, is also broadly confirmed by the present results under the Europe agreement.

The entropy as a measure of industry agglomeration has not been applied to Central and East European data in published literature so far.[132] *Brülhart & Traeger (2003)* applied entropy indices to 7 broad economic sectors across 17 West European countries over the period 1975 to 2000. They found that manufacturing has become gradually more concentrated, although the locational bias towards central regions has become weaker over the period. Concentration measured at the regional level rose for 2 manufacturing sectors for Hungary over the period 1992 to 2004, and declined for the others.

In an effort to measure concentration effects due to the Single Market programme in the EU-15 (14 countries used), *Aiginger & Pfaffermayr (2004)* applied the entropy measure to Eurostat data of value added for 99 NACE 3-digit industries. They found a decrease in concentration for 40% of all industries for the year 1992 - the target year of the Single Market programme - as compared to 1985, one year prior to the Single Market decision. Beyond 1992, they found further dispersion effects up to 1998, with overall decreases of entropy for 66% of all industries. When comparing the end year 1998 to the start year 1985 of that analysis, they found decreases of concentration for 58% of all industries; thus concentration measured by entropy increased for 42% of the industries in that study. Those data are not in line with the publicly perceived wave of mergers and acquisitions sparked by the Single Market programme which are deemed to have fostered concentration processes. Perhaps the broad selection of industries in the study by *Aiginger & Pfaffermayr (2004)* was such that this did not allow for a specific

132 At the time of writing, May 2009.

analysis of the sectors which were subject to explicit and early liberalisation policies under the EU Single Market programme.

4.9 Comparison of concentration indices

In the preceding sections of this Chapter 4, concentration indices have been used to measure manufacturing industries agglomeration. One of the specialities of this research is that it applies 6 different concentration indices to the same data set. Most empirical studies use a single index, or at the most three to four indices.[133] Another main difference is that in this research, regional sectoral data are used, whereas most other studies rely on per-country industry data of a set of several countries. In this section, the six concentration indices shall be compared.

4.9.1 Comparison of results of the 6 concentration measures

The comparison shall be done by taking a "cross section" of all six indices for one industry at a time. First, the chemicals and chemical products industry has been

Figure 36: Comparison of 5 concentration indices and entropy for chemicals and chemical products, value 1992=100; selected years

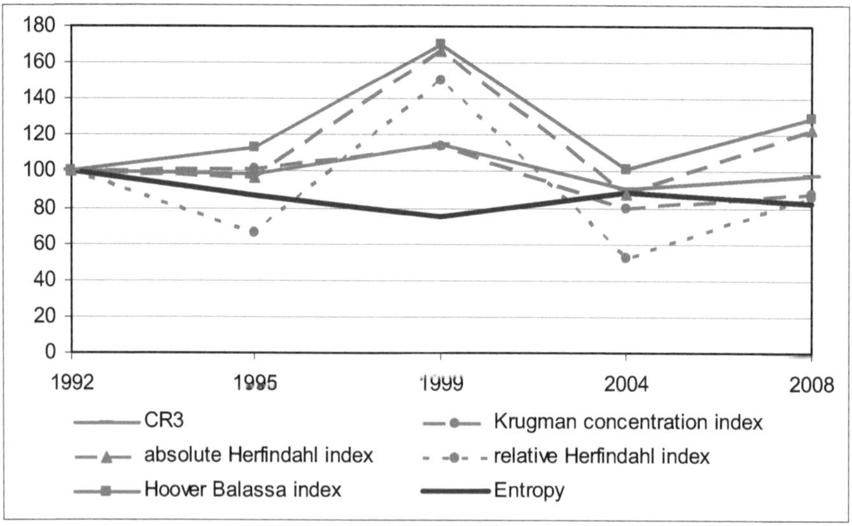

Source: Own calculations; own graphical illustration.
Source of data: *HCSO,* Regional Statistical Yearbook of Hungary, subsequent years, Budapest.

133 *Aiginger & Pfaffermayr (2004)* used 3 measures while *Hallet (2000)* used 4.

chosen, as this industry in general showed the most pronounced rise to a peak in 1999, followed by a decline in concentration. Second, the machinery and equipment industry has been chosen, as this industry contributed most to Hungary's rising exports to the EU, with a share in exports of 66.3% in 2008, and rose to have the largest share in manufacturing output of Hungary, 51.5% in 2008.

Figure 36 shows the development of concentration of the chemicals and chemical products sector based on regional sectoral employment for the years 1992, 1995, 1999, 2004, and 2008. The value for the year 1992 has been set equal to 100, the other values were calculated as an index relative to the base year. This results in the same scale of measurement for all 6 concentration measures which have different numerical values.

The graph shows for the five concentration indices a rise to a peak in 1999, followed by a decline in concentration levels up to 2004. The strongest rise is shown by the Hoover-Balassa index, a relative concentration index, followed by the absolute Herfindahl index, while the Krugman concentration index shows a modest rise. After the peak, concentration of the chemicals index fell rather steeply, to levels below the start level. From 2004 to the 2008 point, concentration

Figure 37: Comparison of 5 concentration indices and entropy for the machinery and equipment sector, value 1992=100; selected years

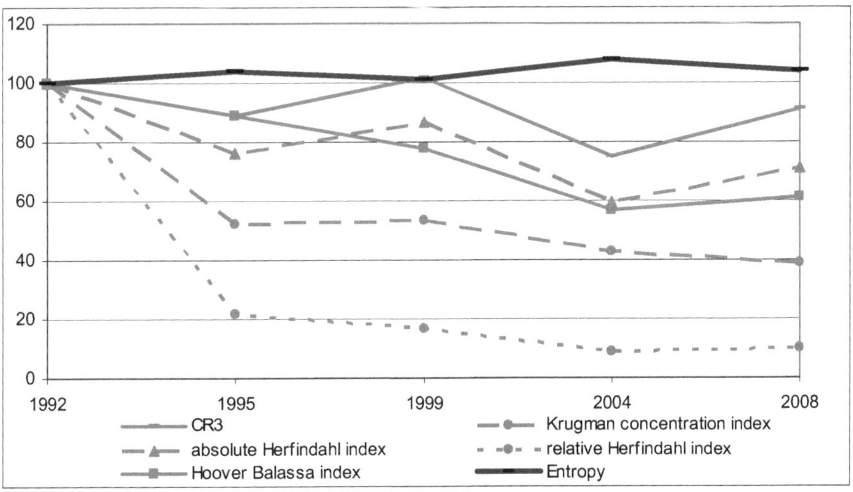

Source: Own calculations; own graphical illustration.
Source of data: *HCSO*, Regional Statistical Yearbook of Hungary, subsequent years, Budapest.

rose to about an intermediate level as that of 1995. The entropy line runs in analogy, but opposite direction as the five concentration measures, as it shows the degree of dispersion in space.

Figure 37 presents the results of the 6 concentration indices for the machinery and equipment sector based on regional sectoral employment data. All indices show a decline in concentration from 1992 to 1995, and an overall decline in concentration from 1992 to 2004. Three indices show an intermediary rise to a peak in 1999, the absolute Herfindahl index, the CR_3 Concentration rate, and the Krugman concentration index. The decline in concentration is shown, however, to quite different degrees by the different indices. From 2004 to 2008, concentration rose as measured by 3 of the 5 concentration indices. Entropy, the degree of industry dispersion, shows a very slight double hub mirroring the development of the five concentration indices.

Figure 38: Comparison of concentration indices and entropy for the machinery and equipment sector in a trend diagram, value 1992 = 100; selected years

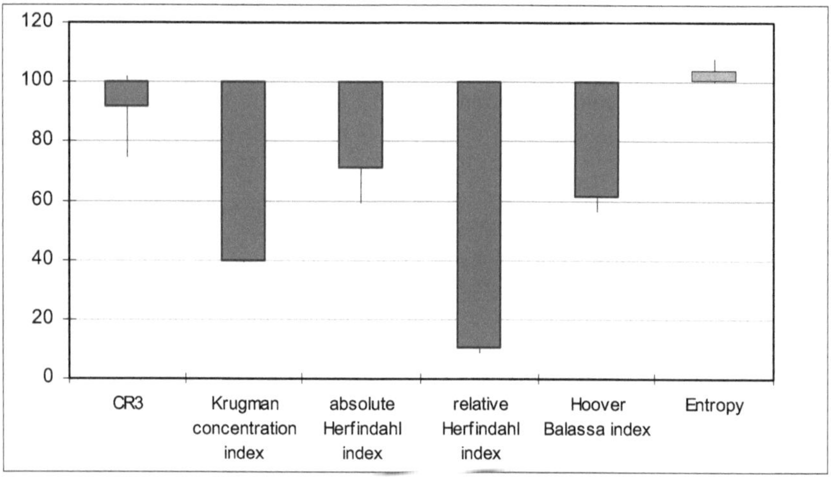

Source: Own calculations; own graphical illustration.
Source of data: *HCSO,* Regional Statistical Yearbook of Hungary, subsequent years, Budapest.

Here again, the Krugman concentration index gives intermediary values, as already for the results of the chemicals and chemicals products sector, i.e. in between those indices with a moderate decline and the index with a strong decline. The Krugman concentration index can therefore be called a "conservative" concentration index. This justifies also why it is later used as the concentration index in the regression analysis (see chapter 6).

Finally, the bar trend diagram in **Figure 38** shows the declining trend in concentration for all concentration indices for data of the machinery and equipment industry for 5 selected years based on employment figures. The year 1992 value was set equal to 100 to make values by the indices comparable. The thin line shows the year 1999-value, the peak in concentration. The relative Herfindahl index shows the strongest decline, followed by the Krugman and Hoover Balassa indices. Entropy shows a rise in the industry's degree of dispersion in space. Here again, the Krugman concentration index is in an intermediate position - as a "conservative" concentration measure.

4.9.2 Concentration indices in other empirical studies

Most empirical studies use only one or two concentration indices to analyse industry agglomeration at the country level based on per-country data for several countries. Of the few studies which use several indices, the one by *Aiginger & Pfaffermayr (2004)* - EU Single Market analysis, EU-14 countries, 99 industries, years 1985, 1992, and 1998 - used the absolute Herfindahl index, CR_3 concentration rate and entropy. Of these three, the authors called entropy their preferred indicator, as in their view, it gives the role of large countries a fair but not dominant share.

In their analysis of 10 CEECs based on a private data base from 1990-1999, *Traistaru et al. (2003)* used two concentration indices, the absolute Herfindahl index and the Krugman index which they called dissimilarity index, as well as a Gini index which only indirectly measures concentration when transposed under a curve. As the country chapters of the book were written by different authors, there is no evaluation contained about which index they preferred.

In their study based on plant level data at the subregional level for Italy, *Di Giacinto & Pagnini (2008)* discuss various concentration indices which require - apart from the Herfindahl index - plant level data. As their analysis is interested in the question whether economic agglomeration spaces ignore regional borders or can form despite them into different areas, they preferred indices taking into account plant level data - which were not available to me for the study of Hungarian agglomeration at the regional level. They also took into account a plant-level index developed by *Devereux et al. (1999)* from their study of the geographic distribution of production in the UK. *Di Giacinto & Pagnini* preferred an Ellison-Glaeser type index to that index which they complemented by some own data in order to take into account spatial autocorrelation measures given by the Moran's I index.

Finally, in their study on 13 manufacturing industries based on per-country output data of 10 CEECs, *Hildebrandt & Wörz (2004)* chose the Hoover-Balassa index as their preferred index, as it measures relative concentration and adjusts for differences in country sizes. To me, the Krugman index is the preferred index as it provides "conservative" estimates for the Hungarian regional sectoral employment data, which should be judged to be the most realistic and reliable.

4.10 Conclusions regarding industry concentration in Hungary and the 6 concentration indices

In order to measure manufacturing industry agglomeration in Hungary, this chapter has described various concentration indices as a tool for obtaining concrete information about the actual developments. Six concentration indices have been selected for the purpose of this analysis, three of them providing an information about the absolute level of industry concentration, three of them relative concentration indices, referring to manufacturing employment as a benchmark.

These six concentration indices have been applied to regional sectoral manufacturing employment data from the HCSO for the period 1992-2008 or selection years. The resulting concentration for 8 manufacturing sectors in Hungary showed that there was a general rise of concentration from 1992 or 1993 to 1999, followed by a decline up to the year 2004. Since the EU membership of Hungary, a new rise in concentration levels set in, but with the end levels in 2008 less high than for the 1999 peak.

For the Krugman concentration index, it was shown that this tendency started to be reversed by 2007 already, when a new decline set in. Furthermore, while the levels in 2004 had in general been below the start levels, the end-levels in 2008 were almost equal to those at the start of the period due to the new rise of concentration since EU accession. That double hub pattern first of agglomeration and then of dispersion, and of newly rising concentration since 2004 was the case for all industries with the exception of the shrinking textiles and apparel industry. Moreover, the changes in the degree of concentration of industries found in Hungary over the period exceeded those observed in the EU during the Single Market process *(e. g. Aiginger & Pfaffermayr 2004)*.

The overall degree of concentration - based on the results of CR_3 - differed greatly between manufacturing sectors in Hungary. The most concentrated manufacturing sector was the non-metallic mineral products sector, which was attributed to the fact of this sector depending on a resource which is located in only a few regions and costly to transport. The chemicals and chemical products sector was second most concentrated, but in this case this was due to the existence of high economies of scale in production prevailing in that industry (as stated in the standard classification by the *OECD (1994)*. Lower concentration levels prevailed in the food, beverages and tobacco as well as the textiles industry, which are both low-wage and rather labour-intensive industries with easily transportable and readily available inputs. The manufacturing industry was rather concentrated at the start of the period and rather dispersed over the country by the end of the period. This was attributed to the large growth in manufacturing output, exports and the large inflow of FDI mainly into this sector. It was also policy-driven to some extent by the Hungarian industrial parks and customs-free zones policies. Moreover, the sector was the main beneficiary of the provisions under the Europe agreement.

The fact that the six concentration measures were applied here to the same set of data allowed for a comparison of indices. This comparison showed that both the Krugman concentration index as well as the entropy provided objective values for the development of actual industry agglomeration. The Krugman concentration index has been singled out as the most "conservative" concentration index to be used later for the purpose of econometric analysis in chapter 6.

The actual development of agglomeration in Hungary's manufacturing industries during the observation period confirms a part of the hypothesis of this research: That there was first a rise in agglomeration up to a point, followed by a decline; and that the peak was reached prior to full membership of Hungary in the EU, namely in 1999 already. Yet interestingly, and despite falling trade costs which should be associated with full EU-membership due to full participation in the Single Market, a second more modest wave of concentration set in among Hungarian manufacturing industries since 2004.

The results are broadly in line with the predictions made by NEG theories for industry agglomeration in the course of economic integration. The model by *Livas-Elizondo & Krugman (1996)* for regional integration modelled in the context of international trade described that an (irreversible) agglomeration would form within the country consisting of more than one region. More in particular, the predictions by *Puga (1999)* about an Ω-shaped relationship between industry agglomeration and declining transport costs during integration have been confirmed by this region-based concentration analysis for Hungarian manufacturing employment data in 1992 to 2008. Further, case 5 of the model by *Ludema & Wooton (1997)* predicted (less than complete) agglomeration to form at some intermediate level of trade costs, followed by dispersion, as trade costs between regions within the country decline even further in the course of proceeding integration. This has also been the case for Hungary.

The evaluation of the results in the light of previous empirical studies has confirmed the special character of this research, namely that it relies on regional data to calculate country-level concentration per industry. Most other studies used country-level data of a set of various CEECs to calculate industry agglomeration for the whole of Central and Eastern Europe. Of the few studies that use regional data, comparability is restricted by the fact that these either relied on output, production or value added; or that they used different concentration indices; or that they rely on total employment as a benchmark instead of manufacturing employment, which has been chosen as the focus of this study for the reason that the Europe agreement with Hungary, the main pre-accession policy, comprised almost exclusively the manufacturing sectors in its trade provisions.

As industry concentration and regional specialization are two concepts which are linked in that they rely on the same or similar data sets, and that both can be put in context with spatial developments in the course of regional integration, the following chapter 5 shall analyse the actual development of regional specialization in Hungary in the pre- and post-accession phase.

5. Regional Specialization of the 20 Hungarian Regions

This research analyses industry agglomerations and regional development in Hungary in the context of European integration from 1992 to 2008. The previous Chapter 4 has analysed agglomeration of the manufacturing industries in Hungary. In this chapter, the focus shall be on regional development, more precisely on regional specialization with respect to manufacturing industries of the 20 planning-statistical regions in Hungary (the Nuts-3 level).

For clarification, the difference between agglomeration and specialization shall be recalled here.

Concentration	looks at the <u>industry</u>, a sector of manufacturing, at the degree of its agglomeration or dispersion in space.
Specialization	looks at the <u>region</u>, at the structure of sectoral employment, whether only a few sectors are dominant, or whether a region is highly diversified.

With respect to specialization, this research looks at the hypothesis whether regional specialization in Hungary has increased or declined in the course of European integration under the Europe agreement, or whether there were both trends and at which stages of the integration process. It also verifies whether there may have been a turning point in the development up to which there was an increase and after which there was a decline. This would be the prediction made by theories of the NEG (e.g. *Venables 1996; Krugman & Venables 1996; Puga (1999); Overman et al. 2008).* The analysis shall also find out whether such a peak point was reached prior to full EU-membership of Hungary.

Here again, the speciality of my research is that it looks at regions and their degree of industrial specialization and not at countries, as most other of the few existing studies on Central and Eastern Europe do.

5.1 Review of previous empirical studies on specialization

The degree of regional specialization in Hungary under the Europe agreement and since full EU membership, namely from 1992 to 2008, can best be measured using an index as a tool for calculations which is applied to the actual data.

Previous empirical studies apply various specialization indices. These have been reviewed in an effort to single out the most suitable index for this study.

In an analysis of country specialization in 10 countries of the EU-15, *Amiti (1999)* applied a Gini index to Eurostat production and employment data of 65 manufacturing industries for the years 1968, 1970, 1980, 1982, 1988 and 1990. Specialization at the country level was found to have fallen in some countries between 1968 and 1990, but all countries in the sample recorded an increase between 1980 and 1990. Increasing specialization was observed in both "richer core" EU countries as well as in "poorer" Southern EU countries.

A potential problem with using the Gini coefficient as a measure of specialization is that it places relatively strong values on changes in the middle parts of the distribution, i.e. industries that are closest to the sample average will get the most weight in the Gini coefficient for the country - or in my case - the region. Thus, this index was not judged as best measure for my purpose.

In a study on intra-industry specialization and trade in the European Economic Space, *Greenaway & Hine (1991)* used the so-called Finger-Kreinin (F-K) index to measure country specialization in 28 manufacturing industries with production and export data. They found evidence of increasing specialization in the early 1980s. The F-K index is a relative measure of specialization which compares one country's distribution of production shares to another. However, this measure of specialization is unsatisfactory when the mean of the sample and the country specialization move in different directions, as it overestimates the result when this is due to large variations in small countries' production shares. For these reasons, this index has also been ruled out for the purpose of my study.

In an analysis of the effects of the European Single market programme, *Sapir (1996)* used the Herfindahl index to measure country specialization based on export data of 100 manufacturing industries.[134] He concluded that specialization remained constant in Germany, Italy and the UK over the period 1977 to 1992, and increased in France since 1986. The inference made in that study from export data to production could be put in question, as in practice exports may change due to domestic consumption and without any changes in production.

The Herfindahl index in the form of an absolute specialization measure was used by *Mafioli (2003)* to analyse regional specialization in Hungary in the period 1992 to 1999. That index ranged between zero and one, where one indicates complete specialization. Calculating country-wide averages, he found that the Herfindahl

134 The Herfindahl index adjusted for measuring (export) specialization is defined as $Hj=\Sigma i(sij)^2$.

remained virtually constant at 0.17 during the 1990s which was evaluated as being "relatively low". He further found that the three most specialised regions were regions in the Western part of the country in 1999, the end-year of that study. As the Herfindahl index tends to overestimate the shares of the largest countries (or regions), however, it is not chosen as the best index for the purpose of my study.

In a paper by *Aiginger & Davies (2004)* the aim of which was mainly methodological, the authors used an adjusted entropy index as a measure of country specialization. They based their methodological analysis on nominal value added data for 14 EU countries for 99 3-digit industries and the years 1985 to 1998. In their results, they only showed average specialization for the group of 14 countries. They found that average specialization increased, which they interpreted in that specialization had increased in most countries. Overall, even taking their methodological considerations into account, this measure does not appear suitable for my analysis.

In a book edited by *Traistaru et al. (2003),* a group of authors apply a so-called dissimilarity index based on *Krugman* to a (private) data base for country studies of Bulgaria, Estonia, Hungary, Romania and Slovenia. That dissimilarity index was calculated for regions of those countries based on manufacturing employment and total employment data from 1990 until 1999 only. Taking the average specialization for each country, that study found that average specialization levels in Bulgaria, Estonia and Hungary were in a lower group, and that they were rising in Hungary up to 1997/98, while average regional specialization in Romania was at a higher level, and that of Slovenia, shown for only four years, was comparatively highest.

Mafioli (2003) calculated relative specialization of regions using a Balassa-type index based on the same data set as *Traistaru et al. (2003)* for the period 1992 to 1999. By means of that relative specialization measure, he found out that the regional specialization pattern for the manufacture of mineral products differed significantly from the national pattern in Hungary during the 1990s.

Given this overview and the advantages and disadvantages of each index, the Krugman specialization index has been chosen for this study as the most suitable index for measuring regional specialization in Hungary. The details will be explained in the next section.

5.2 The Krugman specialization index

The Krugman specialization index is a relative measure of regional specialization and was introduced in international economics by *Krugman (1991a)*, comparing the industrial structure of the USA and Europe. In its original set-up, the index summed up the absolute difference of the industrial structures of the two respective regions. The index is zero if the two regions have the same industrial structures. Its maximum value is 2 which is reached if the two regions do not have any common industries at all.

The Krugman specialization index has also been selected here for the purpose of consistency with Chapter 4 which worked with the Krugman concentration index, and Chapter 6 will use both the specialization and concentration indices for econometric analysis. Moreover, the Krugman specialization index is a tool in line with the predictions made by the theories of Krugman regarding the development of regional specialization in the course of integration *(Krugman & Venables 1996; Venables 1996)*. Finally, the Krugman specialization index provides a conservative estimate of actual developments - the equivalent has been shown for the Krugman concentration index in the comparison of indices in section 4.9. Thus, the results obtained here for regional specialization in Hungary will be a good basis for the validity of this research.

5.2.1 Formula of the Krugman specialization index

The formula of the Krugman specialization index used here is the following:

$$SPEC_j = \sum_{i}^{N} \left| s_{ij} - x_i \right|$$

where the index i refers to the industry sector (8 manufacturing sectors), j to regions (20 Nuts-3 regions). The term in the absolute value brackets is the difference of the share of industry i's employment in region j in total manufacturing employment of region j minus the share of industry i's employment in Hungarian manufacturing employment; the specialization of region j takes the sum of this term over all 8 industries i.[135]

135 The notation of this formula according to *Traistaru et al. (2002a),* but is applied here to 20 Hungarian regions and to manufacturing employment only. Those authors applied the index to a (private) database for 5 Central and East European countries with output and total employment data for the years 1990-1999 (even though the initial years 1990, 1991 and to some extent 1992 can be regarded as distorted by the end of communist regimes data collection).

This index shall be calculated based on regional employment data for manufacturing employment by subsectors, i.e. for the 8 manufacturing industries and each of the 20 regions (data as provided by HCSO). These data have also been the basis of the previous calculations of concentration developments presented in Chapter 4. The index takes the value 0 if a region j has an industrial structure identical to the rest of Hungary, and takes a maximum value of 2 if it has no industries in common with the rest of Hungary.

5.3 Results for regional specialization in Hungary

The results of the calculations of the Krugman specialization index for the 20 Nuts-3 regions in Hungary based on detailed employment figures of the 8 manufacturing industry sectors are complex. To facilitate the analysis, various aspects and results have been selected and will be discussed with the help of figures and graphical illustrations.

5.3.1 Regional specialization

In this first section, the results of the calculations of the Krugman specialization index shall be presented for the period 1992 to 2008. As 20 lines for all 20 regions would have led to a confusing graph, 7 typical regions have been selected for the purpose of presentation.

Figure 39 shows the development of regional specialization for 7 typical regions. At a first glance, a double hub can be seen: the first hub in the lines is around the year 1998 or 1999, while a second hub is visible in the latter years since EU accession. All of these regions show a rise in specialization up to a peak in 1999: For some regions, this started from 1993 onwards, for others like Tolna and Csongrád one or two years later. After the 1999 peak, specialization declined, for some regions with an intermediate point around the years 2000 and 2001 until a down-point in the year 2004 (2005 for Zala region) which is lower than the start level.

Interestingly, regional specialization started to rise again since 2004 or 2005, coinciding with the EU accession of Hungary on 1st of May 2004. The second peak formed around the years 2006 and 2007. Since then, for Baranya and Zala regions a diversification set in again, depicted in falling specialization lines in Figure 39. The regions with the highest specialization in this set are Fejér and Tolna, while Csongrád region is about in a middle position with respect to specialization levels.

Figure 39: Regional specialization in Hungary from 1992 to 2008, Krugman specialization index based on employment data, selected regions

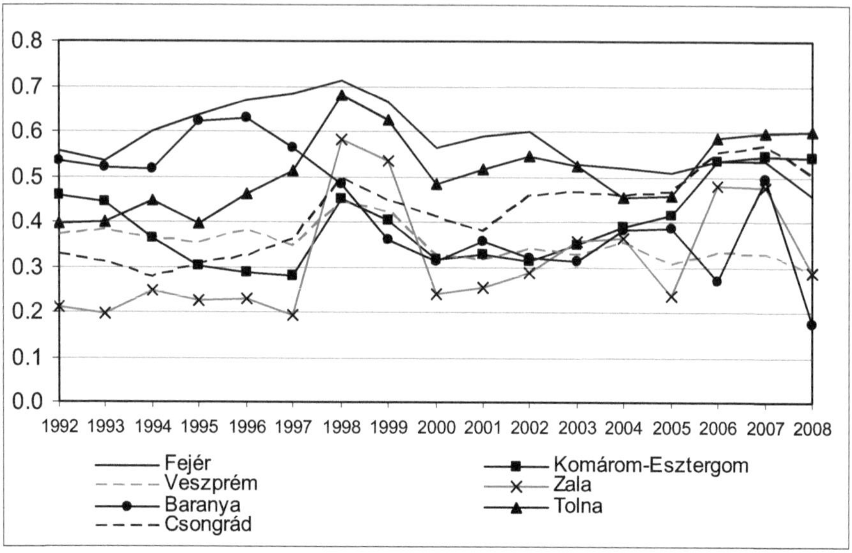

Source: Own calculations; own graphical illustration.
Source of data: *HCSO,* Regional Statistical Yearbook of Hungary, subsequent years, Budapest.

Figure 40 shows a trend diagram for the 20 Hungarian Nuts-3 regions based on the values of the Krugman specialization index for the years 1992, 1995, 1999, 2005 and 2008. The value for the year 1992 was set equal to 100 to make developments comparable. The thin line pointing to the top of the bars for most regions shows the value for the peak year 1999. The bar shows the trend in specialization over the period.

The majority of regions - 12 out of 20 - experienced an overall decline in regional specialization levels over the period up to 2008. That decline ranged from a value of 32 the start level (set = 100) for Baranya, 64 for Pest and between 71 and 77 for 6 other regions. Eight regions show an overall increase in specialization levels compared to 1992. Szabolcs-Szatmar-Bereg, the Eastern-most region bordering Ukraine, increased to 145. The specialization level of Csongrád region increased to 154 and of Hajdú-Bihar even to 205 of the start level. Both of these regions are located in the Great Plain area at the border with Romania. Hajdú-Bihar is one of the least developed regions of Hungary. These border regions have suffered from a loss of jobs in particular in the logistics, textile and shoemaking industry. Many firms of these industries delocated to Romania in the early years of the current decade due to the minimum wage level in Romania which is only half that of the minimum wage in Hungary.[136]

Figure 40: Trend in regional specialization of the 20 regions, Krugman specialization index based on employment data, 1992=100, for selected years

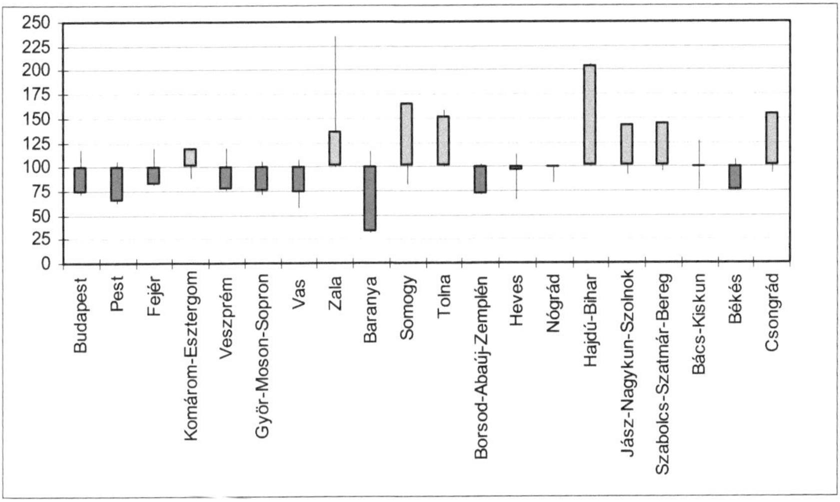

Source: Own calculations; own graphical illustration.
Source of data: *HCSO,* Regional Statistical Yearbook of Hungary, subsequent years, Budapest.

The thin line shows the 1999-peak levels in specialization compared to the start year. The majority of regions show an increase in specialization levels to around 125% of their start level. Exceptions with much higher increases were Zala Hajdú-Bihar, and Tolna regions.

5.3.2 Analysis of the turning point in regional specialization

In this section, the development of regional specialization with respect to the year of the highest specialization as measured by the Krugman specialization index, the year 1999, shall be analysed. This peak year was the turning point for most regions during the observation period of this study; i.e. up to 1999, regional

136 This information was obtained by interview from Hungarian experts during the 4-day BRIT 6 border regions conference which took place in Hungarian border regions in October 2003, in which the author Cordula Wandel participated.

specialization levels rose and fell thereafter up to 2004, the date of Hungary's accession to the EU.

These results clearly indicate that the provisions of the Europe agreement had a profound effect on regional structures in Hungary. This pre-accession policy, intended by the EU mainly as a trade policy measure,[137] induced a profound restructuring of manufacturing industries which changed the location of agglomerations over the country and had deep effects on regional income and employment as well as on the development of regional disparities. The turning point around 1999 coincided with the largest inflow of FDI to Hungary in the year 2000.

Figure 41: Percentage change in regional specialization, 1999/1992; Krugman specialization index based on employment data

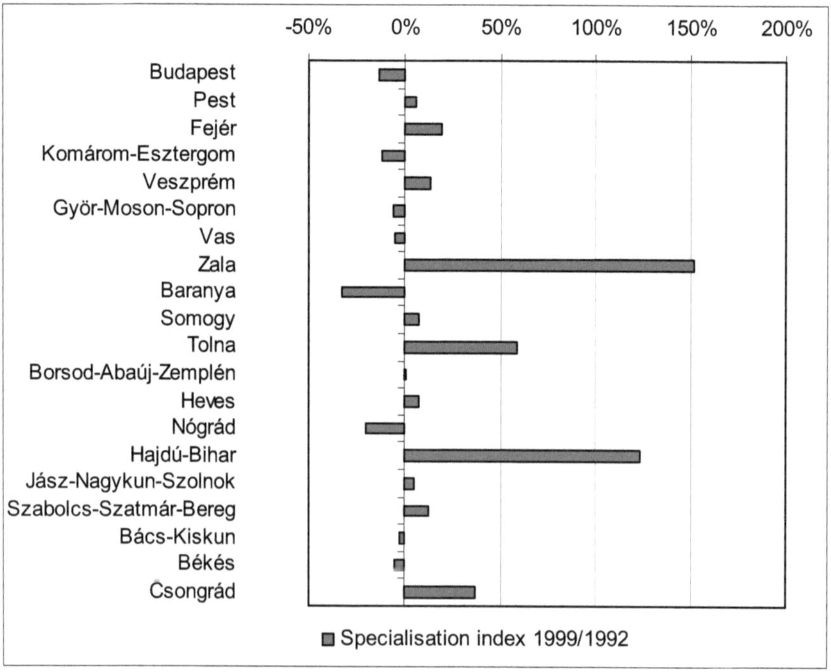

Source: Own calculations; own graphical illustration.
Source of data: *HCSO,* Regional Statistical Yearbook of Hungary, subsequent years, Budapest.

137 The Europe agreement was also seen to some extent as a political insurance to Hungary of the EU's willingness to consider full membership as the ultimate goal.

Figure 41 shows the relative increases in specialization for the 20 regions in the year 1999 as compared to the start year 1992. The values for the year 1992 were set equal to 100 as to make relative increases in 1999 comparable. Overall, the relative increases in regional specialization in 1999 over 1992 were much stronger than the relative decreases. Increases outweighed decreases not only by the number of regions, 12 of them, but also by magnitude, and this by far. Thus, there was an overall trend of a strong increase in regional specialization of the 20 Hungarian Nuts-3 regions in the year 1999 as compared to the start of the period. This is broadly in line with the predictions made for increasing economic integration by *Puga (1999), Venables (1996)* and *Krugman & Venables (1996)*, namely that regional specialization would first increase to a certain point, then decrease as trade costs fall even further.

The strongest increase in specialization - to a value of 150 of the start level - took place in Zala, a Western region at the border of Slovenia (54.1 km) and Croatia (42.0 km).[138] Further strong relative increases took place in Hajdú-Bihar, to a value of 122, in Tolna, a Western internal region, and in Csongrád, a region with borders to Serbia (60.5 km) and Romania (40.5 km). 8 regions had modest increases in specialization levels. Some regions also showed decreases in specialization in 1999, i.e. against the general trend. These were Baranya, a region bordering with Croatia, by -32%, and Nógrád, a Northern region, by -19%. 6 regions had very slight decreases in specialization relative to the start year.

For Budapest, there was a slight decrease in specialization, by 13.2%. As this capital region has a strong agglomeration of all 8 manufacturing sectors (see analysis of CR_3 in section 4.4.2 and 4.4.3 of Chapter 4), relative increases or decreases in specialization can occur without there being a major change in the industrial set-up. Total manufacturing employment in Budapest was 168,500 in the year 1999, the highest of all regions or a share of 22.6% of the total for Hungary. The capital also had the most inhabitants of all 20 Nuts-3 regions, about 1.8 million of the 10.0 million in Hungary. In the next section, the results shall be analysed by groups of regions.

5.4 Analysis of the results by groups of regions

Regarding the development of regional specialization, it would in particular be interesting to see whether there may have been a difference in the development of specialization regarding internal regions located near the capital Budapest, on the

---

138 Values for the length of borders were provided by the Hungarian expert for Schengen implementation in Hungary, Prof. Dr. habil Janos Sallai, Colonel, Budapest. His information is gratefully acknowledged.

one hand, and border regions, on the other hand. Further, it would be interesting to look at regions located near the gravitation centre of Hungarian external trade, i.e. in the Western part near the EU market, versus those regions located further away in the Eastern part of the country. Finally, it shall be analysed whether the neighbouring country group made a difference with respect to regional specialization. Here in particular, a distinction shall be made regarding regions bordering the EU (BEU), regions bordering other CEECs (BCE), and regions bordering external countries (BEX).[139]

5.4.1 Specialization of Western regions versus Eastern regions

In his article on the development of Hungarian regions in the 1990s, *László Faragó (1999)*[140] described territorial development axes in Hungary. During the communist era, the axis went from the North-East - with heavy industry and mining - to the South-West, crossing through the capital area. Since the 1990s, the new development axis in Hungary is a North-South axis crossing through Budapest which divides the country in a growing Western half and a declining Eastern part. This axis starts in the North-Centre, passing along Pest and Budapest regions, Bács-Kiskun and in the South along Csongrád region's border. According to this line, 13 regions are in the Western part and 7 of the 20 Nuts-3 planning-statistical regions are in the Eastern part of Hungary.

In the analysis of Figure 42, this regional division has been applied to my data set. The expected outcome would be lower specialization levels for Western regions than for Eastern regions. The reasons for this are a thinner industrial base and less population in the Eastern part than in the West, which has more manufacturing jobs in absolute terms, a broader industrial structure and more agglomeration centres than in the Eastern part.

Figure 42 shows the actual values of the Krugman specialization index calculated with manufacturing employment data for the period 1993 to 2008.[141] Unlike what

139 For the purpose of classification of regions in this Chapter 5, the largest time span of the reference period has been taken as basis and the classification held constant even beyond EU accession, i.e. for BEU the EU-15 and for BCE the accession candidate countries. This makes also some economic sense, as existing business ties between companies of neighbouring countries probably continued for some time beyond EU membership.

140 Faragó (1999): "Regional „Winners" and „Losers" ", in: Regional Processes and Spatial Structures in Hungary in the 1990s, by Zoltán Hajdu (ed.), Hungarian Academy of Sciences, 1999.

141 The values for each group of regions have been calculated as simple averages of the regions in that category. Calculations per group with the values weighted by each region's population have also been tried. As those results were only marginally different from the

was expected, the two groups - Western and Eastern regions - are rather similar with respect to their levels of specialization. The average specialization of Western regions was only slightly lower than that of Eastern regions. As a reminder, the formula of the specialization index does not take account of the quantity of industry located in a certain area, but rather of the shares of each sector contributing to overall manufacturing employment there. This result can be interpreted in the way that despite the thinner industrial base in the Eastern part of the country, there seems to be a certain mix of sectors as in the West of Hungary.

Figure 42: Regional specialization levels for Western and Eastern regions, Krugman specialization index based on employment data, 1993 to 2008

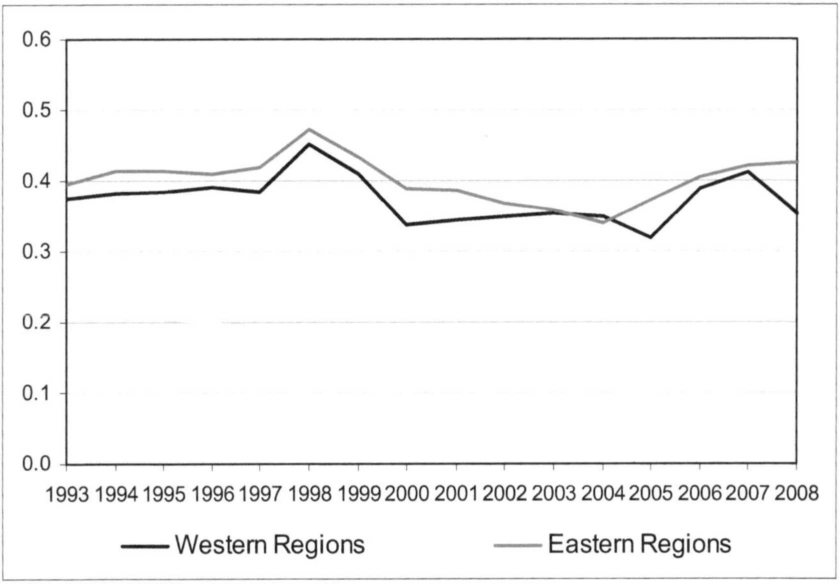

Source: Own calculations; own graphical illustration.
Source of data: *HCSO,* Regional Statistical Yearbook of Hungary, subsequent years, Budapest.

As to the pattern of specialization during proceeding integration, the lines exhibit a double hub structure. Both Western and Eastern regions show first an increase in specialization levels up to a point, in 1999, then a decrease until 2004 or 2005, to levels below the start level. For the latter years of the period, i.e. since the EU accession of Hungary, a second rise in specialization has been observed, although

ones presented here, however, it has been decided to stick with the simple average for clarity.

the peak level is lower than in 1999. For the Western regions, specialization started to decline again from 2007 onwards, while specialization for Eastern regions was still on the rise in 2008. This is broadly in line with the predictions made for increasing economic integration by *Puga (1999), Venables (1996)* and *Krugman & Venables (1996)*, namely that regional specialization would first increase to a certain point, then decrease as trade costs fall even further.

5.4.2 Analysis of internal regions versus border regions

In this section, it shall be analysed whether there was a difference in the development regarding regional specialization for internal regions versus border regions. 7 of the 20 Hungarian regions are located in the middle of Hungary, thus are internal regions, bordering with other Hungarian regions only.[142] One of the 7 internal regions is the metropolitan region of Budapest, which has been taken out of the group and called "INT w/out Budapest" to abstract from the capital region effects. 13 regions are border regions (the latter group and subgroups shall

Figure 43: Regional specialization for internal regions versus border regions, Krugman specialization index for the years 1992 to 2008

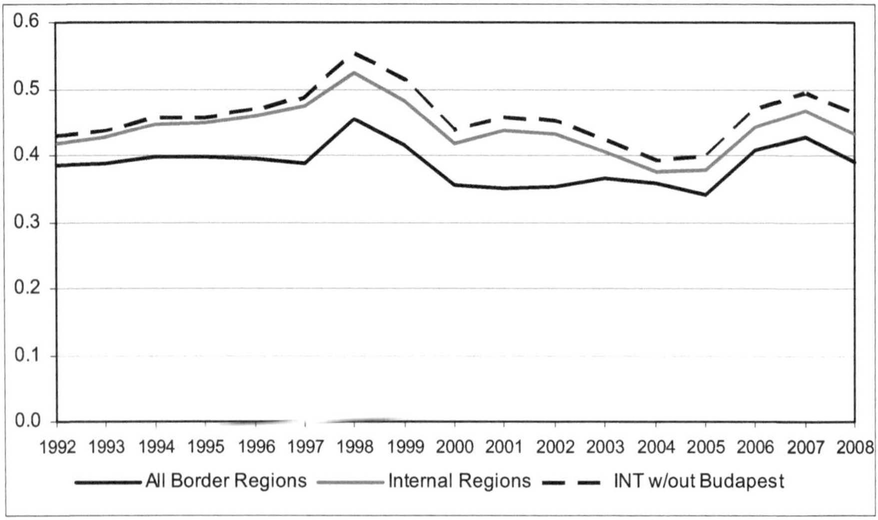

Source: Own calculations; own graphical illustration.
Source of data: *HCSO,* Regional Statistical Yearbook of Hungary, subsequent years, Budapest.

142 Pest region has also been counted into this group, as its overwhelming nature is characterised by its borders with other Hungarian regions, and it only has a very short border with Slovakia; see also map in Chapter 3.

be analysed more in detail in section 5.4.3). The expected outcome would be to find the lowest specialization levels for internal regions including Budapest, as the economic weight of the capital - one fifth of the country's population and the largest regional shares for the 8 manufacturing sectors in country-wide employment[143] - would allow for a good diversification of industry structure.

Figure 43 shows the development of regional specialization of Hungarian border regions and internal regions according to the Krugman specialization index based on regional sectoral employment data for the years 1992 to 2008.[144] Unlike what was expected, border regions show lower specialization levels than internal regions including Budapest. The specialization for internal regions without Budapest is the highest of these groups. This points to a thinner industrial structure in the other internal regions and indicates that they cannot benefit from the capital effect, despite the relatively small size of the country.

Interestingly, here again the pattern of a double hub structure is visible over time, depicted by all three groups of regions: a first hub around the year 1999, and a second smaller hub since 2004 until 2007 when it started falling again up to 2008. The end level was about the same as in 1992, but higher compared to the lowest point in 2004 just before EU membership. This is broadly in line with the predictions made for increasing economic integration by *Puga (1999), Venables (1996)* and *Krugman & Venables (1996)*, namely that regional specialization would first increase to a certain point, then decrease as trade costs fall even further.

5.4.3 Differentiation among different groups of border regions

In this section, a differentiation shall be made among border regions in order to analyse whether there may have been an influence on regional specialization by the nature of the neighbouring country. For the purpose of this analysis, a distinction shall be made in 3 groups:

- regions bordering with the EU (**BEU**): 2 regions, bordering with Austria[145];
- regions bordering with other CEECs, which became member of the EU either in 2004 or 2007 (**BCE**): 6 regions, bordering with Slovenia, Romania, or Slovakia; and

143 These data were taken from Chapter 4, section 4.4.3., on the regional structure of the CR_3 measure.

144 The values have been calculated by taking the average of the regional specialization of regions contained in each group. Here again, as calculations also made with weights by population resulted only in marginal differences from these values, average data are used here for consistency.

145 Please, see the first footnote of section 5.4 regarding Eastern enlargement of the EU.

- regions bordering with external countries, i.e. which did not become member of the EU yet, but might become member at some time in the future (**BEX**): 5 regions, bordering with Ukraine, Croatia, and Serbia & Montenegro.

In the case where a region had a border with two countries, the length of the longer border measured in kilometers was decisive for the category into which it was put.[146] This was the case for 4 regions: Csongrád[147] (BEX), Szabolcs-Szatmar-Bereg[148] (BEX), Zala[149] (BCE), and Györ-Moson-Sopron[150] (BEU).

Figure 44: Regional specialization for EU border regions (BEU), for border external countries (BEX) and for border CEECs (BCE), years 1992 to 2008

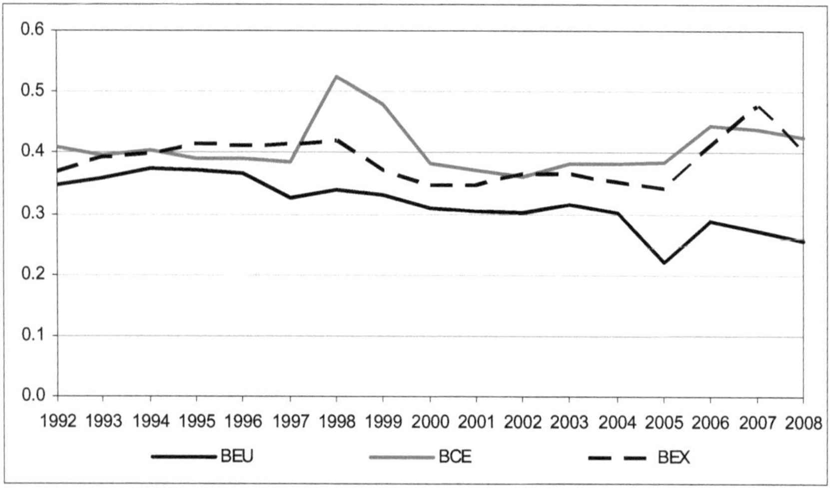

Source: Own calculations; own graphical illustration.
Source of data: *HCSO,* Regional Statistical Yearbook of Hungary, subsequent years, Budapest.

Figure 44 depicts graphically the results for the three groups of border regions BEU, BCE and BEX regarding regional specialization for the years 1992 to 2008. The values for each group of border regions have been calculated by taking the average of the Krugman specialization index of the regions in each group. As

146 The length of borders for those regions with two neighboring countries was provided by a Hungarian expert for Schengen border implementation, Prof. Dr. habil *János Sallai*, Colonel, Budapest.
147 Serbia 60.5 km, Romania 40.5 km
148 Romania 93.5 km, Ukraine 136.7 km
149 Slovenia 54.1 km, Croatia 42.0 km
150 Austria 156.6 km, Slovakia 81.7 km

calculations weighted by population resulted only in marginal differences from these values, average data are used here for continuity.

The graph in Figure 44 shows that the specialization is lowest for the border regions of the EU (BEU), i.e. these have the most diversified industrial structure. For BEU, specialization first rose slightly to a peak in 1995, then fell until 2005, when it was 36% lower than at the start. A slight rise followed after the EU accession of Hungary, yet specialization decreased even further up to 2008.

For the second group of regions, the regions bordering external countries (BEX), specialization developed almost in parallel to that of BEU, only that the decline until 2004 was more modest than for BEU. Again, there is a second hub in specialization in the post-accession period. Specialization levels for the BEX regions were generally higher than for BEU.

Finally, regional specialization for the last group of border regions, BCE, was highest of all three for most years. There was a clear rise to a peak in 1999, followed by a decline until about 2003. The peak was about 17% higher than the year 1992. Since 2005, a second rise in specialization is shown clearly, yet again to lesser levels than 1999, with a decline towards the end of the period. The peak for the BCE-group in 1999 could be attributed to the following: As Romania is the main neighbouring country in question, and due to the rise in minimum wages in Hungary at the turning of the century, many jobs migrated from the Hungarian border regions to Romanian border regions due to the delocation of firms in certain industries such as transport and logistics, textiles and shoe-making.[151]

5.5 Analysis of the results in light of NEG theories

In this section, the results obtained for regional specialization by calculating Krugman specialization indices based on sectoral regional employment data shall be evaluated in the light of the predictions made by NEG theories. The authors of NEG models which include statements on regional specialization also make predictions about the development of regional specialization changes in the course of economic integration, and these shall be recalled here.

The NEG model by *Livas-Elizondo & Krugman (1996)* for regional economic integration in the context of international trade formulated that (irreversible) agglomeration would form within the country consisting of more than one region.

151 This information was obtained by interviews with Hungarian experts during the BRIT 6 border regions conference which took place in Hungarian border regions in October 2003, in which the author *Cordula Wandel* participated.

Trade liberalisation would tend to break up geographical concentration within the economy, thus enabling agglomeration in either region, or the decentralized equilibrium. This implies that with falling trade costs, regional specialization will first rise, then fall again as geographical concentration of industry is breaking up.

The model by *Puga (1999)*[152] predicts a low degree of industry agglomeration for the start of integration processes and initially high trade costs, i.e. the dispersion of industry in space, coupled with low levels of regional specialization; with medium trade costs exercising stronger clustering forces, industry agglomeration increases up to a peak; centre-periphery structures prevail, and regional specialization increases to the highest point; in a further stage of integration with low trade costs, some firms relocate to regions with lower wages, dispersion takes place; regional specialization is decreasing.

Venables (1996) makes similar predictions about regional specialization in the course of integration. In this model, where labour is assumed immobile and manufacturing firms are in an upstream-downstream relationship, agglomeration forms in the course of economic integration in one region; this region then becomes specialised in manufacturing. The agglomeration coupled with high regional specialization is, however, not sustainable at low levels of trade costs, when the development is reversed again, associated with a decline in regional specialization.

In the model by *Krugman & Venables (1996)*, manufacturing firms are no longer in an upstream-downstream relationship, but their products can either be used as input or for final consumption, and each industry uses inputs from the other sector as well. Labour is assumed internationally immobile, but can move between different sectors. In this set-up, agglomeration will become necessary for trade costs at very low levels, such that each region (country) will lose its presence in one of the industries; thus specialization is increasing to high levels. This outcome is subject to the condition that input-output links and the consequent cost and demand linkages are stronger within each of the industries than between them. If this condition is relaxed, then the outcome is that each location will always have some of each industry, as firms then derive more benefit from proximity to firms in the other industry than their own. Thus each region will be less than completely specialised.

The results of the calculations of regional specialization by means of the Krugman specialization index broadly confirm the predictions made by these NEG models

152 To recall from Chapter 2, this model without labour migration across regions takes each region's labour endowment as fixed; the requirement that in equilibrium real wages must be equalised across regions is dropped.

(Livas-Elizondo & Krugman (1996), Puga (1999), Venables (1996), Krugman & Venables 1996). For the majority of regions, regional specialization followed the pattern of a double hub structure: first an increase from 1992 to 1999, then a decrease up to 2004, to levels below the start (see Figure 39). A second slighter rise in specialization levels followed the EU accession, with a decline already setting in towards the end of the period. The same development was illustrated by Western regions versus Eastern regions, as depicted in Figure 42. These two groups show a rise in specialization levels to a peak in 1999, followed by a decline, and a second hub from 2004 until 2008.

Further, the specialization pattern in border regions versus internal regions - a double-hub pattern again, as illustrated in Figure 43 - confirmed the theoretical predictions. Finally, the analysis differentiating among groups of border regions according to their neighbouring countries - as in Figure 44 - can be taken as a confirmation of the theoretical models. All of the three groups of border regions, BEU, BEX and BCE, exhibit the double hub structure: a peak in specialization around the year 1999, followed by a decline, and a second hub since the EU accession of Hungary. In my view this is clear proof of the fact that the pre-accession trade policy of the EU, incorporated in the provisions of the Europe agreement, had profound effects on the regional structure regarding specialization and manufacturing agglomerations in Hungary.

5.6 The results on regional specialization in light of previous studies

Country specialization in the EU-15 was analysed by *Midelfart-Knarvik et al. (2000)* for various industries. The authors found an increase in country specialization either upon EU accession or with a lag of about 6 to 7 years. This research, however, looks at regional specialization – not country specialization - during European integration. Thus, the results cannot be seen in relation to each other.

Few empirical studies exist on regional specialization either in the EU (generally the EU-15) or - even less - in the CEECs. *Hallet (2000)* analysed regional specialization in the EU-15 over the period 1980 to 1995 based on gross-value-added data of 17 branches for 119 regions using a relative specialization index which takes the respective EU-15 average as a benchmark and divides the resulting sum by one half. He found a moderate decline in specialization for all regions taken together from 1980 to 1995. Specialization levels in the Southern peripheral regions were somewhat higher than in the EU core regions of the so-called "blue banana" in 1995, a fact which he attributed to their smaller economic base.

The paper by *Hildebrandt & Wörz (2004)* - while being entitled "industrial specialization and concentration in CEECs" - only deals with concentration and developments of individual industries, taking per-country concentration data as basis (see discussion in Chapter 4, section 4.7.4). Specialization is referred to by the authors as "the other side of the coin", without performing any explicit analysis of it though.

In a study by *Traistaru et al. (2003),* a group of authors applied a so-called dissimilarity index based on Krugman to a (private) data base used for country studies of Bulgaria, Estonia, Hungary, Romania and Slovenia. The dissimilarity index is calculated there with reference to total employment as a benchmark. In the Hungary chapter by *Mafioli (2003),* the period examined was 1992-1999, i.e. it ended in 1999, the year which was found to have the highest specialization in my analysis. This means that the more interesting decline in regional specialization in the course of European integration, or the double hub including the rise after EU accession, are not captured by that study. A comparison of their results for selected regions showed for the overlapping period that values obtained by their dissimilarity index - based on total employment figures - tended to be somewhat higher than those of the Krugman specialization index calculated with manufacturing employment data only, and this, however, by varying distances. Neither did their figures exhibit a clear trend or a specialization peak in the course of integration. Thus, it was apparently a wise choice to concentrate on manufacturing employment rather than on overall employment in my study.

5.7 Conclusions regarding regional specialization

The present chapter has analysed the development of regional specialization of the 20 Nuts-3 planning-statistical regions of Hungary in the period 1992 to 2008. Regional specialization was calculated in this chapter using the Krugman specialization index based on regional manufacturing employment data for the 8 industries as provided by the HCSO.

The hypothesis of this research with respect to regional specialization in Hungary was that there was first an increase of specialization up to a peak or turning point, followed by a decline; and that such a turning point was reached prior to full EU-membership of Hungary. This hypothesis was confirmed by the results of the calculations presented in this chapter, the turning point having been around the year 1999. The results added to that, however, in that there was a second wave of rising regional specialization following the EU-accession of Hungary, and that the second turning point for specialization levels was in 2007 to start falling again.

Furthermore, the hypotheses of this research stated that the Europe agreement - consisting mainly of trade provisions - had an impact on industry agglomerations and regional development in Hungary. The empirical results on regional specialization in this chapter are clear proof in my view that the pre-accession trade policy of the EU, incorporated in the provisions of the Europe agreement, had indeed profound effects on the regional structure regarding specialization and manufacturing agglomeration in Hungary.

Furthermore, this chapter made a differentiation between various groups of regions with respect to their specialization levels.[153] As a first group, a distinction between Western regions and Eastern regions according to the development shed described by *Faragó (1999)* revealed that specialization levels for Western regions were only slightly lower than for Eastern regions, despite the broader economic base and more numerous manufacturing agglomerations in the West (see section 5.4.1). Both Western and Eastern regions exhibited a double hub pattern in specialization levels, a peak in 1999, followed by a decline, and a second (smaller) rise in the post-accession period.

The next distinction showed that specialization levels for internal regions were generally higher than those of border regions, and for internal regions disregarding the capital region Budapest were highest of this group (see section 5.4.2). The rise in specialization for these groups up to the 1999 turning point took place almost in parallel, as did the decline up to 2004, followed by a second rise in specialization since the EU-accession of Hungary up to 2007 when the trend was reversed again.

Finally, a differentiation between groups of border regions according to their bordering neighbours (see section 5.4.3) showed that regional specialization for regions with a border to the EU-15 was the lowest, that of regions bordering external countries (BEX) was intermediate, and that of regions bordering EU accession states[154] (BCE) was highest of these three, yet it showed the steepest rise in specialization to a peak and turning point in 1999. This was attributed to delocation developments in certain sectors such as transport and logistics, textiles and shoe-making to border regions in Romania following the rise in the minimum wage level in Hungary at the turn of the century. All three groups of border regions showed a second, yet slighter rise in specialization since 2004 until 2007 when a new decline set in.

---

153 Specialization for each group of regions was calculated taking simple averages for clarity, as a weighting by population – which had also been tried - would result only in marginal differences.

154 Most CEECs became EU member jointly with Hungary in 2004, while Romania (together with Bulgaria) acceded to the EU in 2007.

The comparison of the results with NEG theories revealed that the calculations obtained were a broad confirmation of the predictions made. Especially the models by *Puga (1999), Venables (1996)* and *Krugman & Venables (1996)* predicted a rise of regional specialization levels, as agglomeration formed or increased in the course of economic integration; then a peak or turning point for regional specialization ensued; finally, with proceeding integration a dispersion set in coupled with a disolution of centre-periphery structures resulting in lower regional specialization levels. This pattern was observed twice in Hungary during the 1992 to 2008 period, not only for the 20 Nuts-3 regions as a whole, but also for the groups of regions just described in the preceding paragraphs of this section.

A review of other empirical studies on regional specialization showed that the results obtained by my calculations for Hungary's Nuts-3 regions in the 1992 to 2008 period are most accurate and have not been obtained nor published in any similar way before.

In chapter 6, the development of manufacturing industry concentration in Hungary during European integration as well as the specialization of Hungary's 20 Nuts-3 regions shall be analysed by means of econometric analysis.

6. Econometric Analysis of Influences on Agglomeration and Regional Specialization

The current chapter 6 will analyse by means of regression analysis the part of the hypothesis about the influences working on industry agglomeration and those relevant for regional specialization in Hungary. The results obtained so far for agglomeration and regional development in Hungary point to a trade-off between the overall catching-up process at the country-level due to increasing trade integration under the Europe agreement, on the one hand, and the increase of regional disparities in the pre- and post-accession phase, as shown by the results from regional specialization and other indicators, on the other hand.

In view of the factors influencing agglomeration and regional specialization processes, two regressions have been generated after a longer modelling process. One will be on the question: Which influences worked on concentration of manufacturing industries in Hungary? This will be the subject of section 6.1 and subsections. The other regression will deal with the question: Which influences shaped the degree of regional specialization in Hungary? That will be the subject of section 6.2 and subsections. The analytic tool which has been used is the programme Eviews 6.0. The two regressions have been formed by way of panel estimation in order to have a sufficient number of observations as base.

6.1 The question for regression 1 on agglomeration

This research analyses agglomeration processes in the manufacturing sectors in Hungary during proceeding European integration, notably during the pre-accession phase governed by the trade provisions of the Europe agreement as well as in the post-accession phase five years after Eastern enlargement of the EU.

The question analysed by regression 1 regarding agglomeration is the following:

> Which influences were relevant for an industry's concentration in Hungary in context with industry characteristics and European integration?

As dependent variable for this regression for modelling agglomeration, manufacturing industry concentration as measured by the Krugman concentration index was chosen. This index - calculated based on employment figures - proved to be the most conservative estimate of concentration, as was shown in Chapter 4 in the comparison of the 6 concentration measures (section 4.9). The industries were the 8 manufacturing industries of the Hungarian classification (based on TEÁOR and NACE) which were used throughout this study and for which data were available from HCSO since 1992 up to 2008:

- **Food**, beverages and tobacco;
- **Textiles**, wearing apparel, leather and fur products;
- **Wood**, paper and printing, publishing;
- **Chemicals** and chemical products;
- Other non-metallic **mineral** products;
- Basic **metals** and fabricated metal products;
- **Machinery and equipment**
(n.e.c., electrical and optical equipment, transport equipment);
- **Other** manufacturing **industries/ recycling**.

The observation period for this regression was chosen as 1993 to 2008, as the data for 1992 proved to be somewhat blurred with respect to certain industry characteristics, which may be due to the break-down of the communist system and the transition process to a market economy still going on with a certain vigour.

The number of observations for regression 1 was 120[155]. This is in the normal range for regression analysis on CEECs due to the short period of availability of reliable data (e.g. *Hildebrandt & Wörz (2004)*).

6.1.1 Selection of independent variables and description of data

As the regression model, the following linear panel regression was formulated:

$$\mathbf{CONC_{i,t} = a0C + a1Expr_{i,t} + a2Impr_{i,t} + a3FDI_{i,t} + a4Prod_{i,t} + a5Lent_{i,t}}$$
$$\mathbf{+ a6Scal_i + a7Hitec_i + a8Medtec_i + a9Low_i + a10Hiw_i + resid}\ \varepsilon_{i,t-1}$$

In this section, the variables will be explained, the data for the variables which entered into the regression 1 shall be described, and an expectation for the signs of the coefficients of the independent variables shall be given in light of relevant theories.

$CONC_{i,t}$ is the dependent variable. It stands for the degree of agglomeration of a manufacturing industry i at time t, where an industry's concentration is measured by the Krugman concentration index (4 digits after the comma).

---

155 120 observations: concentration for 8 industries over 15 years (1994 to 2008), as 1994 became the start year due to the AR correction term which was lagged by 1 year.

The dependent variable had a mean of 0.4189 and a standard deviation of 0.125. The data calculated for the Krugman concentration index per industry have been described in detail and evaluated in the relevant theoretical and empirical context in chapter 4, section 4.3.

The independent variables:

C The constant was included in this linear multiple regression.

$Expr_{i,t}$ This first variable for integration with the EU was an industry's exports to the EU in that year, in million HUF. The EU as export destination was taken in its contemporary form for each year, i.e. EU-25 for 2004 until 2006, EU-27 for 2007 and 2008. The 50 relevant SITC categories were converted systematically into the 8 industries according to a conversion table developed by myself and based on the detailed industry specification in SITC and TEÁOR statistics (the latter has a NACE correspondence). This allowed to then put exports of industry i to the EU over output of industry i for a given year, in million HUF - thus any inflation built in over the years would disappear. The resulting percentage, e.g. 0.120, was multiplied by 100 and then entered into the regression (as 12.0).

It would also have been conceivable to use the logarithm of the value of an industry's exports to the EU, or alternatively to use the share of exports to the EU in total exports to the world. The choice of exports to EU over output has been made as it is an even more concise parameter for integration with the EU than those other measures would have been.

The data for this variable showed a rise of the export rate to the EU (over output) for all industries over the years 1993 to 2008. Certain industries had low export rates, such as wood and paper (33% in 2008), while others such as machinery and equipment (including transport equipment) had high export rates (up to over 85%). A special phenomenon was going on in the textiles industry which showed export rates to the EU of up to 126% of national output. This was due to the outward processing trade with EU countries (see *Baldone & Sdogati 1997* on this) which was strongest in 2001 and declined subsequently, as Hungary lost its productivity advantage to other CEECs and to the Far East, mainly China.

Traditional trade theory predicts that industries are concentrated in the countries with a comparative advantage. In New Trade Theory, which includes product differentiation, a reduction in trade costs reduces concentration, as the home bias - originally in large countries - is removed (as in *Helpman & Krugman (1985)*). As increasing European integration went along with the reduction of trade costs, and as the share of Hungary's exports to the EU rose steadily during the process, the expected sign for the coefficient of the export variable with respect to concentration is negative.

$Impr_{i,t}$ The second integration variable chosen is an industry's imports from the EU in a year, in million HUF. This was converted from SITC statistics analogous to exports from the EU with the same conversion table, then set over output of the industry for that year; the resulting percentage entered multiplied by 100.

While an industry's imports could be sourced worldwide, it is a fact that the share of imports from the EU in total Hungarian imports increased significantly and almost in parallel to exports over the period 1993 to 2008 (see graph in Fig. 21 in section 3.7 of Chapter 3). As this research is interested in the effects of integration with the EU, imports from the EU were chosen here as variable. That import rate (over output) was between 29.7% for minerals and 85.3% for metals and metal products in 2008. Again, the textiles industry as well as other industries including recycling showed percentages above 100% of national output due to outward processing - the latter is a hint to a new division of labour among West European and the new Central and East European member states after Eastern enlargement.

For the same theoretical reasons as given for $Expr_{i,t}$, the expected sign for the coefficient of the import variable is the same as for $Expr_{i,t}$, that is negative: more imports from the EU are expected to lower the degree of agglomeration in Hungary and encourage the dispersion in space.

$FDI_{i,t}$ As a further variable for integration with the EU, foreign direct investment (FDI) in an industry was entered into the regression. This was taken as the FDI stock (from world) in million HUF present in an industry at time t. The variable was entered taking the logarithm (lg) of this value (base 10). To take FDI stock (from world) is seen as appropriate here, as a very large proportion of that FDI in manufacturing - over 50% - originated from EU countries, most prominently among them Germany. Due to the sensitivity of FDI data for the Hungarian authorities, it was not possible to get chronological data by industry according to the countries of origin of the FDI.

The stock of FDI in Hungarian manufacturing industries rose significantly during the period 1992 to 2008[156]. This was shown in detail for the 8 sectors in chapter 3, section 3.8. FDI in Hungarian manufacturing overall rose from 332 billion HUF in 1993 to 5,311 billion HUF in 2008, with the machinery and equipment sector

156 For the FDI stock in 2007 and 2008, provisional data had to be used, as the final data were scheduled to be published after the time of writing.

holding the lion share. After taking the logarithm of the FDI stock (in million HUF), the data ranged from 3.7 for other industries and recycling in 1993 to a high of 6.44 for machinery and equipment in 2008.

The expected sign for the coefficient of the FDI variable is negative: more FDI stock in an industry is expected to lower the degree of agglomeration in Hungary and facilitate the dispersion in space and the location in many possible sites.

In context with FDI and given that the privatisation of the economy had a substantial influence on FDI inflows in Hungary during a certain period (*Kalotay & Hunya 2000*), I also thought about introducing a privatisation variable as a dummy, taking the value one after the sector was included into the state private-sation scheme. But while information on the Hungarian privatisation scheme was readily available in the mid 1990s *(Hantke 1995)*[157], this is no longer the case now when the privatisation scheme of the transition to a market economy has been concluded and Hungary is a full member state of the EU.

$Prod_{i,t}$ This variable was entered in order to model the effect of labour productivity in an industry on its concentration[158]. $Prod_{i,t}$ is the ratio of output of the sector (in million HUF, at constant prices of 1992[159]) over employees of the sector at time t.

Labour productivity in Hungary improved significantly by about the double of the initial level on average for the manufacturing sector over the period 1993 to 2008. Productivity in the chemicals sector tripled, while that in the machinery and equipment sector increased fivefold. Sectors with below average increases were the wood, pulp and paper as well as the recycling and other industries sectors. This overall improvement was a clear sign of the restructuring process during the transition phase initially, until about 1995, and also due to the modernisation of production processes after privatisation and the large inflows of FDI in the latter part of the observation period. The highest productivity prevailed in the chemicals industry, the lowest in the textiles industry.

---

157 During my research in Budapest in the year 1994 for my publication *Hantke (1995)*, officials of various governmental institutions readily provided information for potential investors during the ongoing privatisation.

158 The OECD defines labour productivity as "the ratio of a volume measure of output to a volume measure of input". Volume measures of output are normally … gross value added, expressed at constant prices, i.e. adjusted for inflation, measures of input include the number of employees *(OECD 2002)*.

159 This producer price index is published by the HCSO as an index with previous year =100. In order to take out inflation, I corrected this by holding 1992=100 constant and using a producer price index in terms of prices of 1992 as correction.

In NEG models *(Krugman 1991a, Ludema & Wooton 1997)*, industry tends to concentrate where labour productivity is higher than elsewhere. Therefore, the expected sign for the coefficient of $Prod_{i,t}$ is positive.

$Lent_{i,t}$ This is the number of enterprises[160] of an industry in year t, of which the logarithm was taken. This variable was entered into the model to take account of the third dimension of concentration: where in space it took place. The number of enterprises - as a geographic illustration of the third dimension of concentration, namely where in space - has been described in section 3.4.3 of Chapter 3. This variable shall indirectly reflect the role of "history" - as described in NEG models - for determining industry location and concentration in certain areas, i.e. due to the past presence of certain industries in a production site, new industry is more likely to locate nearby than elsewhere. Further, this variable also implies to some extent the Hungarian government policy of industrial parks under the Széchenyi plan (see section 3.2.4 in Chapter 3) which encouraged industry to locate in these parks which were spread over the country (although two thirds are in the Western part and one third in the less developed Eastern part of the country).

The data for the number of enterprises per sector were lowest for the metals and metal products industry, and for the chemical industry, around 3,500 in 1993, and highest for the textiles industry and machinery and equipment, around 18,000 each. Comparing the year 1995, which showed the highest number of enterprises in all industries, with the end year 2008, a certain consolidation process took place in manufacturing. This process was most pronounced in the textiles industry which reduced active enterprises to less than 40% of that figure. In addition, a low number of enterprises would indicate a high degree of concentration. Therefore, the expected sign for this variable is negative.

To include a government variable such as tax benefits, though perhaps desirable, was not feasible due to language barriers in accessing Hungarian legislative texts; moreover, tax benefits most likely would not have been differentiated by manufacturing industry.

$Scal_i$ This is a dummy variable for the presence and importance of economies of scale in the industry. It takes the value 1 if economies of scale play a role and 0 otherwise. The classification of the OECD *(OECD 1994)* was followed, i.e. scale intensive were 3 industries in the Hungarian data set, namely wood, paper and printing, chemicals and chemical products, as well as metals and metal products, while the other 5 industries formed the reference category.

---

160 Enterprises in the statistics of HCSO: active corporations with 4 or more employees.

In a world with transportation costs, as analysed by the models of New Trade Theory, big countries gain a comparatively larger share in industries where product differentiation and internal or external economies of scale are important *(Helpman & Krugman 1985)*. New Trade Theory postulates that even in the absence of differences in factor endowments, scale economies can induce specialization among countries (regions in this study) and thus affect relative concentration. Further, industries with higher economies of scale may tend to concentrate in relatively central locations or agglomerations *(Krugman 1980; Midelfart-Knarvik et al. 2000)*. Therefore, the expected sign for the $SCAL_i$ coefficient is positive.

$Hitec_i$, $Medtec_i$ These are dummy variables accounting for the importance and level of technology in an industry. Hitec stands for high technology, Medtec for medium technology respectively. They take the value 1 if the industry belongs to that category and 0 otherwise. Again, the classification of the OECD *(OECD 1994)* was followed. The machinery and equipment industry was categorized as high tech (due to electrical and optical equipment, computer equipment); 3 industries were medium tech, namely chemicals and chemical products, metal and metal products, and other manufacturing industries/recycling. The remaining industries formed the reference category (low tech). The OECD classification was judged more accurate and commonly acceptable than the estimates for the importance of scale economies by *Forslid et al. (2002, Table 5)* which were based on input/output matrices for the year 1992 and for the EEA[161] due to the inappropriate country scope and reference year.

Differences in productivity levels between industries are implied to comprise technological differences and thus comparative advantages, which are at the heart of traditional Ricardian trade theory. Large differences in technology levels between industries are expected to have a positive influence on the concentration of an industry. Therefore, the expected signs for the coefficients of the $Hitec_i$ and $Medtec_i$ variables are positive.

Low_i, Hiw_i These are dummy variables accounting for the wage level in an industry, Low for low wage industries, Hiw for high wage industries. They take the value 1 if the industry belongs to that category and 0 otherwise. Here again, the classification of the OECD *(OECD 1994)* was followed. The chemicals and chemical products industry was high wage, while 3 industries were low wage, namely textiles, food, beverages and tobacco, and other industries and recycling. The remaining industries formed the reference category of being medium wage level.

161 The EEA (European Economic Area) comprised the EU-15 plus the EFTA countries, thus no country from Central and Eastern Europe at all.

According to the NEG model by *Krugman (1991a)*, higher real wages prevail in the agglomeration and lower wages in the periphery. Therefore, the expected sign for the coefficient of Low_i is negative, while the expected sign for the coefficient of Hiw_i is positive.

resid $\varepsilon_{i,t-1}$ This AR correction was necessary as in the original regression, errors were auto-correlated as indicated by the value for the Durbin Watson statistic which was lower than the low-sided boundary for that value (0.7236). Consequently, the 8 graphs of the residuals prior to that correction looked very similar to the graphs of the concentration index for each industry.

The significance of the independent variables was not altered by the AR-correction, i.e. those which were significant before remained significant, and those that were not remained insignificant. For one variable, the sign of the coefficient changed though[162]. The value for the adjusted R-squared increased by this correction (as did the Durbin-Watson statistic).

Prior to including the AR correction, it had also been tried to include a linear trend into the regression; this remained insignificant, however, and did not alter the low result of the Durbin-Watson test. So that idea was dropped.

At this point, some lines shall be said about the modelling of trade costs. In most NEG models, the level of trade costs - falling during integration - plays a prominent role in explaining agglomeration processes. I therefore would have liked to include an explanatory variable for the level of tariffs and quotas under the Europe agreement. There were no data available, however, differentiated by industries and for all years, as they were kept secret by the EU administration.

Further, it is acknowledged that NTBs play an even more important role in shaping the level of bilateral trade and economic integration. Regrettably, there are no quantitative estimates on NTBs available for Hungary; just for the EU-15, a series of studies for certain industries was carried out for the EU Commission in context with evaluating the Single Market programme in the mid-1990s.[163] Therefore, NTBs could not be included here either.

---

162 This variable was Lent, which had a negative sign for the coefficient prior to the AR correction, and a positive sign afterwards.

163 *European Commission (1998):* Dismantling of Barriers, Technical barriers to trade, in: The Single Market Review, Subseries III, Volume 1, Official Publications of the European Communities, Kogan Page. Earthscan, May 1998. Subseries I included volumes for: Impact (of the Single Market) on Manufacturing Foodstuffs, (Vol. 7), Chemicals (Vol. 5), and Textiles and Clothing (Vol. 3).

Finally, the time spent in passing borders (waiting time at border controls, and the filling in of customs formalities) could be conceivable as a measure of trade costs. *Bröcker (1998)* estimated this at 100 minutes and 60 minutes for the mid-1990s, and *Niebuhr & Schlitte (2008)* modelled integration by reducing these time penalties. As these are mere estimates or assumptions, they are not deemed appropriate, given the modernisation of border crossing points in accession countries, including Hungary, and the harmonisation of customs formalities which took place financed by EU-funds during the pre-accession period (i.e. under the Europe agreement). Other empirical estimates of trade costs worldwide have been presented in Section 2.2.3 (the latter part) of Chapter 2 but were not suitable to serve as explanatory variable in this model either.

6.1.2 Results of regression 1 - Agglomeration

The results of regression 1 regarding agglomeration shall be presented now. **Table 25** shows the coefficients for the constant and the explanatory variables as well as the error correction term; the p-values are shown beneath in italics and parenthesis. The last column indicates whether the coefficient had the expected sign as well as the significance level.

Regression 1 as presented had an R^2 of 88.7% and an adjusted R^2 of 87.6%. The F-statistic was sufficiently high at 77.61. The constant had a positive coefficient and was significant at the 5% level. The export rate to the EU was highly significant, yet the coefficient was positive unlike the expectation. The coefficient of the import rate to the EU had the expected negative sign, but was not significant at all. The coefficient of the logarithm of the FDI stock was not significant, but had the expected negative sign. Labour productivity was highly significant, and the coefficient had the expected sign. The number of enterprises was not significant, but the coefficient had the expected sign.

The presence of scale economies was very highly significant, yet the coefficient did not have the expected positive sign. The fact that an industry was high tech was very highly significant, yet the coefficient did not have the expected sign. Being medium tech was not significant, nor did the coefficient have the expected sign. The coefficient for being a low-wage sector had the expected negative sign and was very highly significant. Being a high wage sector was highly significant and the coefficient had the expected positive sign. Finally, the residual error correction term was very highly significant.

Table 25: Results of regression 1 on manufacturing industry agglomeration in Hungary, 1993 to 2008

Variable	for	Coefficient *(p-value in italics)*	had expected sign/ significance level
C	Constant	0.758351 *(0.0208)*	*
$Expr_{i,t}$	EU Exports/output ratio	0.000721 *(0.0057)*	**
$Impr_{i,t}$	EU Imports/output ratio	-1.29E-05 *(0.9484)*	✓
$FDI_{i,t}$	Lg of FDI stock	-0.00714 *(0.7151)*	✓
$Prod_{i,t}$	labour productivity	-0.011276 *(0.0017)*	✓ **
$Lent_{i,t}$	Lg number of enterprises	-0.005097 *(0.9442)*	✓
$Scal_i$	Scale economies	-0.229913 *(0.0001)*	***
$Hitec_i$	High tech sector	-0.377893 (0.0000)	***
$Medtec_i$	Medium tech sector	-0.031706 *(0.072)*	
Low_i	Low wage sector	-0.322779 *(0.0000)*	✓ ***
Hiw_i	High wage sector	0.137256 *(0.0004)*	✓ ***
Resid $\varepsilon_{i,t-1}$	AR-correction factor	0.641621 *(0.0000)*	***
R^2		0.887	
adjusted R^2		0.876	
F-statistic		77.61	
Number of observations		120	

* Significant (at the 5% level)
** Highly significant (at the 1% level)
*** Very highly significant (at the 0.1% level)
Source: Own calculations.

6.1.3 Evaluation of the results in view of the hypothesis, NEG models and previous empirical studies

The qustion for regression 1 on agglomeration was: Which influences were relevant for an industry's concentration in Hungary in context with industry characteristics and European integration? The results show that of the integration variables, an industry's export rate to EU over its output as well as the FDI stock, the exports to the EU had a very significant influence on the concentration of that industry in Hungary during the 1993 to 2008 period. The coefficient was positive, that is a higher export rate to the EU on average increased manufacturing concentration. This showed that the export reorientation to the EU turns out to be an important factor for manufacturing industry agglomeration in Hungary. While the FDI stock had the expected dispersing influence on concentration, the coefficient was not significant in this case. The import rate from the EU had the expected sign, but remained insignificant. The importance of trade integration in the sense of export orientation verifies the predictions by the model of *Livas-Elizondo & Krugman (1996)* which predicted agglomeration to form within the multi-region country in the course of integration processes.

Of the industry characteristics, labour productivity was highly significant for the concentration, and the coefficient had the expected sign. While the coefficient for the number of enterprises in a sector had the expected sign, it was not significant for concentration in this data set. Of the remaining industry characteristics all but one were very significant for the degree of industry concentration: the presence of scale economies - in the chemicals and metal products industries - was very highly significant; but contrary to what would be expected from NEG theories, this reduced industry concentration by -0.2299 on average, as compared with the reference category of no scale economies, controlling for other variables. Further, being a high tech sector was very significant. Contrary to what would be expected from NEG theories, this rather encouraged industry dispersion on average, however, as indicated by the negative coefficient. Being a high tech sector on average reduced concentration by -0.3778 as compared with the reference category low tech - food, textiles, minerals and paper industries –, controlling for other variables. Being a medium-tech sector reduced concentration as expected, but the coefficient just fell out of the 5% significance level.

Being a low wage sector had a strong centrifugal influence on industry location, spreading out the industries concerned more over the country: the textiles industry, food, beverages and tobacco, as well as other industries and recycling. This corresponds to the NEG theories, where higher real wages reinforce industry agglomeration *(Krugman 1991a; Ludema & Wooton 1997; Livas-Elizondo & Krugman 1996)*. Being a low wage sector in Hungary reduced concentration by -0.3227 as compared with the reference category medium-wage sectors, controlling for other variables. On the other hand, being a high-wage sector had a strong concentrating influence on the industry concerned, as would be predicted by NEG theories. In fact, the chemical industry had high values for the Krugman concentration index in Hungary over the entire period (see section 4.3.2 of Chapter 4). Being a high wage sector on average increased concentration by 0.1372 as compared with the reference category medium wage sectors, controlling for other variables.

The results of regression 1 shall be put now into context with the relevant literature. Some other authors have run regressions on industry concentration in EU or Central and East Europe countries previously. In their regression for relative industry concentration in 10 countries based on a modified form of the Hoover-Balassa index, *Hildebrandt & Wörz (2004)* also found a negative sign for the coefficient of scale economies, as in my regression 1, both when the concentration (dependent variable) was calculated based on output as well as when it was calculated with employment figures; but that scale variable was not significant in their data. They found a significant influence for the FDI stock, but with a positive sign for the coefficient (unlike in my regression 1). Their technology variable - which was taken as a difference from the mean - had a positive coefficient and was very highly significant for concentration, as in my regression 1. They had included a quadratic time trend to improve the fit of that regression, though, which does not make sense intuitively with respect to the research question. In their regressions for individual industries over the 10 countries, the exports to the EU (exports to the EU over exports to the world in percent) were highly significant for 4 out of 11 industries, the electronics, wood, paper, and food industries. The imports from the EU variable was not significant for the vast majority of industries, except for machinery and wood. Their regressions per industry were based on only 80 observations and had an R^2 around 0.20 for most industries, except for electronics with 0.81.

Brülhart & Torstensson (1998) compared industry Gini coefficients with industry centrality indices for the EU-15 and found a positive correlation between scale economies and industry bias towards the central EU in both 1980 and 1990. *Midelfart-Knarvik et al. (2000)* found that unskilled labour-intensive industries have become more concentrated in the EU from 1970 to 1997, but usually in peripheral low wage countries (thus, this would be a dispersion regarding the third dimension of concentration - where in space: centre versus periphery). During the same period, a number of high and medium tech industries have become more dispersed, i.e. the sign of the coefficient would correspond to the negative sign found in my regression 1.

Finally, in their analysis of concentration effects in context with the Single Market in the EU-15, *Aiginger & Pfaffermayr (2004)* conducted a panel regression on changes of entropy from 1985 to 1992, and from 1993 to 1998, choosing a set of industry variables. Their results showed that skill-intensive industries dispersed faster on average, and that highly globalized (by their exports to world) and capital-intensive industries exhibited a tendency of increasing concentration significantly in the second period only.

Thus, some of the few results of concentration regressions went in the same direction as the results of my regression 1: a negative sign for a scale coefficient, an imports variable not being significant, exports positively correlated with concentration and partly significant and low-wage industries positively correlated with concentration.

The next section 6.2 and subsections will look at regions instead of industries, analysing the subject of regional specialization by means of regression analysis.

6.2 Regression 2 on regional specialization

The part of the hypothesis about the development of regional specialization in Hungary during the period 1993 to 2008 will now be analysed by means of regression analysis. In particular, influences which were relevant for the specialization of a region in context of European integration and region-specific factors playing a role for the specialization of a region shall be the subject of analysis in this part. These questions shall be analysed in regression 2 by means of a panel analysis spanning over the 20 Hungarian regions and the period 1993 to 2008 (300 observations[164]).

The question of regression 2 - on regional specialization - addresses the first of the three dimensions of agglomeration: How strong was the effect of the ongoing manufacturing industry agglomeration on regional specialization in Hungary over the period 1993 to 2008? It does not address the geographic dimension where in space did it happen (due to the panel nature of the regression), nor which industries were involved.

---

164 The number of observations was reduced from 320 to 300 due to an AR-correction factor of the error term which shortened the period to 1994 to 2008 (15 years).

6.2.1 Descriptive statistics and trend regression

Before doing the entire regression analysis, some descriptive statistics and analysis of the dependent variable, specialization of a region as measured by the Krugman specialization index, shall be presented. Specialization was used in regression 2 over the period 1993 to 2008. The variable had a mean of 0.3831 and a standard deviation of 0.1150. The national average for regional specialization was calculated for 1993 - which was 0.3824 - and for 2008 respectively - which was 0.3790. Thus, on average, regional specialization declined by -0.0034, which is a rather slight change overall. As Chapter 5, section 5.3.1, showed, there had been a stronger rise to a peak around 1999 in between, and a second slighter peak around 2006.

Figure 45: Regional specialization in Hungary relative to the national average, 1993 and 2008 in comparison, Krugman specialization index based on manufacturing employment

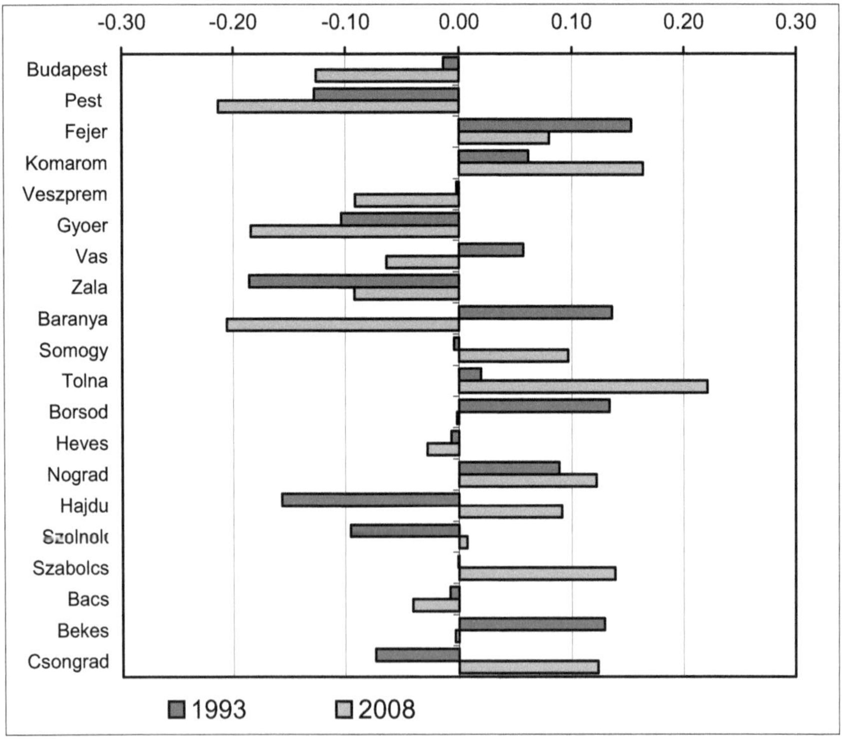

Source: Own calculations; own presentation.
Source of data: *HCSO,* Regional Statistical Yearbook of Hungary, subsequent years, Budapest.

For each region, the regional specialization relative to the national average was calculated for the start year 1993 and the end year 2008. As the bar diagram in **Figure 45** shows, the results are mixed. While 10 regions had a lower than average specialization in 1993 and 10 a higher than average, the result for 2008 was also 10 to 10. Comparing the direction of deviation from the national average, 9 regions had changed their sign from 1993 to 2008, while 11 remained specialised in the same direction. So this does not indicate any clear trend. When looking at the 5 regions with the highest export share, Fejer, Komarom, Györ, Vas, and Somogy, no distinct trend is clear either: while the first two regions had higher than average specialization in both years, Györ had a lower specialization in both years, whereas Vas and Somogy had changed the direction of deviation in opposite sides during the period.

Therefore, in order to get further information, a trend regression was run for the dependent variable, regional specialization. The equation for this regression is shown in the following:

$$\mathbf{SPEC_{j,t} = C + a1*Trend + a2*Resid_{j,t-1}}$$

The residual correction was necessary as without it, errors were auto-correlated as indicated by the value for the Durbin Watson statistic which then was lower than the low-sided boundary for that value (0.3216).

Table 26: Results of trend estimation for regional specialization in Hungary from 1993 to 1999

Variable	For	Coefficient *(p-value in italics)*	had expected sign/ significance level
C	Constant	0.375719 *(0.0000)*	***
Trend	Trend	*0.007102* *(0.0033)*	✓ **
Resid $\varepsilon_{j,t-1}$	AR-correction factor	0.889334 *(0.0000)*	***
R^2		0.7843	
Number of observations		140	

* Significant (at the 5% level)
** Highly significant (at the 1% level)
*** Very highly significant (at the 0.1% level)

Source: Own calculations.

The trend regression was run firstly for the periods 1993 to 1999, during which an increase of regional specialization had been observed up to a peak in 1999 (see section 5.3.1 of chapter 5), secondly for the long period 1994-2008, and thirdly for the period 2004-2008, i.e. since the EU accession of Hungary (80 observations), during which a slight increase in regional specialization had been observed (*ibid*). The coefficient for the latter post-accession period was small and positive (0.0068), it remained insignificant, however, and is therefore not shown here. The results of the first two trend regressions are presented in Table 26 and Table 27.

The trend regression shown in **Table 26** was run for regional specialization over the 20 regions and for the years 1993 to 1999, i.e. with 140 observations. The trend was small and positive as expected and highly significant, as was the constant. R^2 was 78.4%.

Table 27: Results of trend estimation for regional specialization in Hungary from 1994 to 2008

Variable	For	Coefficient *(p-value in italics)*	had expected sign/ significance level
C	Constant	0.404251 *(0.0000)*	***
Trend	Trend	-0.002272 *(0.0075)*	✓ ***
Resid $\varepsilon_{j,t-1}$	AR-correction factor	0.851413 *(0.0000)*	***
R^2		0.7067	
Number of observations		300	

*	Significant (at the 5% level)
**	Highly significant (at the 1% level)
***	Very highly significant (at the 0.1% level)
Source: Own calculations.

The trend regression shown in **Table 27** was run for regional specialization over the 20 regions and for the years 1994 to 2008[165], i.e. with 300 observations. The trend had a negative sign and a small coefficient, as was expected. It was highly significant, as was the constant. R^2 was 70.6%.

165	Initially 1993, but the start year was eliminated due to the AR-correction.

6.2.2 Selection of independent variables and description of data

The model of regression 2 aims at analysing which influences were significant for the degree of regional specialization of Hungarian regions during 1993 to 2008 in context with increasing European integration.

Which influences were relevant for the specialization of a region in context with European integration, and which region-specific factors did also play a role?

The dependent variable chosen was regional specialization, measured by the Krugman specialization index calculated with manufacturing employment data. The explanatory variables were chosen according to what would be desirable to include, on the one hand, and subject to the constraint which data were available from HCSO at the level of the 20 regions and for the entire period 1993 to 2008, on the other hand.

In this section, the selection of the independent variables which entered into the regression 2 shall be described, their data shall be analysed and an expectation as to the sign of the coefficients of the independent variables shall be given in light of relevant theories.

The following equation has been formulated for regression 2:

$$\mathbf{SPEC_{j,t} = a0C + a1INT_j + a2East_j + a3LAct_{j,t} + a4LFDI_{j,t}}$$
$$\mathbf{+\ a5Mig_{j,t} + a6Exsh_{j,t} + a7LGW_{j,t} + resid\ \varepsilon_{j,t-1}}$$

$\mathbf{SPEC_{j,t}}$ is the dependent variable, a region's specialization in manufacturing industries as measured by the Krugman specialization index at time t (4 digits after the comma; see section 5.2.1 for the formula and data base).

The independent variables:

C The constant was included in this linear multiple regression.

$\mathbf{INT_j}$ This is a dummy variable which takes the value 1 if the region is an internal region - which is the case for 8 of the 20 regions -, and 0 otherwise. The reference category was thus being a border region, either with an external country (BEX), or with an accession country (BCE), or with a former EU-15 member state (BEU).

Being an internal region also indicates centrality - in the sense of NEG theories - with respect to the region's location, i.e. closeness to the capital region Budapest with the international airport and other facilities. Therefore, the expected sign of the coefficient is positive, i.e. that internal regions have a higher specialization than border regions.

It had been tried to run the regression with three dummies for these three types of border regions (BEU, BCE, and BEX) and the internal regions as the reference category; these three variables remained insignificant, however, without improving the quality of the regression, therefore including INT_j was the best choice.

$East_j$ This is a dummy variable for the location of a region in the economically less developed Eastern part of the country,[166] which takes the value 1 if the region is located there - which is the case for 7 of the 20 regions-, and 0 otherwise. The expectation for the sign of the coefficient is based on the empirical results derived for the specialization of Eastern regions in Chapter 5, section 5.4.1, namely that their specialization is slightly higher than that of Western regions, which was attributed to their thinner economic and manufacturing base. Therefore, the expected sign for the coefficient of $East_j$ is positive.

$LAct_{j,t}$ This is the economically active population of the region in a year, of which the logarithm was taken. The economically active population was preferred to the population of the region as such due to its higher relevance for manufacturing employment, based on which the dependent variable - regional specialization - was calculated.

For some regions, the economically active population increased over the period 1993 to 2008, as was the case for Györ (+39.0% to 197,900), for some it decreased as for Budapest (-11.5% to 780,800). Taking the logarithm smoothed out the differences in endowment with active population among the regions, improving the results for this variable (not altering the sign of the coefficient though).

A larger number of economically active people are expected to allow for a broadening of the industrial base including manufacturing sectors, i.e. for a greater diversification of the region. Therefore, the expected sign for the coefficient with respect to regional specialization is negative.

166 Division into Eastern part and Western part according to *László Faragó (1999),* as in Chapter 5.

$\mathbf{LFDI_{j,t}}$ This is the share of FDI in enterprises with FDI (minimum 10%) in the region at time t, in billion HUF, of which the logarithm was taken[167]. The FDI capital in enterprises with FDI of a region, in billion HUF, showed an increase from low to higher levels for all regions over the period 1993 to 2008. For Hungary as a whole, this increased from 662.9 to 11,795 billion HUF. The logarithm was taken to smooth values for this variable. A larger FDI stock is expected to allow for a broadening of the industrial base of the region; therefore, the expected sign for the coefficient is negative.

$\mathbf{Mig_{j,t}}$ This is the internal net migration of the region in a year (not in logarithm, as the numbers are sometimes positive and sometimes negative). The data for internal net migration of the 20 regions over the period 1993 to 2008 have been described in detail in section 3.5 and subsections of Chapter 3, and a link has been examined between the balance of internal net migration per region and the regional wage level, verifying what is described in the relevant NEG models (please, see also the tables, maps and graphs in that section). In particular, the model by *Ludema & Wooton (1997)* allows for (partial) internal migration and for regional preferences of manufacturing workers. In case 5 of the equilibria described for the model (see Chapter 2, section 2.1.2.3), which form in the course of integration processes, regional income differences prevail. Both regions have some industry, however, to a different extent.

With a positive internal net migration - such as for Pest region and many Western regions-, regional specialization is expected to decline, whereas with a negative internal net migration, specialization is expected to rise. Therefore, the expected sign for the coefficient is negative.

$\mathbf{Exsh_{j,t}}$ This is the share of exports (to world) in sales of industry located in region j in year t. Even though the variable is based on exports to the world, this points to the EU which had a rising share of around 80% of Hungary's total exports in the latter years of the period. The variable $Exsh_{j,t}$ indicates the degree of openness of a region, and also at which level its economy is internationally linked, to a large extent also through the division of labour with the EU.

Over the period, the figures for the share of exports (to world) in sales of industry by region rose for all regions and for Hungary as a whole. For the year 1993, the export share ranged from 9.8 to 39.1%, whereas for the year 2008, the range was from 28.1 to 89.4%. Five regions have developed into strongly export-oriented

167 The HCSO calls this the "share" of FDI in its statistical publications, even though it should rather be called the foreign "capital".

regions over the period: Fejer, Komarom-Esztergom, Györ-Moson-Sopron, Vas, and Somogy. All of these are in the Western part of Hungary, but only two have a common border with Austria (with the former EU-15).

In the models of New Trade Theory based on a world with transportation costs, big countries gain a comparatively larger share in industries where product differentiation and internal or external economies of scale are important *(Helpman & Krugman 1985)*. New Trade Theory also postulates than even in the absence of differences in factor endowments, scale economies can induce specialization among countries (regions in this study) and affect relative concentration. This is complemented by the NEG model of *Livas-Elizondo & Krugman (1995)* who explicitly modelled a country with two (or several) regions. Therefore, the expected sign for the coefficient of the export variable is negative: a higher share of exports in sales is expected to lower the degree of regional specialization.

$LGW_{j,t}$ This is the (average) monthly gross wage rate in manufacturing industry of the region in year t (in million HUF), corrected by the producer price index for the manufacturing sector[168]. The logarithm was taken of these values. These absolute numbers for the gross wage rates are similar to the regional profile which had been shown in section 3.5.2 of Chapter 3 (Figure 14 illustrated the monthly gross wages in manufacturing per region as percent of the national average for 2005 and 1992).

In the NEG model by *Krugman (1991a)*, higher real wages prevail in the agglomeration, which is the region with high specialization. In the *Ludema & Wooton (1997)* model with partial internal migration, case 5 of the equilibria in the course integration processes describes that regional income differences prevail. Both regions have some industry, however, to a different extent. Therefore, the expected sign for the coefficient of the $LGW_{j,t}$ variable with respect to regional specialization is negative.

resid $\varepsilon_{j,t-1}$ This AR correction was necessary as in the original regression, errors were auto-correlated as indicated by the value for the Durbin Watson statistic which was lower than the low-sided boundary for that value (0.3873). After this correction, the problem was eliminated and the quality of the regression improved (R^2 rose from around 20% to 70%).

168 This producer price index is published by the HCSO as an index with previous year =100. In order to take out inflation, I corrected this by holding 1992=100 constant and using a producer price index in terms of prices of 1992 as correction.

Prior to including the AR correction, it had also been tried to include a linear trend into the regression; this remained insignificant, however, and did not alter the low result of the Durbin-Watson test. So that idea was dropped.

As a variable for the quality of infrastructure of a region which was available from the HCSO data for the entire period, the number of major roads ($RDS_{j,t}$) per 100 km^2 of a region in a year has been considered. The idea behind would be that better infrastructure encourages more industry into the region, fosters the region's diversification and thus reduces its specialization. The data for this variable are such that for some regions, Pest for example (the region surrounding the capital), the figures are around 40, whereas for other regions, like Hajdu and Szolnok, the figures are around 25. The data show hardly any variation over time, i.e. they remain more or less the same, improving only slightly over the period 1993 to 2008. The coefficient had the expected negative sign with respect to regional specialization; but it remained (very) insignificant and did not improve the quality of the regression either. Therefore, it was eliminated in the manual process of stepwise regression.

6.2.3 Results of regression 2 - Regional specialization

The results of regression 2 on regional specialization in Hungary are presented in **Table 28**. The table shows the coefficients for the constant and the explanatory variables as well as the error correction term, and beneath each the p-values in italics and parenthesis. The last column indicates whether the coefficient had the expected sign as well as the significance level.

The regression 2 in its form as presented had an R^2 of 70.58% and an adjusted R^2 of 69.77%. The F-statistic was sufficiently high at 87.27. The constant had a positive coefficient and was significant at the 1% level. The dummy for being an internal region was very highly significant, and the coefficient had the expected positive sign. The dummy for being a region in the Eastern part had the expected sign, but was not significant. The variable for the economically active population of a region (in logarithm) was very highly significant, and the coefficient had the expected negative sign.

The FDI stock of a region (in logarithm) was significant, and the coefficient had the expected negative sign. Internal net migration was very highly significant, and the coefficient - though small due to the fact hat the values were not in logarithm - had the expected sign. The coefficient for the export share of a region had the expected sign (was small though), but was not significant. The gross manufacturing wage of a region (in logarithm) had the expected negative sign, but was not significant either. Finally, the residual error correction term was very highly significant.

Table 28: Results of regression 2 on regional specialization in Hungary from 1993 to 2008

Variable	for	Coefficient *(p-value in italics)*	had expected sign/ significance level
C	Constant	0.959313 *(0.0017)*	***
Int_j	Internal region	0.022274 *(0.0076)*	✓ ***
$East_j$	Eastern region	0.005529 *(0.4933)*	✓
$LAct_{j,t}$	Lg of active population	-0.097088 *(0.0012)*	✓ ***
$LFDI_{j,t}$	Lg of FDI stock	-0.028406 *(0.0631)*	✓ *
$Mig_{j,t}$	Internal net migration	-6.08 E-06 *(0.0000)*	✓ ***
$Exsh_{j,t}$	Export share of the region	-5.24 E-05 *(0.8328)*	✓
$LGW_{j,t}$	Lg of gross manufacturing wage	-0.004222 *(0.9360)*	✓
Resid $\varepsilon_{j,t-1}$	AR-correction factor	0.808182 *(0.0000)*	***
R^2		0.7058	
adjusted R^2		0.6977	
F-statistic		87.27	
Number of observations		300	

* Significant (at the 10% level)
** Highly significant (at the 5% level)
*** Very highly significant (at the 1% level)

Source: Own calculations.

6.2.4 Evaluation of results in view of the hypothesis, NEG models and previous empirical studies

The question for regression 2 on regional specialization was: Which influences were relevant for the specialization of a region in context with European integration, and which region-specific factors did also play a role?

The relevant NEG models which play a role for the interpretation shall be recalled. The model by *Livas-Elizondo & Krugman (1996)* for regional integration modelled in the context of international trade described that an (irreversible) agglomeration would form within the country consisting of more than one region, and that specialization would increase there. The model by *Puga (1999)* predicted an Ω-shaped relationship between agglomeration and trade costs with proceeding integration, with regional specialization reaching its highest level when agglomeration is strongest. The model by *Ludema & Wooton (1997)* predicted (less than complete) agglomeration to form at some intermediate level of trade costs, followed by dispersion as trade costs decline even further in the course of proceeding integration. Finally, in the model by *Krugman & Venables (1996)*, with labour assumed internationally immobile but moving between different sectors, agglomeration will become necessary for trade costs at very low levels, such that each region (country) will lose its presence in one of the industries; thus specialization is then increasing to high levels.

The results of regression 2 show that of the two integration variables - a region's FDI stock and its export share - only the FDI stock was significant with the Hungarian data, reducing regional specialization and allowing for a broadening of the manufacturing industry base in a region.

Of the region-specific factors related to a region's location - being an internal region, and being in the (economically backward) Eastern part - only the first was significant for regional specialization. An internal region had a regional specialization which was 0.0222 higher on average than that of a border region, controlling for other variables.

Of the three region-specific factors related to population, a region's active population (in logarithm) had the largest influence on regional specialization, reducing it by allowing for the broadening of the manufacturing sectors of a region. Internal net migration had a negative influence on specialization. In Pest region, the region with the largest internal net migration (even in absolute terms), regional specialization decreased by -35% from 1993 to 2008, while the cumulative internal net migration was +242,000 (or almost 20% in terms of the region's population in 2005). This would point to the NEG-model by *Ludema & Wooton*

(1997) as the relevant model for the specialization of Hungary's regions in the observation period, as inter-regional migration did play a significant role for the degree of regional specialization, perhaps working through a whole chain of other influences such as the local housing markets. Finally, the gross manufacturing wage of a region did not have a significant influence on regional specialization, unlike the importance it is generally given in NEG models based on the original *Krugman (1991a)* model.

Few other authors have run regressions on regional specialization in the EU or in CEECs in previous empirical literature. While some studies exist on country-level specialization of EU member states, e.g. on decreasing trade specialization *(Sapir 1996)* and decreasing production specialization *(Amiti 1997, Midelfart-Knarvik et al. 2000)*, few dealt with the specialization of regions by way of regression analysis. *Hallet (2000)* estimated a trend regression for regional specialization of EU-15 regions based on production data from 1980 to 1995. The trend line was a linear regression with β = -0.3869 (thus much stronger than in my trend regressions, due to the longer time span and the fact that the sample also included regions of large countries such as Germany) and an R^2 of 43.1%. He did not analyse influences on regional specialization though.

Based on specialization of regions by output, *Traistaru et al. (2003)* showed a trend regression for Hungary over the period 1990 to 1999. This had the very low R^2 within of 0.0074. The time trend had a small negative coefficient -0.0019, but was not significant. Instead of a regression about influences on regional specialization, the authors produced summary statistics for regional specialization and a number of economic indicators (GDP per capita, wages, and unemployment) relative to the national averages and for the years 1990 and 1999. They inferred that border regions (all three categories analysed, BEU, BCE and BEX) were found to be more specialised compared to the national average, while internal regions were less specialised. High specialization was associated with inferior economic performance, while regions with low specialization performed better than the national averages.

Compared with the attempts in previous literature, regression 2 has brought forward some interesting results about region-specific characteristics and the role of proceeding European integration for regional specialization. Based on the empirical results of regression 2 for regional specialization in Hungary during 1993 to 2008, the following general statement can be made: Regional specialization is an attribute of a region which is more transitory in nature than the degree of concentration of an industry is (regression 1). Regional specialization of a given region changes over time, and the direction for a given region can rarely be predicted (as shown in Figure 45 of section 6.2.1.). What can be predicted, however, is the average degree of specialization for a group of regions during proceeding integration processes, based on the NEG models by *Livas-Elizondo & Krugman (1996), Ludema & Wooton (1997), Puga (1999),* and *Krugman & Venables (1996)*, which have been chosen as the analytic framework for this part of the research. Past specialization of groups of Hungarian regions has been analysed empirically in Chapter 5, section 5.4 and subsections.

This concludes chapter 6 about regression analysis of manufacturing industry concentration and regional specialization in Hungary during the 1993 to 2008 period. The final chapter 7 will provide a summary of the results of this research and draw conclusions on the direct effects which pre-accession policies such as the Europe agreement had on agglomerations and regional development in Hungary. Further, it will highlight the role which agglomeration and regional specialization can play in the overall cohesion process. Future options for the reform of European regional policy will be discussed in the face of new needs after Eastern enlargement, based on results for the Hungarian regions. And finally, some policy recommendations will be given regarding future EU enlargement candidates.

7. Policy Implications for an Enlarged EU

In context with the Europe agreement and the Eastern enlargement of the EU, this research deals with the effects of pre-enlargement integration policies and post-accession effects on industry agglomerations and regional development in Hungary. The results for Hungary clearly show that there is a trade-off between the overall catching-up process at the country-level due to increasing trade and economic integration under the Europe agreement, on the one hand, and the increase of regional disparities in the pre- and post-accession phase, as shown by the results for industry agglomeration and regional specialization, on the other hand. This concluding chapter will summarize the main results of this research, derive policy implications and look at recent developments regarding European regional policy in the context of Eastern enlargement, and draw policy conclusions for future enlargement candidates.

Chapter 7 is structured as follows: section 7.1 will summarize the main results of this research regarding agglomeration and regional development in Hungary during the pre- and post-accession period up to 2008. Section 7.2 will derive policy conclusions regarding the role of agglomerations and specialization in the overall cohesion process going on. Given the academic debate with regards to cohesion in the EU, proposals for the next reform of European regional policy will be discussed given the new challenges after Eastern enlargement in Hungary and probably to a similar extent in the other CEEC. The concluding section 7.3 will derive policy recommendations for Hungary, the EU and future EU accession candidates with a perspective on the future economic geography of Europe.

7.1 Review of the main empirical results

Hungary as a transformation economy and the profound economic processes entailed by transition and restructuring have been examined over the time span of almost two decades, much longer than by previous studies on transition countries. Agglomeration in the manufacturing industries and regional development in Hungary's 20 regions have been the focus of this research undertaken in context with increasing European integration. The exact timeframe chosen was 1992 to 2008, the first 12 years having been those governed by the institution of the

Europe agreement with Hungary,[169] while the ensuing 5 year period spanned the time since Hungary's EU accession.

The theories of the NEG based on *Krugman (1991a)*, which have been chosen as the theoretical framework for this research, made certain predictions about the agglomeration of industry and the degree of regional specialization in the course of economic integration processes. A handful of models were singled out as relevant for the processes in Hungary analysed by this research, namely the models by *Ludema & Wooton (1997)* - assuming (less than full) migration of industrial workers between regions of a country - and by *Puga (1999)* - assuming no interregional migration. These were considered jointly with models by *Krugman & Venables (1996)* and *Livas-Elizondo & Krugman (1996)* which modelled integration with falling trade costs between multi-region countries. These 4 models predicted the formation and dispersion of industry agglomerations during proceeding economic integration, going along with a rise and subsequent decline of regional specialization.

Questions posed by this empirical research included: Did the Europe agreement have direct effects on industry agglomerations and regional development in Hungary? Which regional development took place in Hungary during different stages of the European integration process? How did manufacturing industry agglomeration evolve during the period, was there a certain pattern? Where in space did the concentration of manufacturing industries take place? Which influences were relevant for the degree of an industry's concentration, variables of increasing European integration or rather industry-specific characteristics, or both? Which development pattern of regional specialization took place in Hungary? Which influences played a role there? Was there a turning point – perhaps already prior to EU accession - at which the highest agglomeration and specialization levels were reached?

These hypotheses were tested based on empirical analyses using regional sectoral employment data from the Hungarian Central Statistical Office for 8 manufacturing sectors and the 20 Nuts-3 regions from 1992 to 2008: This is a relatively long time series - as compared to previous studies on CEECs after 1989 - and was the longest available and reliable at the time of writing.

With respect to industry agglomeration, most of the previous empirical research on Central and Eastern Europe was based on the country-level for a group of countries (CEECs), while the present research used regional-level data to analyse

169 The trade provisions of the Europe agreement, which this study is mainly interested in, have indeed been in force for this entire period, from 1992 until 1994 under the provisional name of "Interim Agreement between ... the EU.. and Hungary".

agglomeration for the country chosen, namely Hungary. With reference to the tools, a unique contribution of this research is that it applies six different concentration indices for measuring manufacturing industry agglomeration to the same set of data, thereby allowing for a comparison of them. Regression analysis on the influences working onto industry concentration and especially on regional specialization has rarely been performed before nor been based on data from Central and Eastern Europe.

Chapter 3 introduced the main characteristics of the 20 regions in Hungary, including the location and geographic situation, main economic sectors as well as structural problems of each region. By means of key indicators such as population, per-capita income, unemployment, internal net migration, and growth, the main winners have been identified as well as regions falling behind over the almost two decades. The analysis of Hungary as a transformation economy and the profound economic processes brought about by the transition entailed a changing role of economic centres over the country, some on the winner side and others on a declining path. Whilst in the pre-1989 period, the heavy industry in North Hungary and the metropolitan area around Budapest were the drivers of economic growth, since the mid-1990s, the former industrial regions have been in decline[170].

The new development divide in Hungary is rather an East-West axis, with the regions in the West near the border of Austria (EU-15) and the Centre advancing in terms of per-capita income, while the Eastern part including the agricultural Great Plain is in decline, as characterized by lower and declining income levels and persisting unemployment. New agglomerations of manufacturing industry have located in the Western part near the EU-15 markets, such as the automobile industry in Györ-Moson-Sopron and neighbouring regions. This pointed to a rise in specialization levels in those regions and to a shift in agglomerations towards the West. Alarmingly, regional disparities at Nuts-3 level based on per-capita GDP in purchasing power standards increased over the period from 31% to over 40% of the EU average; these disparities were the largest among large CEECs.[171] This pointed to new challenges regarding the EU's regional policy in bringing about cohesion, not just within Hungary but also with respect to the EU average, which will be discussed in section 7.2 of this chapter.

The analysis of the balances of internal-net migration per region showed that the Western regions as well as Pest tended to register positive balances, whilst regions in Northern Hungary, towards the Eastern border with Ukraine and in the

---

170 The metropolitan area of Budapest had exceptionally high and still advancing per-capita income, 213% as compared to the country-average in 2005.

171 Data for Poland at Nuts-3 level were not available at the time of writing.

Great Plain area tended to have negative balances over the period 1992 to 2008. The level of migration was judged as rather low - whether due to housing market constraints or socio-economic attachments is not clear, except for Pest region with a high positive balance. These results left it somewhat ambiguous whether to prefer the NEG model by *Krugman (1991a)* based on no migration predicting the emergence of non-reversible agglomeration, or that by or *Puga (1999)* or *Ludema & Wooton (1997*) based on the assumption of partial labour migration, predicting agglomeration for intermediate levels of trade costs and dispersion during further integration.

The analysis of Hungary's foreign trade with the EU countries for the period 1992 to 2008 - based on an own conversion matrix from SITC to the 8 Hungarian manufacturing sectors[172] - showed that the machinery and equipment sector contributed a share of over 70% by the end of the period within the rising share of exports to the EU in total exports to the world. The contributions of the 8 manufacturing sectors to EU exports of Hungary corresponded broadly to their shares in manufacturing output. In the high stock of FDI in Hungary - the highest in any of the CEECs –, machinery and equipment again attracted the lion share of manufacturing FDI, followed by the chemicals industry and food, beverages and tobacco. This was taken as a first hint towards tangible effects of these two integration variables on concentration in these manufacturing industries.

With respect to the regional structure, five regions located mainly in the Western part of Hungary developed especially high shares of exports in sales of manufacturing industry over the period. The bulk of FDI was found to be concentrated in the Western part of Hungary and the capital region, indicating a geographical advantageous effect of proximity to EU-markets. The presence or enhanced formation of manufacturing agglomerations in this part of the country raised questions on whether regional specialization increased there at a certain time as well.

Further, in Chapter 4 the development of industry agglomeration was analysed empirically by means of 6 different concentration indices, the Krugman concentration index, the concentration rate CR_3, the (absolute) Herfindahl index, the relative Herfindahl index, the Hoover-Balassa index, and the entropy. For each of the 8 manufacturing industries, the degree of concentration was calculated based on sectoral employment data from the 20 regions in Hungary for the period 1992 to 2008. Interestingly, the results showed a common pattern best described as a "double hub", with some variations for the sectors and depending on the index. From 1992 until 1999, concentration levels were rising to a peak, the highest over

172 The Hungarian Central Statistical Office used TEÁOR, which summarizes several NACE sectors under one heading.

the 17 year period. This was followed by a decline in concentration levels until 2004.

The EU accession of Hungary spurred a new, but slighter increase in industry concentration which was already reversed from 2007 onwards. These empirical findings confirmed predictions of the *Puga (1999)* model about an Ω-shaped relationship between industry agglomeration and declining transport costs during economic integration processes as well as those modelled by *Ludema & Wooton (1997)* who predicted (less than complete) agglomeration to form at some intermediate level of trade costs, followed by dispersion as trade costs decline even further in the course of proceeding integration.

The highest absolute concentration levels - as measured by the Herfindahl index - prevailed in the chemicals industry, followed by the mineral products and basic metals sectors, the lowest in food, beverages, and tobacco. The machinery and equipment sector showed a decrease in overall concentration levels from the start to the end of the period. Regarding the spatial aspect of agglomeration, the calculations upon which the CR_3 measure was based revealed a prominent role for Budapest and Pest region, as they were among the 3 largest regions for each of the 8 manufacturing sectors. This indicated a high degree of diversification of these regions and pointed to a low specialization - which was confirmed by the analysis of chapter 5 (for detailed summary, please see below).

The comparative analysis of the six concentration measures revealed that the Hoover-Balassa index tended to overestimate changes in concentration levels, while CR_3 underestimated them. The Krugman concentration index was found to be a "conservative" measure of the development of industry agglomeration in Hungary and was therefore selected for the econometric analysis of chapter 6.

The empirical analysis of regional specialization in Chapter 5 was done based on the Krugman specialization index for regional manufacturing employment in the 8 sectors over the 17-year period. Interestingly again, the majority of regions taken individually as well as groups of regions exhibited a common pattern similar to that observed for agglomeration: a double hub with two peaks in the pre- and post accession periods. Regional specialization for the majority of regions first increased from 1992 to 1999, when a peak was reached, then decreased up to 2004 to levels below the start. A second slighter rise in specialization levels followed EU-accession, with a decline already setting in towards the end of the period. The same development was illustrated by Western regions versus Eastern regions, where Eastern regions showed a slightly higher degree of specialization overall.

Further, the development of border regions versus internal regions confirmed the double hub pattern of specialization levels during proceeding European integration. Among this group, internal regions showed higher specialization levels than border regions, the more so when leaving out Budapest. Finally, the analysis differentiating among three groups of border regions according to their neighbouring countries — BEU, BEX and BCE - exhibited the double hub structure, with the peak in specialization around the year 1999, followed by a decline, and a second, slighter hub since the EU accession of Hungary having surpassed its climax in 2008 already. BCE showed the highest specialization levels among this group, while BEU was the most diversified on average.

The predictions made by the relevant NEG models *(Livas-Elizondo & Krugman (1996), Puga (1999), Ludema & Wooton (1997), Venables (1996), Krugman & Venables 1996)* are broadly confirmed by the results of the calculations on regional specialization in Hungary over the 1992 to 2008 period. The hypothesis of this research with respect to regional specialization in Hungary was confirmed, namely that under the Europe agreement, there was first an increase of specialization up to a peak, followed by a decline, and that the turning point - in 1999 - was reached prior to full EU-membership.

Regarding the econometric analysis, the first regression analysed influences of relevance for an industry's concentration in Hungary, based on a set of integration variables and other industry characteristics. The results of the panel regression analysis showed that the integration variable export rate to the EU had a very significant (yet positive) influence on industry concentration. The export variable endorsed the strong influence which the Europe agreement had on agglomeration processes in Hungary. On the policy side, this showed that the strong export orientation pursued by Hungary towards the EU and the pursuit of FDI-attracting location policies - which increased productivity - turned out to be important factors for manufacturing concentration in Hungary. The importance of trade integration verified empirically the model of *Livas-Elizondo & Krugman (1996)* who predicted agglomeration to form within the multi-region country in the course of integration processes.

The FDI stock, the second integration variable, was not significant as such, but indirectly decisive for the increase in productivity, an industry variable which turned out to be highly significant and positive with respect to industry concentration. Of the industry characteristics, the majority was very significant for the degree of industry concentration: the presence of economies of scale (yet negative sign), and being a high tech sector (also negative signs), although contrary to what would be expected from NEG theories, these two characteristics on average rather encouraged industry dispersion. With respect to the wage level, being a low wage sector had a strong centrifugal influence on industry location, while being a high-wage sector had a strong agglomerating influence. These empirical results confirm the predictions by NEG theories, where higher real wages reinforce industry agglomeration *(Krugman (1991a), Ludema & Wooton (1997), Livas-Elizondo & Krugman (1996).*

The second panel regression analysed influences on regional specialization in Hungary, based on a set of integration variables and region-specific characteristics. The results of regression 2 showed that of the two integration variables - a region's FDI stock and its export share - only the FDI stock was significant, reducing regional specialization and allowing for a broadening of the manufacturing industry base. With respect to the influence of a region's location on specialization - being an internal region, and being in the (economically less developed) Eastern part - only the first was significant for regional specialization. An internal region on average had a higher specialization than a border region, controlling for other variables.

Of the three region-specific characteristics related to population, a region's active population was very highly significant for regional specialization, the negative sign is indicating a diversification on average with respect to the industrial structure. Internal net migration was very highly significant and had a negative influence on regional specialization. In Pest region, the region with the largest internal net migration (even in absolute terms), regional specialization decreased by -35% from 1993 to 2008, while the cumulative internal net migration was +242,000[173]. This points to the NEG-model by *Ludema & Wooton (1997)* as the relevant model for the specialization of Hungary's regions during the observation period, as inter-regional migration did play a significant role for the degree of regional specialization, perhaps working through a whole chain of other influences such as the local housing markets. Finally, the gross manufacturing wage of a region did not have a significant influence on regional specialization, unlike the importance the wage level is generally given in NEG models based on the original *Krugman (1991a)* model.

The results of regression 1 - agglomeration - and regression 2 - regional specialization - allow the following general statement: Regional specialization is an attribute of a region which is more transitory in nature than the degree of concentration of an industry is. Regional specialization of a given region changes over time, and the direction for a given region can rarely be predicted (see Figure 45 of section 6.2.1). What can be predicted, however, is the average degree of specialization for a group of regions during proceeding integration processes, based on

173 This corresponds to about 20% of the region's population in 2005.

the framework provided by NEG models (*Livas-Elizondo & Krugman (1996), Ludema & Wooton (1997), Puga (1999),* and *Krugman & Venables (1996))*. The predictions for the future development of regional specialization in Hungary are made in the following section 7.3. (The past development of the specialization of groups of Hungarian regions has been analysed empirically in Chapter 5, section 5.4 and subsections).

Overall, the results of this research on manufacturing agglomeration and regional specialization in Hungary contribute an empirical confirmation for one of the key propositions emerging from NEG called for by *Head & Mayer (2004)*: That trade induces agglomeration - a reduction in trade impediments from relatively high initial levels will promote greater spatial concentration. And further, regarding the spatial aspect of concentration, some empirical evidence was added towards the idea of NEG that a temporary shock to economic activity in a location can permanently alter the pattern of agglomeration, as was the case for the 3 regions of Northern Hungary, flourishing due to the concentration of heavy industry in the socialist era, but in decline after the break-down of the CMEA (the shock) from the early 1990s onwards (see sections 3.3. and 3.4).

Policy implications ensuing from the results of this research will be derived in section 7.2 and subsections in context with regional policy in an enlarged EU, and policy recommendations for Hungary, the EU and future accession candidates will be formulated in section 7.3.

7.2 Policy implications

In context with the Europe agreement and the Eastern enlargement of the EU, this research deals with the effects of pre-enlargement integration policies and post-accession effects on industry agglomerations and regional development in Hungary. The results for Hungary have shown that there is a trade-off between the overall catching-up process at the country-level due to increasing trade integration under the Europe agreement, on the one hand, and the increase of regional disparities in the process, as shown by the results for regional specialization and other indicators, on the other hand.

The field of potential policy implications is wide. Therefore, one policy, namely European regional policy was chosen as the focus here, notably for three reasons: Firstly, the results of this research identified a trade-off between pre-accession policies and increasing regional disparities, which points to a need for reform of European regional policy after Eastern enlargement. Secondly, regional policy has considerable resources with a financial envelope amounting to one third of the EU budget. And thirdly, future regional development in Hungary has a chance to be (substantially) influenced by interventions co-financed by the European Structural Funds, given the sizable amount of transfers from the EU which will amount to about 4% of Hungary's GDP.[174]

The remainder of section 7.2 will proceed as follows: Section 7.2.1 will get a view on the role which agglomerations and regional specialization can play in concepts for regional growth, with a view to the results of chapters 4, 5 and 6. Agglomerations in this chapter will be understood in the brought sense of the term, including the concentration of population in towns, cities and metropolitan areas, not mere concentration of manufacturing industry, as in the previous chapters. Some interesting concepts regarding the role of agglomerations for regional development and the chances lying in a certain way of specialization will be brought forward. Given the increase of regional disparities in Hungary over the period 1992 to 2008, namely in the pre-and post-accession periods, the economic rationale for a European cohesion policy will be recalled in light of empirical evaluations of the cohesion process in the EU. Section 7.2.2 will point to the main economic challenges regarding regional policy in Hungary, review regional policy in Hungary in its past and present institutional set-up as well as present the current strategies for the period up to 2013; this is done exemplary for other CEECs which exhibit similar challenges with respect to regional disparities in the post-accession period. Section 7.2.3 will describe areas for improvement of European regional policy, taking into account the current political developments at the European level concerning ideas for the next reform of European regional policy for the period beyond 2013.

7.2.1 Rationale for a European regional policy and role for agglomerations and specialization

The results of this research on agglomerations and regional development in Hungary have shown that there is a trade-off between the overall catching-up process at the country-level due to increasing trade integration, on the one hand, and the increase of regional disparities in the process, as shown by the results from regional specialization and other indicators, on the other hand. While Hungary has been able to catch-up with average EU income at the country level

---

174 In addition, the author Cordula Wandel has previous work experience in the field, namely in the Cabinet of Commissioner Dr. Monika Wulf-Mathies, the Commissioner in charge of Regional Policy, from May 1997 until December 1999, a period during which the Agenda 2000 was designed, the third Cohesion Report published, a reform of the Regional Policy brought forward, the new Financial Perspective for 2000-2006 with the Structural Funds budget negotiated, and the new regulations governing the implementation in the new period passed.

under the Europe agreement, regional disparities in Hungary have widened not only during the pre-accession phase, but also in the first five years since full EU membership. This development is exemplary for the growth of regional disparities in other CEECs. It points to new challenges for European cohesion policy after Eastern enlargement. This section shall discuss these in light of the empirical results obtained for Hungary and of the current academic and political debate regarding European regional policy.

There is agreement among economists and policy makers about what is needed to reduce regional disparities, as for example *Baldwin & Martin (2001), Barrios & Strobl (2005), Giannetti (2002), Tondl & Vuksic (2003)*, namely an appropriate stimulus for economic growth, both for country-level and for regional growth. Commonly agreed drivers of growth include: Physical capital (including FDI), human resources, agglomeration and concentration of industry in clusters, a suitable environment (business, institutional, natural, and physical), innovation and the importance of a favourable macroeconomic context - the latter is stressed even more in the face of the current world economic crisis.

Summarizing the most recent debate regarding economic growth with a policy perspective, economists and policy-makers have become more cautious as regards both the explanations for growth and for disparities between places and about which measures can or should be taken to stimulate growth.[175] The experience of the last two decades has frustrated the expectations of policy advisers who thought they knew which policy ingredients promote growth, according to *Rodrik (2005)*. There is a strong consensus on one aspect, however, namely that "agglomeration" is one of the key drivers of growth and development. A policy of strategic specialization, which will be defined later in this section, can also contribute to regional growth strategies. These two are relevant with regards to the subject of analysis of this research.

In the context of European integration, cohesion means a catching-up process of poor regions with average per capita income in the EU. So-called "beta-convergence" is required for a reduction of regional disparities. This term refers to a process in which poor regions grow faster than rich ones and therefore catch-up on them in terms of per-capita income. The concept of beta-convergence is directly related to neo-classical growth theory based on *Solow*. *Perroux (1970)* has added the concept of "growth poles" and stressed their importance for the overall development of a country. Growth poles in the EU of today are often associated with agglomerations and networks of smaller towns and cities.

175 See Rodrigues-Posé & Fratesi (2004) for a critical view based on their economic evaluation of past cohesion.

Scholars of NEG *(Krugman (1991a), Fujita et al. (1999), Thisse 2000*[176]*)* and endogenous growth *(Romer 1986)* have in common the idea that there are local economies of scale and increasing rates of return. In such context, economic growth will tend to concentrate in a few places in a self-sustained, spatially selective and cumulative process. Under these assumptions, economic growth fosters regional divergence rather than convergence. Several of these theories also argue, however, that beyond a certain level, due to congestion or social effects, agglomeration can reduce efficiency, that is increasing returns come to an end.

Agglomerations - in the broad sense - are defined as the concentration of consumers, workers and businesses in a place or area, together with the formal and informal institutions that make an agglomeration cohesive, which has the potential to produce externalities and increasing returns to scale[177] *(Fujita et al. 1999*). In Europe which is highly polycentric, the growth of the metropolitan region around the capital city has often exceeded growth elsewhere, as is the case of Budapest for example. Agglomerations are initiated by chance and by natural events or by supra-local public action. The prevailing distribution at any given point in time is not necessarily superior to other possible distributions in terms of efficiency. Nor does the existence of an agglomeration necessarily mean that it is efficient, due to limits after which diseconomies rise.[178] A concentration of activity is neither a necessary nor a sufficient condition for growth. The limits to agglomeration lead to adverse effects such as congestion, pollution, and price increases, the latter effects are manifested in Budapest in 2009. The *OECD (2006)* argued that for metropolitan regions of over 6 million people, the relationship between income and population size is negative.

Regarding the role of trade as growth driver for agglomerations, *Martin & Ottaviano (2001*) showed that trade integration-driven agglomeration lowers the cost of innovation in one region and thus favours innovation and growth. They see a circular causation arising between growth and agglomeration: where two regions are initially identical (no agglomeration), when the aggregate economy starts growing, the only steady state outcome is one in which one of the two regions gets all the innovation activity and most of the industrial production (an agglomeration). The positive correlation between agglomeration and aggregate growth of economic activities comes as a natural consequence of the economic forces at

---

176 The title of *Thisse (2000)* may serve as an indication of his message: "Agglomeration and regional imbalance: Why? And is it bad?".

177 An overview of economies of scale based on *Pratten (1988)* has been presented in Chapter 2, section 2.1 of this research.

178 This is inferred from a model by *Puga (2002)* which explicitly takes account of the (unintentional) side-effects of firms' decisions to move.

work. *Ottaviano et al. (2002)* broadly endorse these findings regarding the important role played by trade for the process of agglomeration.

Opportunities for growth also exist in areas where there is less concentration of economic activity, however (e.g. *European Commission 2007).* Thus, although agglomeration is a driver of growth and development, it is not the only one. In particular, growth for a region often requires "network effects" to be at work, i.e. enabling it to benefit from the growth occurring elsewhere because of transport, energy, ICT and other connections. In Europe where space for large agglomerations is limited and polycentrism is high, economies of scale and growth can best be generated by networking between major agglomerations and their hinterland and by dense networks of big or middle sized cities (this is commonly agreed among policy makers in the field, see for example *Hungarian Development Agency 2007*).

Moreover, political decisions with spatial effects are simultaneously taken with private agents' decisions on whether to invest capital and whether or not to move. Public and private decisions go together and reinforce each other. Whether there is too much or too little agglomeration in the absence of regional policy interventions is not clear. This means, that - given the lack of relevant information - any public action with spatial effects needs to be cautious, whether promoting, mitigating or forestalling an agglomeration process. Such caution is very necessary because of inter-dependencies between regions. The movement of labour and capital away from regions with untapped resources, often rural areas on the periphery, to thriving agglomerations - the "centre" in NEG theories - could reduce the potential output of the former region by more than they raise the potential output of the latter.

Further, mass movement away from rural areas can have negative consequences on the sustainability of overall growth at the country-level by depriving certain landscapes of the people taking care of it, warned the *European Commission (2007)*. The resulting impoverishment of rural areas might reduce the capacity of the overall economy to react to changes and shocks, including the effects for migrant workers then deprived of a place to return to and of alternative sources of income there.

Nevertheless, there are certain risks involved in any attempt to "balance" the spatial distribution of economic activity by investing in the peripheral regions. The supposed "untapped potential" of the periphery might turn out not to exist, as was the case for certain regions in Greece, as past regional policy experience has shown since the mid-1990s. Furthermore, interventions might end up constraining an efficient agglomeration process while failing to achieve results in the periphery. Along the line of these arguments regarding areas of agglomeration, what would be required in my view is taking a country-wide perspective on economic development and growth, singling out growth poles, agglomerations and networks of cities making a positive contribution to overall development, and then making visible policies by all government levels working towards this strategy locally to all actors in a place potentially concerned by them.

Turning towards the second issue of relevance for this research, that of specialization, *Romer (1987)* modelled a scenario of endogenous growth based on increasing returns due to specialization. Under the notion of "smart specialization" in the narrow context with innovation, the *Barca (2009)* report, which is discussed in detail in section 7.2.3 of this chapter, brings forward an aspect of interest with respect to the topic of this research. Regions should embark in a "smart specialization", that is for each region, a limited number of sectors should be selected in which innovation can most readily occur and a knowledge base built up, in accordance with the concepts for a European Research Area. To avoid that local actors - such as universities, firms, or research centres - benefit unduly from public intervention, member states should create incentives along the lines sketched out in the policy paper by *Foray & Van Ark (2007)* in order to ensure the reaching of the objectives, and public funding should be made conditional upon the commitment to using these incentives.

The relevant policy question which should be posed with regards to the results of this research regarding regional specialization in manufacturing industries is the following: Would it make sense for policy makers to pursue a strategic specialization with respect to single industries as a development and employment strategy for a region? For example, in my view it would make sense for the region Györ or the Nuts-3 region Györ-Moson-Sopron to favour the location of firms in the automobile sector, including manufacturers of components; or for Borsod-Abaúj-Zemplén in Northern Hungary to favour the location of the electrical machinery industry in the effort to build on previous strengths of the region, namely a large manufacturing workforce, yet to enhance a future-looking orientation.

Strategic specialization as a regional development strategy, when targeted at a growing, future-oriented sector, is better than diversification, which in turn is a better strategy than specialization in a declining sector (such as heavy industry for Northern Hungary up to the early 2000s). Given that Hungary has pursued a policy favouring the electrical machinery and engineering sector successfully at the national level,[179] a policy of strategic specialization at the regional level would very well make sense in my view. Examples of concrete measures could include

179 See also *Hildebrandt & Wörz (2004)* on this.

the provision of industrial park sites especially opened for firms from the favoured industries, or the construction or renewal of other infrastructure essential for that industry, or the facilitation of research centres, programmes and other innovation sites of importance for that industry.

Given the increase of regional disparities in Hungary over the period 1992 to 2008, the economic rationale for a European cohesion policy shall now be recalled in light of economic evaluations of the past cohesion process. In the EU, inequalities in GDP per capita as measured by a Gini index are over 60% higher across EU regions than across US States *(Puga 1999)*.[180] Only 7% of the overall EU population lives in cities of over 5 million inhabitants, as against 25% in the United States. Europe maintains a relative balance between urbanisation – including polycentric urban structures - and rural areas, which contributes to the European way of life.

Eastern enlargement of the EU has led to a widening of the economic development gap, a geographical shift in the problem of disparities towards the East, increasing disparities within the CEECs - as illustrated for Hungary in this research - and a more difficult employment situation. The average GDP of the EU has decreased by 12.5% upon Eastern enlargement, while socio-economic disparities have doubled (see for example *Monfort 2009*). At the same time, the whole of the EU faces challenges arising from an acceleration in economic restructuring as a result of globalisation, trade opening, fast technological progress, an ageing population, the development of the knowledge economy and society, and a growth in immigration. The consequences of the economic downturn resulting from the world economic crisis and the turbulences on the financial markets since autumn of 2008 have to be added to that list.

The EU is the suitable level for such a regional policy because it responds to expectations of EU citizens to deliver results tangible for them, it is the best suited level to tackle externalities spanning beyond national borders, and it is able to redistribute resources collected from all member states to benefit the poorest regions - cohesion - and those parts of the population the most in need.

The main rationale for regional policy measures is to provide public goods in response to market failures such as incomplete information and externalities. This expression also includes public goods in the sense of goods from whose benefits it is costly to exclude an individual and it is also undesirable since there is no marginal cost of an additional individual to enjoy it. Examples for public goods in

180 This number refers to the EU-15, thus it would even be higher for the EU-27 after the increase in regional per-capita income labels due to Eastern enlargement.

response to market failures are environmental care and contract enforcement as well as other goods like education, health care, and transport.

Regional policy interventions in the sense of "public goods" take the form of providing integrated bundles of goods and services. Examples for these are infrastructure such as bridges, motorways, water sewage systems, as well as innovation and the research that can lead to it. The latter in particular tends to be under-produced by society due to well-recognised market failures, or due to asymmetries of information. Climate change is also an extraordinary example of market failure. Meanwhile, despite controversy and persistent uncertainty about the exact magnitude of the potential effects, a broad consensus has emerged about the need for public action, though there is disagreement about what nature and size this should be and who should bear which share of the cost.

Furthermore, there is a rationale for encouraging cross-border cooperation as part of EU cohesion policy, as the most meaningful economic regions can span beyond local, regional and national borders of several member states (see *Di Giacinto & Pagnini 2008).* The border regions in the EU represent 40% of the territory and account for 25% of its population.[181] Many of the cross-border economic areas can be meaningfully targeted only by European actions coordinated at a wider EU level and with the entire perspective in view.

Regional policy in this section does not have the same meaning as industrial location policy. Regional policy has as content the inter-regional redistribution of resources which could either be production factors or income. Regional policy can meaningfully be conducted by administrative levels which have an influence both on benefiting as well as on charged regions. Industrial location policy, on the other hand, aims merely at strengthening the advantages of one location as compared to another, while its instruments are limited to its own location.[182] This chapter shall discuss only regional policy in the former sense.

Regional policy could also be used with the aim to increase the political acceptance of proceeding economic integration (e.g. *Krieger-Boden 1995).* This was of particular relevance in winning the endorsement by referendum for the EU accession treaty in several CEECs during the Eastern enlargement in 2004 and 2007, and it will certainly play a role for future enlargement candidates. This effect is achieved by measures dampening the adjustment processes painful to some regions or population groups. Regional policy in this case is using distributive instruments in order to support an economy-wide efficiency goal, namely the

181 Regions are defined at the Nuts 3 level here; figures according to the *European Commission (2007).*

182 For a discussion of these two policy strands, see also *Lammers & Stiller (2000).*

better provision with goods due to proceeding economic integration. Examples from EU regional policy include support to declining textile regions in Portugal suffering from the liberalisation under the Multifibre agreement of the Uruguay Round.

The tasks conferred to European regional policy by the EC Treaty are threefold (see Table 29): to promote "harmonious development", to tackle "disparities of regions", and to deal with "regional backwardness" by means of cohesion policy. This section will look in particular at disparities. The basis is in the treaty which calls for a reduction in disparities between "the levels of development of the various regions and the backwardness of the least favoured regions or islands, including rural areas" (art. 158 of the *EC Treaty*). It is certain that the reduction of the disparities following Eastern enlargement will require long-term sustained efforts in the form of exogenous, spatially aware public interventions.

Table 29: Tasks conferred to European regional policy by the EC Treaty

The tasks conferred to European regional policy by the EC Treaty are threefold: (i) to promote "harmonious development", (ii) to tackle "disparities of regions", and (iii) to deal with "regional backwardness" by means of cohesion policy.

Source: Art. 158 of the EC Treaty.

Which lessons can be drawn from economic evaluations of the cohesion results under European regional policy for the particular challenges present in Hungary? Evaluation of the performance or outcome of European cohesion programmes is often a question of indicators (macro, micro). Although the European Commission provided some practical guidance regarding the use of some indicators for measuring the success of EU cohesion policy,[183] there is no common set of micro indicators agreed among all member states. With respect to macro indicators, GDP per head is still the most commonly used for allocating funds (at the Nuts-2 level), although perhaps not the best one. Eurostat currently has the mandate to develop new indicators suitable for evaluation of regional policy. Which ever they

183 European Commission (2006b): The New Programming Period 2007-2013. Indicative Guidelines on Evaluation Methods: Monitoring and Evaluation Indicators, Working Document No. 2; and European Commission (2006c): The New Programming Period 2007-2013. Methodological Working Papers – Draft Working Paper 'Indicators for Monitoring and Evaluation: a Practical Guide, January.

will chose, it will be difficult to find a consensus among member states, as each country looks at them with the perspective of how it can benefit for their regions the most.

An illustration shall be given based on a recent evaluation by *Monfort (2009).* When looking at the Nuts-2 level, namely GDP per head and growth levels in the EU-27 from 1995 to 2005 - taken relative to the EU-27 average, he found evidence for a catching-up process.[184] Based on these figures, where poor regions tended to grow faster than rich ones, convergence was taking place. When the figures were taken relative to member states' average GDP per head, however, instead of the EU-27 average, there was no longer a significant relationship between the two variables. This left the conclusion that convergence is much less likely within a country as - most often in the new EU member states - the poorest regions seem to be left out of a rapid development process.

Summarizing academic evaluations of past cohesion, one common finding is that a convergence process is taking place among EU regions (at least when considering EU-15 or EU-27), but that the process is rather slow. More recent contributions introduced a spatial dimension in the formulation of the problem. The proxymity and numerous linkages between neighbouring regions imply that regional economic variables are likely to be inter-dependent. In general, the inclusion of spatial effects is found relevant and tends to reduce the estimated speed of the global convergence process while highlighting that the speed of convergence is higher for the poorest regions of Europe. *Straubhaar (1998)* discussed convergence processes in context of relevant theory and the economic policy context, identifying a meaningful role in context with globalisation and proceeding European integration. He points out that the motives of regional policy need to be set out clearly and the instruments well-targeted, as otherwise the economic results could be mixed, which is a clear hint towards Hungary which currently has a rather mixed regional policy line (see summary in section 7.2.2). *Bräuninger & Niebuhr (2005)* found a lower steady state income for urbanised and rural areas of the EU than for highly agglomerated regions. Their findings are in line with newer models which combine endogenous growth models with an NEG framework. These state that there might be convergence "clubs", agglomerations and rural peripheral regions possibly converging towards different steady state equilibria.

Getting a more global perspective, the *World Bank (2008a)* recently recognised that specialization and trade - facilitated by fewer international divisions - are central to economic development, which goes along with spatial transformations. Geography matters greatly in deciding what is needed, what is unnecessary, and

184 The relationship was found to be significant and negative, with an R^2 of 0.2009, and an equation of $y = -0.0001x + 0.014$ (Monfort 2009).

what will fail. By calibrating the blend of these policies, developing nations can, according to the *World Bank (2008b),* "reshape their economic geography, much as today's high income economies did in the past. Economic growth is seldom balanced, and efforts to spread it out prematurely will jeopardize progress. If, however, developing nations blend this policy mix well, their growth will still be unbalanced, but their development will be inclusive".

Turning back to Europe, what should European cohesion policy aim at regarding regional development from a future-looking point of view? The challenges after Eastern enlargement have grown larger, as illustrated by the decline in average GDP in the enlarged EU, by -12.5% upon enlargement, and the dramatic growth of regional disparities at the Nuts-3 level, which was experienced between regions in Hungary and similarly in other CEECs in recent years (as shown in section 3.4.2). The formation of industry agglomerations in Hungary during the almost two decades analysed in this research, influenced by the institution of the Europe agreement in the pre-accession period, has contributed to a non-deniable extent to this development. The rise and decline in regional specialization which occurred among the Nuts-3 regions in Hungary between 1992 and 2008 illustrated the challenges posed at the regional level by proceeding European integration.

In this context, European cohesion policy should aim to achieve primarily efficiency, given the relatively large but limited financial means it can dispose of in the foreseeable future. Efficiency for a region can be defined as the achievement of full capacity or potential, meaning the value of output that, given the immobile resources of a place, would be achieved if all the economic and institutional opportunities were exploited and every feasible agglomeration or network effect was at work *(Barca 2009).* Full capacity is the result of private and public action which either increases the utilisation of current capacity at a given point in time, the static aspect, or expands capacity itself over time, the dynamic aspect. Full capacity is determined not by given technological conditions but through the interaction of economic and political decisions and institutions.

A second conceivable objective for European regional policy - apart from the primary goal of achieving efficiency - could be about equity of such a policy, meaning that regional policy should reach a person's well-being irrespective of where they live. This would include various aspects making a life worth living, comprising opportunities to achieve what an individual considers relevant and to widen their set of options regarding labour skills, health, education, housing, security, income, working conditions, self-respect, a role in decision-making and so on. The political notion for this policy objective is "social inclusion". This can be defined as "the extent to which, with reference to multi-dimensional outcomes, all individuals and groups can enjoy essential standards, and the disparities between individuals and groups are socially acceptable, while the process through which these results are achieved is participatory and fair" (definition according to *Barca 2009*).

Cohesion can - in a certain sense - be called an aspect of the social dimension of European integration, as *Wagener, Eger & Fritz (2006)* pointed out. Indeed, the tasks conferred to the EU include a social policy with a European Social Fund (Art. 3 EC Treaty). The goals formulated for that policy are: fostering employment, improvement of the living and working conditions, adequate social protection, social dialogue, improvement of the potential labour force, and combating exclusion. There are, however, clear limits to what the EU can do in this field. Social policy is usually associated with budget-consuming redistribution schemes. Indeed, the size of national welfare expenditures reached between 15% and 31% of GDP for 6 of the EU-15 member states in 2001. Therefore, the welfare supporting and demand-side policy functions of the welfare state remain in the domain of the member states, while the EU concentrates above all on the improvement of the supply side.

A concrete example of such a policy target would be the social inclusion of children.[185] Faced with the situation of increasing child poverty, several EU member states do not have a policy specifically aimed at children, but seek to reduce their risk of social exclusion through policies on education, housing, childcare, and health. Since Eastern enlargement of the EU, social discrepancies have increased, not only in the CEECs but also in the old member states. My view on such demands shall be expressed in section 7.2.3., in context with the discussion of the *Barca (2009)* report.

Given these remarks on the current academic debate regarding the empirical results of European cohesion policy so far, about the rationale for a regional policy at the EU level, and about suitable goals for European regional policy, the next section 7.2.2 shall deal with concrete challenges for regional policy in Hungary for the coming years.

---

185 Family circumstances matter for childhood deprivation. Children in large families (with 3 children or more) have a risk of poverty rate of 25%, as opposed to 19% for all children, and those in lone parent households a rate of 34%, an alarming figure, given that the share of children not living with both their parents increased from 14% to 19% during the 1990s. In these households too, as in others, the risk of poverty of children is strongly affected by the education level of parents and their labour market situation. On average across the EU, for over 30% of children at risk of poverty, neither of their parents had an upper secondary level of education as opposed to 16% in the case of all children; Barca (2009).

7.2.2 Current challenges for regional policy in Hungary

Which is the track record of Hungary regarding regional policy? Which are the current challenges regarding regional development? And what are the priorities set by the policy makers for using the funds of the EU regional policy up to 2013? Which role is foreseen for agglomerations, which for regions specialised in certain sectors or industries? This section shall provide answers to these questions.

Whilst still being a relatively centralized state - also due to the weight of the capital Budapest relative to the rest of the country[186] -, Hungary has an experience in regional policy prior to 1989 and starting earlier than in most other CEECs. A tradition of regional development policy started in the early 1970s, although it was dominated mainly by sectoral interests then. In the year 1985, the Hungarian national parliament passed a decree on longer-term regional policy goals and tasks, although policy measures were restraint to only two of the 20 regions up the year 1989. Due to the limited financial and institutional means (a rather bureaucracy-shaped regional policy), they remained without any remarkable influence on the economic structures of the regions concerned.[187] While a separate ministry for environmental and regional policy was set up in 1990 and a regional development fund was started in 1991, it took until the mid-1990s for Hungarian regional policy to be reshaped. In 1993, a "resolution" defined goals and instruments of regional policy for the first time since the break-down of communism. Regional crisis management and economic reorientation as well as the implementation of selected infrastructure projects in peripheral regions were enumerated as key tasks for the Hungarian regional policy.

The "law on regional development and spatial planning" passed in the year 1996, the first law of its kind in any of the EU accession countries, was the starting point for a greater decentralisation in Hungarian regional policy - an orientation at the principles prevailing in EU structural funding which Hungary then started to prepare for. The law set up the territorial units for regional policy which are the 20 planning-statistical regions as the Nuts-3 level in Hungary as well as 7 Nuts-2 regions comprised by between 2 to 3 Nuts-3 regions. The new, rather centrally-steered concept aimed at economic restructuring saw as key goals the support of a market-orientated development in all regions of the country, the establishment of the prerequisites for a lasting and self-supporting economic growth in the regions, the reduction of income differences between Budapest and the rest of the country, as well as of economic differences between well advanced and less developed

186 Budapest has a population of just under 2 million, thus roundabout one fifth of the 10 million inhabitants of Hungary.

187 For an account of the history of regional policy in Hungary prior to 1989, see *Dreyhaupt-von Speicher (2002)*, pp. 250-251.

regions, but also the favouring of regional and local initiatives in line with the national development goals. The "national regional policy concept" passed by the national parliament in 1998 added the missing main strategy line to the 1996 law *(Horváth 2000)*.

Regional governments have an important role to play in ensuring the successful implementation of European regional policy, which is based on partnership between the EU level and the national, regional and local level. While Hungary is the country among CEECs in which local authorities enjoy the largest independence from the national level and the most far-reaching competences (such as the provision of public services), the level of Nuts-3 regions has been substantially constrained in their influence after 1990. There are no exclusive competences at the level of Nuts-3 regions. Among shared competences at the Nuts-3 level are land use planning, environmental issues and tourism. The Nuts-3 level has no own tax revenues, only transfers from the central government budget.

The Nuts-2 level of the 7 regions - which is the level at which funds from the European regional policy are allocated - are merely "planning-statistical regions" for which no administrative structure existed prior to their design, neither did they have the right to self-government. Regional policy experience in the EU shows that the administration of funds under the objective-1 is typically done better and more efficiently at a larger regional level (although this is not a prerequisite for receiving EU funds at all). The example of Greece - where objective-1 regions exist merely as statistical planning units - shows, that the EU Regional funds were used by far not as efficiently and successfully there as in those countries where objective-1 regions and administrational levels handling the EU funds corresponded.

The pre-accession aid received first in the context of the PHARE programme since 1991, later on specifically under the pre-accession instruments ISPA (for regional policy) and Sapard (for agricultural policy) shall not be described here for lack of space. The first funds under the 2004-2006 regional policy budget shall also be left out here for that same reason. The current situation in Hungary shall rather be given attention regarding the main economic challenges and the role foreseen for agglomerations and specialization in the context of regional development.

The current situation in Hungary with regards to regional development is still characterized by increasing regional disparities at the Nuts-3 level relative to the EU-average which have not been diminished in the past two decades, in spite of the efforts of the national regional development policy.

The spatial differences are pervasive at different levels:

- between Budapest and the rest of the country;
- between the regions in the Western part of the country, and those lagging behind in the Eastern part, Northern Hungary and some regions in South Transdanubia (bordering with Serbia);
- at the level of micro-regions, where the rise or decline of industries - sometimes of individual firms - and geographic endowments shape the situation;
- at the local level between city agglomerations and the country side;
- and between central regions and border regions in a peripheral situation.

The majority of the territory of Hungary is rather rural in nature. More concretely, of Hungary's 20 Nuts-3 regions, 6 can be classified as predominantly rural, remote regions, and 5 more as predominantly rural, close to a city.[188] While only Budapest is a predominantly urban region, 7 regions are classified as "intermediate" regions, according to the *European Commission (2008b).*

Apart from the above weaknesses, the main driving force of regional growth in Hungary has recently been stemming from the growth of county seats[189] (i. e. the administrative seat of the country administration) and some medium-sized cities, which are the most dynamic parts of the Hungarian urban system. There is a well developed system of cities between Budapest and the Lake Balaton, thus along a development axis from the North-East to the South-West, and also along the axis between Budapest and Vienna, while a few other well-developed cities are more island-like *(National Development Agency 2007).*

The empirical results of this research on agglomeration have shown that industry is relatively concentrated in Hungary, as compared to the EU-15, and that agglomerations are located primarily in the Western part of the country and around the capital of Budapest. Moreover, while the degree of agglomeration has increased and decreased again in a double hub over the 1992 to 2008 period, the start and the end levels in context with proceeding European integration were more or less the same. Given the relatively strong concentration of production and

---

188 This is defined in that study as "at least 50% of the population of the region lives at less than 45 minutes road travel time from a city of at least 50,000 inhabitants".

189 County seats are the administrative seat of the Nuts-4 regions; the 20 planning-statistical regions of the Nuts-3 level are comprised each by between one and up to three Nuts-4 regions, called counties. Only these counties have a grown administrative structure. The smaller organisational structures for the Nuts-3 regions – data collecting and policy implementing - were created in Hungary to comply with the requirements for receiving EU Regional Policy funding.

services in agglomerations and the disadvantages of remote rural areas, a balancing out between regions is therefore what is needed in Hungary.

Investments as well as research and development expenditures are concentrated in Budapest and surroundings. Due to the good accessibility of the markets of Western-Europe, advanced infrastructure and skilled labour, the Northern and Western parts of Transdanubia and the county seats, especially Pécs, Szeged, Debrecen and Miskolc, are functioning as regional and economic knowledge centres and growth poles. On the side of weaknesses, the growth rate of the majority of the most disadvantaged micro regions is far below the average and with a negative trend. If the current tendencies remain, these regional differences can increase and result in significant social tensions, according to the Hungarian authorities *(National Development Agency 2007)*. Well-developed regions of the country have a relatively good infrastructure whereas the lack of infrastructure in peripheral regions far away from Budapest hinders development to a large extent. A special problem of these regions is that available jobs (in country centres or major towns) cannot easily be accessed by public transport.

Furthermore, significant inequalities persist between the development of traditionally industrialized regions, on the one hand, and agriculture-oriented regions, on the other. Most of these previously leading industrial regions (mainly in Northern Hungary) have not recovered from the transitional shock after the collapse of heavy industries, which is manifested in high unemployment, thus high inactivity persists, combined with a bad health status of the population. The situation of rural areas is dull as the agricultural sector has lost its major markets, therefore the profitability of agricultural production has dramatically decreased.

The labour demand of agriculture is seasonal, and falling: most of the previously rural production facilities have gone bankrupt, and there has not been any reorganisation. Thus, unemployment in rural areas is extremely high. Regarding North Hungary and parts of South Transdanubia, the least developed micro regions are such regions which are peripheral, border regions and regions without urban centres and with small villages, which cannot easily be accesses by public transport. The development of these regions is also hindered by their geographical setting, as they are situated in hilly regions, with poor transport capacities. Most of their population does not have legal employment which means no legal income, therefore they need social support from city councils, or low-level, pension-type income from the national level.

With respect to higher education and research institutions, regional centres have developed such facilities, yet the most advanced knowledge intensive businesses still operate in Budapest agglomeration. The majority of people with a diploma graduating from institutions in rural areas move away from there - most of them to Budapest because they cannot find an appropriate job in line with their qualification or if they could, they would earn less otherwise. Looking at regional differences in terms of employment, the greatest disparities exist at the level of micro regions which function as local labour markets *(Fazekas 2003)*. Regions with high unemployment are typically characterised by a bundle of problems: the rate of low-skilled people is higher than average, the proportion of long-term unemployed is higher, and the inactive population is marginalised from the labour market as are those receiving social assistance. This has lead to an increase of the regional concentration of inactive and marginalised people.[190]

Against this background of weaknesses and opportunities in Hungary, two key challenges of regional development policy are seen for 2007 to 2013[191]:

- to sustain long-term growth, and
- to increase employment.

Sustained long-term growth is to be achieved through a widening of the economic base, measures to improve competitiveness, and the development of the business environment. Increasing employment shall be attained mainly by improving employability and labour market activity in order to increase labour supply.

Hungary has been allocated 25.3 billion Euro from the EU budget for the 2007 to 2013 period, the Hungarian contribution (co-financing) will be 4.4 billion Euro. The EU-transfers amount to an equivalent of 4% of the GDP of Hungary. Six of the seven Nuts-2 regions fall under the convergence objective[192], while Central Hungary (with Budapest) is a phasing-in region for competitiveness and employment funding[193]. The industrial sector is continuing to undergo restructuring processes which were analysed in this research for almost the past two decades. The decline of heavy industries located primarily in Northern Hungary affects the economic base of these regions. Similarly, the decline of the textiles sector brings challenges to certain local labour markets. The entire country qualifies for the

---

190 A particular minority problem is seen by the National Development Agency (2007) with regards to the Roma population which make up 1.86% of the population in Hungary. According to the 2001 population census, there were 189,984 Roma (gipsy) living in Hungary; HCSO: Statistical Yearbook of Hungary 2004, Budapest 2005. Their employment rate fell back from 75% in 1980 to 30% in 2007 indicating their social marginalisation, and the few regions in which this population is concentrated, Cserehát, Ormánság, or Budapest slums, are underdeveloped micro-regions with deep poverty.

191 This timeframe is due to the timeframe of funds under the Financial Perspective of the European Community 2007 to 2013, which had been finalised by the European Council in December 2005.

192 Objective 1 regions, those receiving the highest support under EU Regional Policy.

193 Former Objective 2, funded by the European Social Fund (ESF).

cohesion fund financing project in the environmental protection, energy and transport sectors.

Which development can be forecast for Hungary concerning industry agglomerations and regional development in the nearer future, based on the empirical results of chapters 4 and 5 and on the predictions of NEG theories? The process of decreasing agglomeration in manufacturing industries, which started in 2007, looks set to continue for some years. Similarly, overall declining regional specialization, which has begun in 2007, will prevail for several years more.

As regards regional development, support under the "New Hungary" development strategy is planned to be given to regional growth poles, rural development and the realignment of disadvantages micro-regions. These objectives were translated into six thematic and territorial priorities *(National Development Agency 2007)*:

1. Economic development;
2. Regional development;
3. Transport development;
4. Social renewal;
5. Environment and energy development; and
6. State reform.

Examples of concrete projects are the partnerships in 112 industrial parks, the industrial grass project for the paper industry in the Southern Great Plain, and green energy provision for modernisation of Szeged hospital.[194] Projects funded by the European Cohesion fund include the reconstruction or construction of 500 km of roads and 500 km of railroads, the improvement of waste water management in 10 major towns (including Debrecen, Szeged, Pécs, and Györ) and the creation of a complex waste management system for more than 1,000 settlements. All counties of Hungary are involved in at least one environmental project funded by the Cohesion Fund. These projects affect almost 6.5 million people (of the total population of 10 million).

Furthermore, Hungary is benefiting from funds for cross-border cooperation among EU-member states, namely for its border regions with Austria, Slovakia, Romania[195], and Slovenia. In addition, the co-operation instrument for

---

194 The details were taken from the Website for Regional Policy of the *European Commission*, under the Heading "Success Stories", date of download: 23.4.2009.

195 The operational programme for Hungary-Romania for 2007 to 2013 was endorsed by the Commission on 24 April 2009. It encompasses 4 Hungarian Nuts-3 regions and 4 Romanian regions and has a budget of 224 million Euro, representing approximately 2.6% of the funds for cross-border cooperation under the Cohesion Policy budget for 2007 to 2013. MEMO/09/196 of the *Spokesmen Service*, http://europa.eu.

pre-accession assistance is benefiting Hungary's border regions with Croatia and Serbia-Montenegro. Border disparities in terms of the quotient of GDP per head were greater than 2.5 at Hungary's border with Serbia, between 1.25 and 2.5 at its borders with Ukraine and Austria, and less than 1.25 at the other borders *(European Commission 2008b)*.

The expected impact of the new cohesion policy is to achieve an increase of more than 10% in the added value generated by enterprise and a 4% increase in the number of employees outside the public sphere by 2015 *(EU Regional Policy 2008a)*. Hungarian spending on the ear-marked Lisbon categories is expected to increase by another 10% in the 2007 to 2013 period (46% during 2004-2006).[196]

This seems much too optimistic in my view, given the lack of experience of most actors involved in the implementation of regional policy. The very low portion of funds paid by invoice for the 2004-2006 period - only 21.37% by May 2007, according to the *National Development Agency (2007)* – to my mind clearly indicates that Hungary is experiencing coordination problems of the kind explained above. Part of the slow use of funds could be due to little experience of the administrative staff in handling the implementation of programmes and projects of European regional policy, as the scope of the pre-accession instrument ISPA in Hungary - although certainly a useful preparatory tool - was very limited and so was the training effect for administrative staff.

Further, the lack of a coordinating administrative structure at the Nuts-2 regional level is likely to raise serious coordination problems. The fact that the New Hungary Development Plan 2007-2013 foresees objectives to be implemented at the level of micro-regions goes in line with the lack of any capable administrative structure at the Nuts-2 or Nuts-3 level. Last but not least, the current economic crisis and severe fiscal constraints on the Hungarian government budget in the wake of the IMF conditionality agreement signed in October 2008 could seriously endanger these goals, expressed in the difficulty to raise the required national co-financing.

7.2.3 Reforming regional policy after Eastern enlargement

This section will look at European cohesion policy with respect to present or past weaknesses and suggest solutions for improvement, in particular for tackling the

196 It should be recalled that these projections were made prior to the world economic crisis which has lead the state of Hungary to the verge of insolvency in October 2008. This situation and the IMF Conditionality agreement signed then required the new government under G. Bajnai in power since April 2009 to take austerity measures reducing public spending *(FAZ 18.4.2009)*.

challenges due to the new realities after Eastern enlargement to an EU of 27 member states, as illustrated in this research at the example of Hungary. This will be done taking account of the current political debate at the European level. Recent proposals for reforming European regional policy for the period after 2013 will be discussed, with an attention given to the role foreseen for agglomerations and the policy option of strategic specialization as a regional development strategy.

Cohesion is about overcoming distance, division and inequality. A suitable regional policy needs to address the three dimensions of cohesion:

(1) Economic cohesion;

(2) Social cohesion; and

(3) Territorial cohesion.

The first notion, economic cohesion, implies a convergence of the regions in terms of GDP per capita, a narrowing of the disparities between the richest and the poorest regions in these terms. The second notion, social cohesion, includes a balanced labour market, and avoiding people from being marginalised from the labour market and from access to social services. And the third notion, territorial cohesion, calls attention to themes such as sustainable development and access to services. This underlines that many issues do not respect administrative boundaries and may require a response from several regions or countries, while others need to be addresses at a local or neighbourhood level.[197]

The EU's cohesion policy for the period 2007 to 2013 has a total budget of 347.410 billion Euro[198]. These sizeable transfers correspond to 0.3% of the GDP of the EU-15 member states[199], and to 3% of the GDP of the new Member States (CEECs) in 2013. From 2011 onwards, the funds earmarked for the new member states will be higher than those for the EU-15[200]. The Community Strategic Guidelines for the period 2007 - 2013 set out three priorities for regional policy: (i) improving the attractiveness of regions and cities in the member states;

---

197 To give an example from remote rural areas, in the EU on average 40% of people live further than a 30-minute drive from a hospital and 43% live more than one hour's drive from a university.

198 In prices of 2007.

199 The entire budget of the European Union corresponds to about 1% of the GDP of the EU; the Cohesion budget is about one third of the EU budget, agricultural policy takes about 45%.

200 Planned cohesion expenditure in the 12 new member states will exceed that in the (old) EU-15 from 2011 onwards during the 2007-2013 programming period, according to *European Commission (2007)*, Forth Cohesion Report, p. xxxviii.

(ii) encouraging innovation, entrepreneurship and growth in the knowledge economy; and (iii) creating more and better jobs. The first of these explicitly foresees a role for agglomerations, including various dimensions of urban policy: the role cities can play as motors of regional development and centres of innovation; the need to improve the internal cohesion of urban areas; and the need to promote a more poly-centric regional development and a balanced development of urban and metropolitan areas.

The overall priorities of the EU regional policy are to be achieved through three objectives in 2007 to 2013: the convergence objective (former objective 1, the regions whose GDP is less than 75% of the EU average) which gets 81.5% of the funds; the regional competitiveness and employment objective (former objective 2), with 16% of the funds; and the European territorial cooperation objective (cross-border cooperation[201]) receiving 2.5% of the funds.

This section in this study primarily deals with the design of regional policy in "normal" times from a forward-looking perspective. Nevertheless, in the face of the severe economic recession since the fall 2008, the contribution by European regional policy towards alleviating the financial tensions of member states and supporting their counter-cyclical fiscal policy efforts shall not pass unnoticed. In the so-called "European Recovery Plan" passed by the European Commission in December 2008, the most important contribution of regional policy is the increase in the advance payments to member states for the 2007 to 2013 programmes. These additional advance payments will provide immediate cash injections of 6.25 billion Euro in 2009 for investments, within the financial envelope agreed for each member states for the 2007 to 2013 period.[202] This change would bring the total of advance payments to 11.25 billion Euro in 2009 (for all member states), or from 671.3 million Euro to 996.8 million Euro in the case of Hungary. Other measures include the extension of the deadline for use of funds from the 2000 to 2006 operational period[203] - this benefits especially the new member states little

201 The main Community Initiative is INTERREG with three different strands; PEACE also goes under this heading, it is the Community initiative for cooperation between the border regions of Northern Ireland (UK) and the Republic of Ireland.

202 The EU budget – which is not allowed to run deficits - is financed by contributions of the member states paid in at the beginning of the year. The advance payments provide up-front liquidity to member states. The remainder of the amount is paid out only after satisfactory documentation – including for the amount of the advances - about the implementation and actual costs of the projects has been provided to the payment authorities and approved by the European Commission.

203 This means a relaxation of the n+2 rule, under which funds decay (cannot be used any more) if no satisfactory documentation about the implementation of the programmes is presented by the end of the second year after the programming period, which would have been 31 December 2008 for the 2000 to 2006 period.

experienced with European regional policy, including Hungary - and a relaxation of state aid rules, although this benefits all economic branches to some extent.

Which weaknesses of European regional policy have been identified in the recent academic and political debate? Which initiatives have been taken by the European institutions, and which views brought forward by other actors? How are these to be judged in the context of agglomeration and regional specialization in Hungary? The next paragraphs will deal with these issues.

At their recent informal Council under the *Czech Presidency (2009),* the Ministers in charge of regional policy shared the view that the major increase of inter-regional disparities within the EU following the recent Eastern enlargements has emphasized the relevance of the cohesion policy. Ministers believed that the primary focus should be put on the convergence of less prosperous areas. The funds of the regional policy - one third of the EU budgetary resources - should stimulate public investment and leverage additional public and private resources, which is particularly relevant during the current global economic crisis. Furthermore, the Ministers endorsed the core principles of cohesion policy: multi-annual programming, partnership, concentration, co-financing and additionality, monitoring and evaluation. As preconditions for the success on the ground, they recalled: subsidiarity and multi-level governance, partnership, including public-private partnerships, shared management, and proportionality[204]. Ministers also called for significant improvements towards real simplification and reduction of the administrative burden for the current and the next programming period, including more alignment in the rules of the different cohesion policy funds involved, in order to ensure a greater effectiveness, while maintaining sound financial management.

As to the European Commission, its Collège adopted a "Green Paper on Territorial Cohesion" in October 2008, aimed at achieving a better and shared under-

204 This refers to the proportionality of effort and benefit (also in reference to programme and project size). The principle of proportionality regulates the exercise of powers by the European Union, seeking to set within specified bounds the action taken by the institutions of the Union. Under this rule, the institutions' involvement must be limited to what is necessary to achieve the objectives of the Treaties. In other words, the extent of the action must be in keeping with the aim pursued. This means that when various forms of intervention are available to the Union, it must, where the effect is the same, opt for the approach which leaves the greatest freedom to the member states and individuals. The principle of proportionality is laid down in primary law under Article 5, third paragraph, of the Treaty establishing the European Community (TEC). A Protocol on the application of the principles of subsidiarity and proportionality, annexed to the TEC by the Treaty of Amsterdam, sets out the criteria for applying both of these principles.

standing of territorial cohesion and its implications for the future of the EU's regional policy, and opened a public consultation on this.[205]

The Commission stressed three main territorial challenges, the first of which deals with the role of agglomerations:

(i) Overcoming differences in density. Agglomerations can foster both positive and negative effects. For instance, there can be increased focus on innovation and productivity and at the same time, more pollution and deeper social exclusion. The Green Paper suggests that better coordination is key to enabling cities and their surrounding regions to complement their strengths to ensure that each territory can maximise its contribution to the prosperity of the European Union as a whole.

(ii) Overcoming distance. Access to public services, efficient modes of transport, reliable energy networks, and broadband Internet remain unevenly distributed across the European Union. In remote rural areas, on average 40% of people live further than a 30-minute drive from a hospital and 43% live more than one hour's drive from a university. And

(iii) Overcoming administrative borders in order to cooperate on common issues such as environmental problems, associated with climate-change, flooding, biodiversity loss, or commuting do not respect borders and better cooperation is needed to meet these challenges. Although cohesion policy already promotes cooperation through the INTERREG programmes, the Green Paper underlines that much needs to be done, for instance in the Baltic Sea Region and Danube River Basin cooperation areas, where stronger cooperation is seen as crucial to tackle environmental problems and to boost competitiveness.

The Committee of the Regions (CoR) of the EU[206] in its opinion on the subject *(CoR 2008)* judged the Green Paper as showing lack of ambition, as a clear definition of territorial cohesion is missing in it. The issue of territorial cohesion is seen all the more urgent given the additional costs generated by the lack of territorial cohesion in Europe: additional environmental costs mainly due to congested urban areas and climate change; additional social costs created by the spatial concentration of social problems, and hampering effects towards the smooth functioning of the European Single Market. On the operative side, the

205 The debate on territorial cohesion began in the early 1990s and led to the adoption by Member States of the European Spatial Development Perspective (ESDP) in 1999.

206 This is an institution of the EU in which the regional governments of the EU are represented (for large member states such as Germany only a selection of them) and which is consulted in the EU legislative process on issues of relevance for the regional level.

CoR believed it to be necessary to broaden the political scope of the concept of territorial cohesion at the Community level, and called on the Commission to specify the means of implementing the objective (in a White Paper); at the same time the Commission should develop relevant indicators for specific types of regions, where necessary, at sub-regional level.

Taking position on the Commission's Green Paper on Territorial Cohesion, the Academy for Spatial Planning and Research (ARL) in Hannover called for emphasis to be given to development dynamics, on the one hand, and to different types of territories, on the other hand *(ARL 2008)*. Unlike the Green Paper, the ARL called for a broadening of the scope to all territories and their fragilities, not just the territories disadvantaged by geological factors. The new kind of cohesion policy would require two types of indicators: indicators describing the need for support, and indicators identifying the best way of making use of resources available (including support), taking into account territorial potentials. The issue of solidarity within the EU would need to be further stressed, while maintaining what the ARL describes as a "bottom-up top-down" way of handling the regional policy in practice. Finally, the ARL called for lean bureaucracy in an environment of shared competences and for a lightening of the complexity of multi-governance processes.

A specific policy issue arises with respect to rural areas, agriculture and territorial cohesion. It should be recalled that half of Europe is predominantly rural, home to around 20% of the population, with CEECs being characterised by an even higher share of rural areas. These have to face the challenges of migration and modernisation at the same time. Throughout the EU, rural regions display the greatest variations in GDP per capita. According to Commission forecasts, 5 million farm jobs will be lost by 2014 *(EU Regional Policy 2008b)*. The Common Agricultural Policy (CAP) has an undeniable territorial dimension, particularly when considering the Less Favoured Area status,[207] agro-environmental measures, and various types of production strongly linked to geography. Complications experienced by the member states are probably due in part to an unclear distribution of the objectives and scope between cohesion and rural development policies. Rural areas face multiple challenges, some of which are at the heart of the CAP and

207 In place since 1975, the aid to farmers in Less Favoured Areas (LFA), it is a long standing measure of the Common Agricultural Policy. In areas designated as "less-favoured", agricultural production or activity is more difficult because of natural handicaps, e.g. difficult climatic conditions, steep slopes in mountain areas, or low soil productivity in other less favoured areas. Due to the handicap to farming, there is a significant risk of agricultural land abandonment and thus a possibility of loss of biodiversity, desertification, forest fires and the loss of highly valuable rural landscape. To mitigate these risks, the LFA payment scheme is an important tool, implemented by all the member states although it is not a compulsory measure.

cohesion policies. That being the case, the central question regarding the right policy for rural areas is: Should there be one European policy solely devoted to rural issues? Or should the territorial dimension of the CAP be reinforced, in order to explicitly contribute towards the cohesion goal?

A further issue is that of an increase in cross-border cooperation in the context of cohesion policy, given the important share of EU population living there, namely 39.4%, which would be desirable in my view. The aim should be to work on a symmetric, multi-polar and balanced Europe. New cross-border regions have been added after Eastern enlargement, including borders between countries which have been political enemies and subject to differing economic systems for decades. In addition, new entities of regional development, so-called "meta-Regions" like the Baltic Sea region, start playing a role. In the face of these new challenges, the rapporteur from the European Parliament, *van Nistelrooij*, proposed to boost this objective. The leverage of interregional and cross-border co-operation is huge, and should be more profiled.

Another issue is that of measuring the success of such co-operations while economic indicators are nearly missing in this area. A successful example, according to *Bedoya Vega*[208], an actor from the ground, is transnational cooperation in the South-West Europe area, where more than 500 organisations set in motion common cooperation projects, even when no previous experiences of cooperation were recorded. He posed the question: How can trans-European cooperation be strengthened to facilitate connectivity and territorial integration?

An impediment for advancing the role of cross-border cooperation is the political economy side of it in my view. While member states are primarily interested in the extent of their own influence (see also *Bindseil & Hantke (1997)* on this)[209], they may find it difficult to believe that cooperation between regions can improve competitiveness and the lives of their citizens. For those policymakers already convinced, the problem is rather about how to assess the impact on the ground which cross-border cooperation is having. The most frequently used indicator, GDP, is not capable of describing the situation in fine enough detail. Indicators may have normative or descriptive functions. In the first category, GDP is and will remain central because of its robustness. In the second category, the European

---

208 Mr. Bedoya Vega is Deputy Director-General of Economy in the Cantabrian Regional Ministry of Economy and Finance, and head of the Managing Authority of the cooperation region South-West Europe, interview in: EU Regional Policy (2008b).

209 The article of *Bindseil & Hantke (1997)* deals with the power distribution in decision making among EU member states using a game-theoretic approach to policy making in the Council of the European Union, modelling various enlargement scenarios and determining therefy the influence in decision making which each member state can exert.

Commission is working with Eurostat to improve understanding of the dynamics. Whatever they will come up with will not please every one; indicators are a real problem, because every member state tries to work out what is in it for them.

A further problem in cross-border cooperation is about how to maintain financial accountability and to control for sound financial management. Finding a new modus vivendi in this field would be particularly beneficial for Hungary which has 13 border regions among the 20 Nuts-3 regions. As European tax payers' money is involved, the EU has allocated a certain amount of money from the cohesion policy budget to each member state (this is typically done at the European Council which decides on the financial perspectives), and has transferred oversight for the execution to the managing authorities, monitoring committees and the national courts of audit. In cross-border programmes, this responsibility is blurred due to the blend of funds and the cross-border nature of projects. Therefore, the European Commission and most EU member states have an interest to limit money spent in cross-border cooperation. This is quite unfortunate for Hungary which has a large proportion of border regions and 7 neighbouring countries. Thus, while consent is rising among policy makers on the desirability of enhanced cross-border cooperation, an increase of funds is hindered by the institutional structure of the EU for the time being.

With respect to policy coordination, an issue playing a role in current developments is the interaction between cohesion policy and the targets of the Lisbon process with respect to research, communication and information technologies. The cohesion policy as a whole, with its objectives and tools, supports the Lisbon strategy (see also *Wandel (2004)* on this) which was renewed at the March 2005 European Council with the adoption of the partnership for growth and jobs and the corresponding national action plans. In the New Hungary Development plan (the programming document for cohesion policy in Hungary from 2007 to 2013), for example, an entire section deals with the coherence between the National Action Plan drafted in context of the Lisbon process with the New Hungary Development Plan *(National Development Agency 2007).*

A further issue raised in this context is the notion of "smart investment". Smart investment includes investing in energy efficiency, clean technologies, environmental services, infrastructure and interconnections, broadband networks, to develop forecasting regarding future labour market needs and matching skills with future demand, or opening up new finance for SMEs especially, as research-intensive and innovative SMEs would be considered to fall in this field of "smart investment".[210] The EU's new scheme regarding energy efficiency in the residen-

210 "Smart investment" was also recommended to the member states in the Commission's European Recovery Plan for their review of regional programmes due by the end of 2009,

tial sector also goes into this direction.[211] The questions arising in this context of improving regional policy with regards to the Lisbon goals are: Which innovation policies need to be put in place in order to avoid a technological divide between territories with potential and those which are less advanced? And how can more money be allocated to "smart investments"?

The ex-post evaluation of cohesion policy programmes of the period 2000 to 2006 identified certain weaknesses while finding mixed success of programmes at the macro level *(Evaluation Network 2007)*. Among these weaknesses were an only limited concentration of expenditure in many cases - contrary to the agglomeration recommendation; and only limited expenditure on research, technological development and innovation, contrary to the Lisbon targets. Compliance of regional development strategies with recommendations was found difficult to determine because of lack of advice on which of the various drivers of growth to focus on and the relative priority to be given to each. Further difficulties arose because of insufficient recognition of differences in regional characteristics and circumstances. The issues with respect to agglomeration which are emerging in the evaluators' view are: How can the importance of agglomeration and a concentration of expenditure be reconciled with to goal of balanced regional development? And how can the innovation capacity be strengthened in lagging regions?

In summarizing the debate up to this point, the following elements should be retained for a forward-looking European regional policy taking account of the new challenges after Eastern enlargement:

- More concentration of resources on the less prosperous member states and regions in order to enhance solidarity and advance with cohesion;[212]

whether priorities could be modified in order to include more "smart investment" than initially planned.

211 Regarding energy efficiency, the Commission has launched a scheme allowing for European co-financing of national programmes targeted at low-income households national, regional or local schemes for insulation of walls, roofing and windows (double-glazing), solar panels, and replacement of old boilers for more energy-efficient ones. As the residential sector is responsible for a quarter of energy consumption and 40% of greenhouse gas emissions in the EU, this additional policy line is a "win-win measure", according to Commissioners Danuta Hübner, Regional Policy, and Andris Piebalgs, Energy; IP/08/1874 press note of the *Commission's Spokesmen Service (2008)*.

212 Planned cohesion expenditure in the 12 new member states will exceed that in the (old) EU-15 from 2011 onwards during the 2007-2013 programming period, according *European Commission (2007)*, Forth Cohesion Report, p. xxxviii.

- A polycentric and balanced policy for agglomerations and networks of towns and cities, as agglomeration is acknowledged to be one of the key drivers of growth and development;
- Tailor-made regional strategies based on a diagnosis of strengths and weaknesses at the regional level, including the option of a strategic specialization as a regional development policy;
- Better integrated strategies for rural areas; and finally
- A stronger accent on performance and quality, coupled with new and better indicators for evaluating results.

The *Barca* report published by the European Commission on 27th of April 2009 was intended as a starting point for reflections towards the next reform of European regional policy for the period beyond 2013.[213] The report suggests for the next period of regional policy that around 55-65% of the funding should be concentrated on three or four core priorities. Criteria for the allocation of funding would remain much as now, i.e. based on GDP per capita. One or two core priorities should also address social inclusion.

This proposal of a 55-65% allocation means a dramatic watering-down of funds destined towards the cohesion process of the poorest regions in the EU. The share of funds concentrated on the convergence objective, the poorest regions with a per-capita GDP less than 75% of the EU-average, amounts to 81.5% in the current period 2007 to 2013. The regional competitiveness and employment objective, covering basically the remainder of the EU territory, currently receives 16.0% of the funds. Its share would go up to 35-45% if the *Barca (2009)* proposals were followed, taking account of whatever share would be left for territorial and cross-border cooperation (currently 2.5% of the funds).

It is a fact that regional disparities have grown in the pre- and post-accession phase, for the EU-27 as a whole and especially in the CEECs. Another fact is that personal income inequalities have increased largely since the Eastern enlargement of the EU. This has led to rising demands towards an added social dimension of European regional policy. Moreover, in the face of dwindling scope in strained government budgets due to the current severe economic recession, demands for a European social policy coupled with the redistribution scheme of European cohesion policy emerge more and more. While all these are plausible causes which could have led to the drastic proposals by *Barca (2009)*, they are unjustified and in the wrong place in my view. This would mean to give the richer regions

213 The report was written by Fabrizio Barca, an external expert, upon request of Commissioner Danuta Hübner, in charge of Regional Policy, and is based on the current debate and a series of policy hearings and seminars.

making up the larger territory and population in the EU more of the funds than now, while reducing the help for the poorest and problem regions. European regional policy should be concentrated on convergence of the poorest regions, in my view, providing them with integrated bundles of public goods and services to enable them to grow appropriately. Social policy should be left to national governments and their budgetary resources, as in line with the principle of subsidiarity, the bulk of it – apart from the coordinating tasks foreseen by the Treaties - is clearly not an issue for the EU level.

Apart from that, *Barca (2009)* called above all for a "place-based approach" to regional policy[214]. The notion of "place-based" is more or less a synonym for the term "with territorial aspects" used by the European Commission in context with the third dimension of cohesion - the territorial one - and the Green Paper on Territorial Cohesion. The two main objectives of such a "place-based" cohesion policy that are singled out by the *Barca* report are "efficiency" and "social inclusion", which should be pursued by separate measures or instruments.[215] The efficiency objective is about realising the full utilisation of the potential of every place or region. The social inclusion objective is about ensuring equal opportunities for individuals irrespective of where they live.

Such a placed-based policy would be more expensive to implement - higher management costs - than the current policy, as the *Barca (2009)* report admitted. These higher costs could only be justified if they delivered better results, such as a more equitable outcome regarding social inclusion and sustainable growth. The relevant unit for allocating funds of the EU regional policy under such a "place-based" approach could still continue to be the Nuts-2 level - as Nuts-2 regions are the closest approximation to places for which homogeneous and reasonably updated economic data are available for an allocation to be made *ex-ante.* But the measures and programmes should be focussed and targeted to smaller places within the Nuts-2 regions.[216]

---

214 By choosing the term "place-based" rather than "region-based", the author wanted to make the statement that in some circumstances, the most meaningful spatial unit for a targeted action can either be smaller and more localised than a region, or also spanning beyond regional or even national borders, such as in the case of economic agglomerations in border regions of several member states.

215 For any progress made by pursuing the efficiency objective might help the pursuit of the equity objective, but this need not be the case.

216 *Barca report (2009)*, p. 113: "The present arrangement by which resources are pre-allocated to NUTS 2 Regions (and, for the cohesion fund, to member states), leaving the lower level of government to allocate it internally, is thus coherent with the policy model." This sentence has been inscribed into the report by the Commission official (Eric van Bresca) or the Cabinet of the Commissioner in my view in order to ensure the feasibility of the reports' conclusions regarding the future operability of EU Regional

Beyond that the *Barca* report postulated that every policy, whether at national or regional level and in what field so ever, should be made with a territorial perspective in view, i.e. policy makers should make a territorial impact assessment at the stage of its design and well ahead of its implementation. Many policies even at the national level are said to be made with specific locations or problems in mind. For example, a national labour market policy in Hungary targeted at long-term unemployed miners would primarily benefit the 3 regions Nógrád, Heves, and Borsod-Abaúj-Zemplén in Northern Hungary where heavy industry was concentrated under the CMEA socialist planning system.

Moreover, the implementation of a reform of regional policy along the lines proposed by the *Barca (2009)* report would require a strong political compromise to take place during 2010. It would also require some changes to be anticipated in the current programming period and, more difficultly, changes to the structure of the budget negotiation on cohesion policy in order to allow for simultaneous agreement on resources, governance and goals[217]. Whether such a major political concession would come about in the face of the deep economic crisis prevailing since the autumn of 2008 is extremely unlikely, in my view.

A final word shall evaluate the relevance of the *Barca (2009)* report with respect to the results of this research on industry agglomerations and regional specialization in Hungary. Agglomerations are acknowledged to be among the "key drivers" of economic growth and development. A country-wide perspective to economic development should be taken because of the strong inter-dependences between regions, as the movement of labour and capital away from regions with untapped resources to thriving agglomerations can reduce the potential output of the former region by more than they raise the potential output of the latter[218]. Public actions intervening in the agglomeration process should therefore take the form of a transparent process for private and business actors.

The notion of "smart specialization" for regions is a second concept of interest for this research. The notion as used in *Barca (2009)* alludes to a specialization of a region with respect to innovation policies. Along the lines and in accordance with the research results of this research, it would rather make sense to broaden the concept to strategic specialization as a regional development strategy. Policy

---

Policy after the next reform. The initial draft by Barca would have been more radical and rather academic in nature; that is my impression.

217 This would mean a simultaneous agreement on 3 relevant documents: the financial framework, the European strategic development framework, and the regulation on cohesion policy (rules for use of the grants).

218 See also the main statement of *World Bank (2008a)* on this, discussed more in detail earlier in this chapter.

makers should then pursue a policy of "strategic specialization" with respect to specific manufacturing industries as a development and employment strategy at a regional level.

Hungary and its regions are clearly on the recipient side of EU regional policy, in need of solidarity by the more prosperous member states, given that six of the seven Nuts-2 regions in Hungary need support under the convergence objective, and that the country has almost the largest personal income disparities among CEECs. In this respect, Hungary would rather benefit from a further concentration of funds on the cohesion goal than from the watering down of funds which the *Barca (2009)* proposals seem to imply. Given the large economic disparities in the Central and East European member states, more means should go towards this objective rather than less. The equity objective referred to as "social inclusion" could also be reached as a side objective, but not as a binding objective within the European regional policy. Social policies ought to be left to national member states in my view, as the national context with regards to the composition and needs of the population as well as the social systems vary greatly from country to country.

A word of caution shall conclude, namely that it should not be forgotten that Hungary still struggles with the implementation of current programmes according to the EU rules, as administrations handling the regional policy interventions are often little experienced in this field - despite the attempt of preparation made by ISPA and the phasing-in during the 2004-2006 period. In addition, a coordination problem among micro-regions, which are implementing the actions, seems to exist due to the lack of an administrative structure at the Nuts-2 regional level in Hungary, as indicated by the low portion of funds paid by invoice (only 21.37% for 2004-2006). Thus, despite the potential benefits which European cohesion policy may bring for Hungary, the advancement on the ground is slow and in need of further institutional improvements, training efforts, information, and exchange of good practice.

7.3 Conclusions, forecast for Hungary, and policy recommendations for further EU enlargements

In context with the Eastern enlargement of the EU, this research dealt with the effects of pre-enlargement integration policies on industry agglomeration and regional development in Hungary. In the framework of NEG models, the development of manufacturing industry agglomerations as well as specialization of the 20 Hungarian regions were analysed empirically and by means of regression analysis for the period 1992 to 2008. The regression results for agglomeration and regional specialization show that the integration variables exports and FDI had a significant influence, and that regions have succeeded to different degrees to cope with structural transformations and the additional adjustments required by the accession process. The results for Hungary clearly show that there is a trade-off between the overall catching-up process at the country-level due to increasing trade integration under the Europe agreement, on the one hand, and the increase of regional disparities in the pre- and post-accession phase, as shown by the results from regional specialization and other indicators, on the other hand.

Agglomeration went through certain phases during the process of proceeding European integration. The results with respect to manufacturing industry concentration in Hungary can best be described as a double-hub, a first peak around 1999 in the pre-accession phase, and a second slighter hub since the EU-accession. A similar development could be observed in the regions. Periods of high industry concentration tended to go along with a rise in specialization, and dispersion processes of industry with a diversification at the regional level. The double-hub structure of regional specialization also held for groups of regions. Internal regions tended to have higher specialization levels than border regions and a thinner industrial base than in border regions. Among border regions, those next to the EU-15 countries were the most diversified and also performed better. This coincided with the fact that most agglomerations were located in the Western part of the country and around the capital.

A particular strength of this research was that it combined concrete empirical research with policy relevance in light of practical work-experience gained in European policy making. With respect to the empirical analysis of industry agglomeration, most previous research was based on the country-level for a group of countries (EU or CEECs), while the present research used regional-level data to analyse agglomeration for the country chosen, namely Hungary. With reference to the tools, a unique contribution of this research is that it applied six different concentration indices to the same set of manufacturing data, thereby allowing for a comparative analysis. Regression analysis on the influences working on industry concentration and especially on regional specialization had rarely been performed before nor been based on data from Central and Eastern Europe.

The theories of the NEG chosen as theoretical framework made certain predicttions about the formation and development of agglomeration as well as about regional specialization during an integration process. The results of this research on manufacturing agglomeration and regional specialization in Hungary contributed an empirical confirmation called for regarding a key proposition of the NEG: that trade induces agglomeration.

Which future development can be forecast for Hungary concerning the areas of this research - agglomeration and regional development - in context with European integration? The process of on average decreasing agglomeration in manufacturing industries which started in 2007 looks set to continue for some years. Similarly, overall declining regional specialization, which has begun in 2007, will prevail for several years more. The border regions will benefit from a further deepening of integration in the EU, in particular the Western border regions due to the location of agglomerations there and due to their proximity to the high-income markets Austria and to a lesser extent Slovenia.

The empirical results regarding the effects of pre- and post accession policies on Hungarian manufacturing industries and regional development have certain policy implications. Policy conclusions which emerge from the *Ludema & Wooton (1997)* model with partial inter-regional migration - a realistic assumption in the case of Hungary - include the following. To counter growing regional disparities during integration processes, policy makers should lower transport costs between regions in a country. And they should seek to increase the degree of (partial) mobility of industrial workers by mobility-supporting and encouraging measures.

Agglomerations are acknowledged to be among the "key drivers" of economic growth and development. In Hungary where space for large agglomerations is limited and polycentrism is high, economies of scale and growth can best be generated by networking between major agglomerations and their hinterland and by dense networks of big or middle sized cities. Based on the empirical results regarding agglomerations in Hungary and along the line of the academic discussion, the following policy should be recommended with regards to agglomeration: Taking a country-wide perspective on economic development and growth, identifying growth poles - either certain agglomerations by themselves, or networks of cities and towns - which are giving a positive contribution to overall economic development, and then making policies in a coordinated fashion among all government levels, which are working towards this strategy, making them visible to all actors potentially concerned at the local level.

The tool of strategic specialization for a region seems to be an interesting option for policy makers interested in regional development based on this research. In particular, it might make sense to pursue a strategic specialization of a region with respect to growing, future-oriented manufacturing industries as part of a development and employment strategy for a region. This implies building on the strengths and taking account of the weaknesses of a region. Through such an approach, the most could be made of the present diversity of industrial agglomerations and networks, while their openness beyond regional or national boundaries would be promoted.

The pre-accession policy perspective should now be opened up towards further enlargement candidates of the EU such as Croatia in the nearer future and Ukraine further away on the horizon.[219] The challenges are threefold, firstly at the level of pre-accession policies, secondly at the institutional and policy side within the current EU, and thirdly at the level of the accession candidates.

The results of this research have underlined the positive role of integration policies – namely the instrument of the Europe agreement - on agglomeration and regional development. The regression results for agglomeration and regional specialization have shown that the integration variables exports and FDI - both of which increased sizeably over the period (see sections 3.7 and 3.8) - had a significant influence, and that some industry- and region-specific characteristics were relevant factors as well.

Taking an overall picture, the empirical results for Hungary derived in chapter 3 clearly show that there is a trade-off between the overall catching-up process at the country-level due to increasing trade integration under the Europe agreement, on the one hand, and the increase of regional disparities at the Nuts-3 level in the pre- and post-accession phase, on the other hand. Pre-accession policies based on trade liberalisation, as the Europe agreement with Hungary, are nevertheless beneficial for both sides. Hungary's share of exports to EU markets rose from one third to over 80% over the entire period, while trade volumes have tripled in the enlarged EU from 175 billion Euros to 500 billion in the 5 years since the Eastern enlargement. The westward re-orientation of Hungary after the break-down of communism was only possible due to early political integration policies by the EU, the Europe agreement, PHARE aid as well as the ISPA and Sapard pre-accession instruments. Without these integration policies, social unrests at a large scale due to the effects on manufacturing industry adjustments and regional restructuring processes would have interrupted the overall economic growth of Hungary over the period in my view.

Therefore, similar pre-accession instruments - Europe agreements and ISPA-type instruments, or by whatever name they will be called - should continue to be part of any EU strategy towards future accession candidates. Based on the profound

219 The accession of Turkey to the EU is seen as unlikely to ever take place for multiple economic, political and socio-cultural considerations. These include the fact that the application for membership was deposited long ago in 1975, that the economic disparities are enormous, making the extension of European regional and agricultural policies not fundable by EU budgetary means, that Turkey is not a European country except for 5% of is territory, and the fact that the majority of the citizens of the current EU and at least one member states (Greece) are against the accession, because of the general feeling that a mainly Islamic country would not fit into the set of ideals and values by which the Christian Occident is ruled since two millennia.

side-effects which the Europe agreements had on agglomerations and on the regional development processes in the accession countries, namely a widening of regional disparities - as proved by the empirical results of this research-, free trade agreements should be complemented by appropriate policies counteracting this tendency, both at the level of national governments in candidate countries and at the EU level.

Furthermore, European regional policy - as one of the EU's core policies taking up one third of the EU budget - should be reformed in the face of the new realities after Eastern enlargement, as illustrated by the increased regional disparities among Hungarian regions in this research. The economic development gap has widened, the problem of disparities has shifted geographically towards the East, and the employment situation has become more difficult, namely socio-economic disparities have doubled, while the average GDP of the EU decreased by 12.5%.

Cohesion is about overcoming distance, division and inequality. Cohesion policy must be focused on promoting sustainable growth, competitiveness and jobs. A reformed regional policy should result in tailor-made strategies for regional development, taking into account the territorial perspective of cohesion. Means should be more concentrated on a limited number of targets and actions than now. The bulk of funds should continue to go towards the provision of public goods and services in the poorest regions, similar to the percentage in the current period. Furthermore, cross-border cooperation should be given a more prominent role than in the current period. Efficiency in the sense of realising the full utilisation of the potential of every place or region should be one overall goal, while ensuring fair opportunities for individuals irrespective of where they live should gradually become a second objective.

In addition, institutional reforms in the EU are a necessary pre-condition for further enlargements. This includes the ratification of the Lisbon Treaty as one building block[220]. At the same time, the whole of the EU faces challenges arising from acceleration in economic restructuring as a result of globalisation, trade opening, technological progress, and an ageing population, the development of the knowledge economy and society, and a growth in immigration. The consequences of the economic downturn resulting from the world economic crisis since autumn 2008 have to be added to that list. Ensuring the European way of life, including sustainable environmental standards, and aiming at the goals in the area of research, communication and information technologies set by the Lisbon process are viable strategies for a strong EU.

220 At the time of writing, the ratification by Ireland was still outstanding.

More generally, the question should be posed whether the model of integration which the EU has followed in the past – keeping the same level of integration for all, but proceeding at the pace of the slowest member state[221] – will be suitable to cope with future challenges. Concepts discussed in this context include those of "flexible integration" and possibilities of "opting out", as was the case for the Euro. The nature of the political integration will have to evolve in order to take account of new economic challenges and of the method of working and decision making in an EU of 27 or more member states which is necessarily different from than of an EU of 15. As *Bruha & Straubhaar (2000)* pointed out, rigid forms of integration should belong to the past; optimal integration instead of a maximum of it should be the future path for the EU to go, meaning that those areas which are reap for a common policy should be integrated as soon as possible, leaving aside those areas where the interests of member states diverge too far. This could be a viable concept for Hungary and the other new member states as well as for future CEECs in order to participate meaningfully in the project of proceeding European integration.

The EU also needs a strong competition policy including the control of national champions in order to ensure a level playing field for firms and consumers in the now larger European market. The current remarked laxity in face of the economic crisis cannot be continued for long without a lasting damage to the credibility of the European Commission in this field. Single market policies including market liberalisation and further measures for free movement of workers (mutual recognition of degrees and professional qualifications) face new challenges with the accession of new member states. A liberal policy for the migration of qualified workers should continue to form part of such a strategy to create one labour market among EU member states. Fears about mass-migration from East to West following Eastern enlargement have not materialised, less than 1% of the population in working age in the EU-15 countries are working or work-seeking migrants from the new member states,[222] whilst most EU member states have already completely liberalised their labour market for all EU citizens (except for Austria and Germany[223]). In a time-span of about two decades, about 1 to 1.5

221 See *Reichenbach et al. (1999)* for an account of this process and a political analysis of the reasons for phases of fast and of slow progress of European integration.

222 An exception to the less than 1% general figure are the UK with 1.2% and the Republic of Ireland with 5%; according to the communication: „Five years of an enlarged EU", *European Commission (2009b)* and *(2009c)*.

223 The recent decision by the German government is contrary to this line; they decided to prolong the restrictions on the migration of workers from the new member states in Central and Eastern Europe for another two years until the last date, 30 April 2011. This was done mainly for jobs requiring low qualifications and certainly in the face of rising unemployment during the current severe economic crisis expected to top 4.5 million in 2010, more than during the Great Depression which started in 1929.

million people from the CEECs are expected to migrate to the EU-15 countries, taking into account remigration. This corresponds to about half a percent of the EU population, no reason for concern, according to *Straubhaar (2004)*.

This touches also on industrial policy at the EU level, which should continue to gradually eliminate the possible causes of product market malfunctioning in the EU, along the lines sketched in *Ilzkovitz et al. (2008)*. The role of entrepreneurship in the EU should generally be promoted at the national and EU levels,[224] given the important role played by SMEs in employment growth, innovation and jobs.[225]

Secondly, from the example of Hungary lessons can be drawn for policies which a country can usefully pursue prior to EU accession. The Hungarian policy of free trade zones, the majority of which are located in the Western part of the country, has added significantly to the positive effects of trade liberalisation of the Europe agreement. Further, the policy of industry specialization at the country level led by the Hungarian government, namely to favour the machinery and equipment sector, has contributed to this sector's taking the lead in manufacturing output, employment and exports to the EU. Furthermore, the industrial parks policy has fuelled the emergence and growth of new centres of agglomeration in the Western part of the country, benefiting the overall economic development of Hungary. Such location and industrial policies seem fruitful policy lines for further EU accession candidates. Last but not least, Hungary's policy of creating an investor-friendly economic climate and legislative framework and of attracting foreign direct investors - imbedded in privatisation and other schemes - has contributed to the largest stock of FDI in any of the CEECs by the year 2000. The positive roles played by FDI for productivity as well as process and facility renewal in manufacturing and in employment strongly speak in favour of FDI-friendly policies.

Finally, a few words shall be said about the future architecture of Europe. Enlargement of the EU depends always not only on economic considerations, but also on the political will in the current EU and the accession candidates, and to a certain extent on the overall geopolitical climate as well.[226] The Europe of tomorrow will still have the EU as a motor of economic and political stability. Modified

---

224 For a study on the role of SMEs in national growth, see *Nijkamp & van Hemert (2007)* for example.

225 SMEs, i.e. enterprises with a number of employees between 1 and 249, have accounted for 67.3% of jobs in the EU-27 as in 2008; *EU-Nachrichten(7.5.2009)*.

226 The favourable geopolitical climate following the fall of the Berlin Wall in 1989 and the break-down of the communist regimes in the former Soviet Union and Eastern Europe enabled the Eastern enlargement of the EU.

forms of Europe agreements, or whatever they will be called, will continue to link the EU and its European neighbours in an effort to ensure political stability beyond the EU's external borders - the "wider Europe" process of which the new Neighbourhood Policy[227] and the new Eastern partnership inaugurated in May 2009 are building blocks.[228] There will be further, yet smaller rounds of enlargement of the EU-27, such as by Croatia in the nearer future, or by Ukraine and Macedonia in the more distant future.

Yet the nature of the political integration will change from one of equal to one with differing speeds - concentric circles and flexible integration. A core group will continue to be linked under the common currency, the Euro, the other old member states in the next-nearest circle being already well-integrated into the European Single market, while the new member states (CEECs) are still in the process of defining their place in the new division of labour in the enlarged European market. In the participatory democratic and economic process which European integration has been in the past, the future still opens up multiple opportunities for actors from the research community as well as private, public and business fields to participate in shaping the architecture of an ever wider and larger Europe.

227 The European Neighbourhood Policy towards Russia, the Western Newly Independent States, and the Southern Mediterranean disposes of a new financial instrument operating on both sides of the border (EU member states and external countries) which builds on the experience of the PHARE, TACIS and INTERREG programmes; *European Commission (2008c).*

228 The summit meeting of the EU on 7th of May 2009 in Prague inaugurated a new form of cooperation with a diversified group of countries: Ukraine, Moldova, Byelorussia, Georgia, Armenia, and Azerbaijan. In an effort to foster political stability in the area and to secure access to energy resources, the EU intends to create deep and comprehensive free trade zones with these countries.

Bibliography

Sources of data

European Central Bank: Website (for official exchange rates), http://www.ecb.int/stats/exchange/eurofxref/html/index.en.html

Eurostat: Regional data base, Eurostat website.

Eurostat (2008): Portrait of the Regions, drawn from the Eurostat Website on 9th Sept. 2008.

HCSO Hungarian Central Statistical Office: Regional Statistical Yearbook of Hungary, Budapest, series (1992 - 2005); from thereon: data available at the Website, Database Economy.

HCSO Hungarian Central Statistical Office: Statistical Yearbook of External Trade, series (1992 - 2005); from thereon: data available at the Website, Database Economy.

HCSO Hungarian Central Statistical Office: Statistical Yearbook of Industry and Construction, series (1992 - 2005); Budapest.

HCSO Hungarian Central Statistical Office: Statistical Yearbook of Hungary, Budapest, series (1992 - 2005); from thereon: data available at the Website, Database Economy.

HCSO Hungarian Central Statistical Office, Website, Database Economy, http://portal.ksh.hu/portal/page?_pageid=38,122433&_dad=portal&_schema=PORTAL

HCSO Hungarian Central Statistical Office, Website, Stadat System Tables, Regional Data,
http://portal.ksh.hu/portal/page?_pageid=38,122433&_dad=portal&_schema=PORTAL

Publications by international organisations, governments and government agencies

Committee of the Regions (2008): Opinion on the Green Paper on Territorial Cohesion (by the European Commission), version of December 2008, Brussels.

Czech Presidency (2009): Communiqué of the Informal Meeting of EU Ministers for Regional Development, held in Mariánské Lásně (Czech Republic), Council of Ministers, 22-24 April 2009.

Deutsche Bundesbank (2001): Monatsbericht, Oktober 2001.

European Union (2003): Treaty of Accession by the Czech Republic, Estonia, Cyprus, Latvia, Lithuania, Hungary, Malta, Poland, Slovenia and Slovakia to the European Union, AA 2003 final, Brussels, 3 April 2003.

European Commission (1994): The Economic Interpenetration between the European Union and Eastern Europe, European Economy No. 6 - Reports and Studies series, DG Economic and Financial Affairs, Brussels, 1994.

European Commission (1995): White Paper on Competitiveness and Growth, Brussels.

European Commission (1998): Dismantling of Barriers, Technical Barriers to Trade in: "The Single Market Review", Kagan Page. Earthscan, Subseries III: Vol. 1, 1998.

European Commission (1999): Specialization and (Geographic) Concentration of European Manufacturing, DG Enterprise Working Paper No. 1; Background Paper for The Competitiveness of European Industry: 1999-Report, Brussels; experts contributing: Aiginger, K. & Boeheim, M. & Gugler, K. & Pfaffermayr, M. & Wolfmayr-Schnitzer, Y.

European Commision (2001): Evaluation of the 2001 pre-accession economic programmes of candidate countries, DG Economics and Financial Affairs, January 2001, Hungary, pp. 57-65.

European Commission (2006a): Enlargement, two years after: an economic evaluation, by the Bureau for European Policy Advisers and the Directorate General for Economic and Financial Affairs, European Economy, Occasional Papers, No. 24, May 2006.

European Commission (2006b): The New Programming Period 2007-2013. Methodological Working Papers - Draft Working Paper 'Indicators for Monitoring and Evaluation: a Practical Guide, January

European Commission (2006c): The New Programming Period 2007-2013. Indicative Guidelines on Evaluation Methods: Monitoring and Evaluation Indicators, Working Document No. 2.

European Commission (2007): Growing Regions, growing Europe, Fourth report on economic and social cohesion, Communication from the Commission, Brussels, May 2007.
European Commission (2008a): DG Economic and Financial Affairs, country page Hungary.
European Commission (2008b): Green Paper on Territorial Cohesion - Turning territorial diversity into strength, Communication from the Commission to the Council, the European Parliament, the Committee of the Regions and the Economic and Social Committee, Brussels,6.10.2008; accompanied by a staff working document of DG Regional Policy.
European Commission (2008c): European Neighbourhood Policy: Economic Review of EU Neighbour Countries, European Economy, DG ECFIN, Occasional Paper no. 40, August 2008.
European Commission (2009a): Economic Forecast Spring 2009, DG Economic and Financial Affairs, European Economy, 3/2009.
European Commission (2009b): Five years of an enlarged EU - Economic achievements and challenges, Communication from the Commission to the European Parliament, the Council, The Economic and Social Committee, the Committee of the Regions and the European Central Bank, COM (2009) 79/3, Brussels (February) 2009.
European Commission (2009c): Five years of an enlarged EU - Economic achievements and challenges, European Economy No. 1/2009, DG Economic and Financial Affairs, Brussels, 222 pages.
EU Regional Policy (2008a): Cohesion Policy 2007-13 - National Strategic Reference Frameworks, Publications Office of the European Communities, Luxembourg, p. 50f.
EU Regional Policy (2008b): inforegio panorama, no. 28, Office for Publications, Luxembourg.
Eurostat (2008): Portrait of the Regions, drawn from the Eurostat Website on 09.09.2008.

Hungarian Central Statistical Office (2005): Change of course - Hungary 1990 - 2004, Budapest.
Hungarian Development Agency (2007): The New Hungary Development Plan, National Strategic Reference Framework of Hungary 2007-2013, Employment and Growth, Budapest (May 2007).

KfW Kreditanstalt für Wiederaufbau (2004): Die EU-Beitrittsländer auf dem Weg zum Euro, Makroscope Nr. 10, Januar 2004.

OECD (1994): Scoreboard of indicators for manufacturing industry sectors, Paris.

Official Journal of the European Communities (1978): Series L 120/78, Rewe/ Bundesmonopolverwaltung für Branntwein, Jurisdiction No. 1979.

Official Journal of the European Communities (1992): Interim Europe agreement between the EU and Hungary, OJ No. L 116/92, No. L 195/93 and No. 200/93, Corrigendum to the Interim Europe agreement, OJ No. L 13/93 of 21 January 1993.

Official Journal of the European Communities (1994): Europe agreement Establishing an Association Between the European Communities and their Member States, on the one part, and the Republic of Hungary, of the other part, No. L/25, 29 January 1994, Brussels.

World Bank (2008a): World Development Report 2009 - "Reshaping Economic Geography", Washington.

World Bank (2008b): Press release for the World Development Report 2009 - "Reshaping Economic Geography", Washington.

World Trade Organization (1998): Trade Policy Review Hungary 1998, Geneva, December 1998.

References by author

Aiginger, K. & Davies, St. (2004): Industrial Specialization and Geographic Concentration: two sides of the same coin? Not for the European Union, in: Journal of Applied Economics, Vol. VII, No. 2, p. 231-248, Nov. 2004.

Aiginger, K. & Pfaffermayr, M. (2004): The Single Market and Geographic Concentration in Europe in: Review of International Economics, 12 (1), pp. 1-11, 2004.

Amiti, Mary (1997): Specialization Patterns in Europe, Centre for Economic Performance Discussion Paper No. 363, September 1997.

Amiti, Mary (1999): Specialization Patterns in Europe, in: Weltwirtschaftliches Archiv, Vol. 135 (4), 1999.

ARL Academy for Spatial Research and Planning (2008): The Territorial Cohesion Principles - Position paper to the EU Green Paper on Territorial Cohesion, Hanover.

Azhar, A. K. M & Elliott, R. J. R. (2003): On the measurement of trade-induced adjustment, in: Review of World Economics, Vol. 139, No. 3, Springer Berlin/Heidelberg, September 2003, pp. 419-439.

Barca, F. (2009): An Agenda for a reformed Cohesion Policy - A place-based approach to meeting European Union challenges and expectations, independent report prepared at the request of Danuta Hübner, Commissioner for Regional Policy, Brussels, 27 April 2009.

Balassa, Béla (1964): The Purchasing Power Parity Doctrine: A Reappraisal, in: Journal of Political Economy, Vol. 72, December, pp. 584-596.

Balassa, Béla & Bauwens, Luc (1987): Intra-Industry Specialization in a multi-country and multi-industry framework, in: The Economic Journal, 97, December 1987, pp. 923-939.

Baldone, S. & Sdogati, F. (1997): EU-CEECs Integration: Policies and markets at work, Franco Angeli, Milano, 1997.

Baldwin, R. & Martin, Ph. (2004): Agglomeration and Regional Growth, in: Handbook of Regional and Urban Economics, Vol. 4, Elseview B.V., pp. 2671-2711.

Barrios, S. & Strobl, E. (2005): The dynamics of regional inequalities, European Economy, Economic Papers No. 229, July 2005.

Békés, Gábor (2005): Location of manufacturing FDI in Hungary: How important are inter-company relationships?, MND Working Papers, 7/2005.

Bindseil, Ulrich & Hantke[229], Cordula (1997): The Power Distribution in Decision Making among EU Member States, European Journal of Political Economy, Amsterdam, Elsevier, No 13, April 1997, pp. 171-185.

Boudier-Bensebaa, Fabienne (2005): Agglomeration economies and location choice, Foreign direct investment in Hungary, in: Economics of Transition, Volume 13 (4), p. 605-628.

Brakman, S., Garretsen, H. et al. (1994): Congestion and Industrial Location, University of Groningen, mimeo.

Bräuninger, Michael & Niebuhr, Annekatrin (2005): Agglomeration, Spatial Interaction and Convergence in the EU, HWWA Discussion Paper No. 322, 2005.

Brenton, P. & Sheehy, J. & Vancauteren, M. (2001): Technical Barriers to Trade in the European Union: Importance for Accession Countries, in: Journal of Common Market Studies, Blackwell Publishers Ltd., Vol. 39, No. 2, pp. 265-84, June 2001.

Bröcker, Johannes (1998): How would an EU-membership of the Visegrád-countries affect Europe's economic geography? Annals of Regional Science, 32, pp. 91-114.

Brülhart, Marius (2001a): Evolving Geographical Concentration of European Manufacturing Industries, in: Weltwirtschaftliches Archiv, Vol 137 (2), December 2001.

Brülhart, Marius (2001b): Growing Alike or Growing Apart? Industrial Specialization of EU Countries in: The Impact Of EMU In Europe, In: The Developing Countries, Chapter 7, by Charles Wyplosz, Oxford University Press, 2001.

Brülhart, M. & Crozet, M. & Koenig, P. (2004): Enlargement and the EU Periphery: The Impact of Changing Market Potential, HWWA-Discussion Paper No. 270, February 2004.

Brülhart, Marius & Jametti, Mario & Schmidheiny, Kurt (2008): Do agglomeration economies reduce the sensitivity of firm location to tax differentials?, CEPR Discussion paper No. 6606.

Brülhart, M. & Torstensson, J. (1998): Regional Integration, Scale Economies and Industry Location in the European Union, February 1998.

Brülhart, M. & Traeger R. (2003): An Account of Geographic Concentration Patterns in Europe, HWWA Discussion Paper No. 226, 2003.

Bruha, Thomas & Straubhaar, Thomas (2000): Ante-Portas Strategien für die MOEL, in: Erweiterung und Vertiefung der European Union, Hasse, R., Schenk, K.-E. & Wass von Czege, A. (Eds), Nomos Verlag, Baden-Baden, 63-86.

229 *Hantke* is the maiden name of the author of this book, *Cordula Wandel*.

Buigues, Pierre & Ilzkovitz, Fabienne (1988): The Sectoral Impact Of The Internal Market, Commission of the European Communities Document II/335/88-EN.

Buigues, P., Ilzkovitz, F. & Lebrun (1990): Non-Tariff Barriers (NTBs) in the EU, study for the European Commission, Brussels.

Crozet, M. & Koenig Soubeyran, P. (2004): EU enlargement and the internal geography of countries in: Journal of Comparative Economics, Elsevier, No. 32, pp. 265-279.

Csengodi, S. & Jungnickel, R. & Urban, D. (2003): Foreign takeovers and wages in Hungary, Flowenla Discussion Paper No. 3, 2003.

Cseres-Gergely, Zsombor (2003): Residential mobility, migration and economic incentives - The case of Hungary in 1990-1999, Flowenla Discussion Paper No. 26, HWWA, 2003.

Davis, D. R. & & Weinstein, D. E. (1999): Economic geography and regional production structure: An empirical investigation, in: European Economic Review 43, pp. 379-407, Elsevier, 1999.

De Sousa, J. & Disdier, A.-C. (2002): Der Steuerwettbewerb und die Osterweiterung der EU in: Wirtschaftsdienst 2004.

Devereux, M. P., Griffith, R. & Simpson, H. (1999): The Geographic Distribution of Production Activity in the UK, The institute for fiscal studies, Working Paper No. 26.

Di Giacinto, V. & Pagnini, M. (2008): Agglomeration within and between Regions: Two Econometric based Indicators; Bank of Italy Working Paper No. 674, July 2008.

Dixit, A. K. & Stiglitz, J. E. (1977): Monopolistic Competition and Optimum Product Diversity in: American Economy Review, 1977.

Dreyhaupt-von Speicher, P. (2002): Die Regionen Polens, Ungarns und der Tschechischen Republik vor dem EU-Beitritt - Interregionale Disparitäten, Bestimmungsfaktoren und Lösungsansätze, Schriften zur Wirtschaftstheorie und Wirtschaftspolitik, Band 24, Peter Lang Verlag, Frankfurt am Main, 2002.

Eger, Thomas (2003): Institutionen und wirtschaftliche Entwicklung, Hrsg., Schriften des Vereins für Socialpolitik, Jahrestagung 15-17 Sept. 2002, Duncker & Humblot, Berlin, 240 p.

Eger, Thomas (2000): Systemtransformation als umfassender institutioneller Wandel: die fünf Dimensionen der Transformationsprozesse in Osteuropa, Arbeitsberichte, No. 2/2000, Frankfurter (Oder) Institut für Transformationsstudien, 44 p.

Ellison, G. & Glaeser, E. (1997): Geographic Concentration in U.S. Manufacturing Industries: A Dartboard Approach in: Journal of Political Economy, vol. 105, no. 5, 1997.

Ellison, G. & Glaeser, E. (1999): Evolution of the geographic concentration of industry, The Geographic Concentration of Industry: Does Natural Advantage Explain Agglomeration? in: American Economy Review, Vol. 89 H2, pp. 311-316, May 1999.

EU-Nachrichten (2009): Kleine Unternehmen - große Ideen, Woche der KMU, Nr. 16/2009, 7.5.2009.

Evaluation Network (2007): Presentation held at the Evaluation Network meeting, 13-14 November 2008, the network consisting of APPLICA, Ismeri, Wiiw; Source: ec-europa.eu/regional_policy.

Faragó, László (1999): Regional "Winners" and "Losers", in: Hajdú, Zoltán (1999): Regional Processes and Spatial Structures in Hungary in the 1990s, Centre for Regional Studies of the Hungarian Academy of Sciences, Pécs, 1999.

Fazekas, Károly (2003): Effects of foreign direct investment on the performance of local labour markets - The case of Hungary, Budapest Working Papers on the Labour Market, Institute of Economics Hungarian Academy of Sciences, 3/2003.

Fischer, Peter A. & Straubhaar, Thomas (1994): Ökonomische Integration und Migration in einem Gemeinsamen Markt, 40 Jahre Erfahrung im Nordischen Arbeitsmarkt, Verlag Paul Haupt, Bern, Stuttgart, Wien, 323p.

Foray, D. & Van Ark, B. (2009): Smart Specialization in a Truly Integrated Research Area is the Key to Attracting more R&D to Europe, in: Knowledge Economists Policy Brief, No. 1.

Forslid, R. & Haaland, J. I. & Midelfart-Knarvik, K. & Maestad, O. (2002): Integration and transition, Scenarios for the location of production and trade in Europe in: Economics of Transition Volume. 10 (1) 2002, pp. 93-117.

Fujita, M. & Krugman, Paul & Venables, A. J. (1999): The Spatial Economy - Cities, Regions, and International Trade, MIT Press, 1999.

Fujita, M. & Thisse, J.-F. (2002): Economics of Agglomeration, Cities, Industrial Location, and Regional Growth, Cambridge University Press, 2002.

Frankfurter Allgemeine Zeitung (2009): Ungarn ringt mit starker Rezession - Neue Regierung aus Fachleuten will sämtliche Sozialleistungen kürzen, 18.4.2009, p. 13.

Gács, Janos (1993): The Economic Interpenetration between the EC and Eastern Europe: Hungary, International Institute for Applied Systems Analysis, Laxenburg, Austria (March).

Giannetti, Mariassunta (2002): The effects of integration on regional disparities: Convergence, divergence or both? in European Economic Review 64, pp. 539-567.

Greenaway, D. & Hine, R.C. (1991): Intra-Industry Specialization, Trade Expansion and Adjustment in the European Economic Space, in: Journal of Common Market Studies, 29 (6), pp. 603-622.

Grubel, H. G. & Lloyd, P. J. (1975): Intra-Industry Trade, The Theory and Measurement of International Trade in Differentiated Products, The Macmillan Press Ltd. London, 1975.

Guerson, A., Parks, J. & Parra Torrado, M. (2007): Export Structure and Growth - A Detailed Analysis for Argentina, Word Bank Policy Research Working Paper 4237, May 2007.

Haaland, J. I. & Kind, H. J. & Midelfart Knarvik, K. H. & Torstensson, J. (1999): What Determines The Economic Geography Of Europe?, CEPR Discussion Paper No. 2072, February 1999.

Hajdú, Zoltán (1999): Regional Processes and Spatial Structures in Hungary in the 1990s, Centre for Regional Studies of the Hungarian Academy of Sciences, Pécs, 1999.

Hallet, Martin (2000): Regional Specialization and Concentration in the EU, Economic Paper No. 141, EC Commission, Brussels, March 2000.

Hamilton, C. B. & Winters, L. A. (1992): Opening up international trade with Eastern Europe in: Economic Policy, Vol. 4, April 1992.

Hanson, Gordon H. (1998): Regional adjustment to trade liberalization in: Regional Science and Urban Economics 28, pp. 419-444, Elsevier, 1998.

Hantke, Cordula (1993): Zum Stand der wirtschaftlichen Reformen in Ungarn: Der ordnungspolitische Rahmen (1989-1992), Wirtschaftsreformen in Osteuropa, Seminararbeit an der Universität des Saarlandes, Fachbereich Volkswirtschaft, 31. Januar 1993.

Hantke, Cordula (1995): The Europe agreement with Hungary: Trade opportunities and economic challenges, Nomos Verlag, Baden-Baden, Bd. 22 Wirtschaft, 1995, 145 p. (Masters thesis at Universität des Saarlandes, Europa Institut, Saarbrücken).

Head K. & Mayer, T. (2000): Non-Europe: The Magnitude and Causes of Market Fragmentation in the EU, in: Weltwirtschaftliches Archiv, 136(2), pp. 284-314.

Head K. & Mayer, T. (2004): The Empirics of Agglomeration and Trade, in: Handbook of Regional and Urban Economics, Volume 4, ed. by Henderson, H.V. & Thisse, J.-F., Elsevier, chapter 59, pp. 2610-2669.

Helpman, E. & Krugman, Paul (1985): Market Structure and Foreign Trade – Increasing Returns, Imperfect Competition, and the International Economy, MIT Press, 1985.

Helpman, E. & Krugman, Paul (1989): Trade Policy and Market Structure, MIT Press, 1989.

Hildebrandt, Antje & Wörz, Julia (2004): Determinants of Industrial Location Patterns in CEECs, Research Paper commissioned by the Foreign Research Division of the Oesterreichische Nationalbank.

Horváth, G. (2000): Hungary, in: Bachtler, J., Downes, R, & Gorzelak, G. (eds): Transition, cohesion and regional policy in Central and Eastern Europe, Ashgate, 378 p.

Hummels, D. (2001): Time as a trade barrier, Purdue University, July 2001, mimeo.

Ilzkovitz, F., Dierx, A. & Sousa, N. (2008): An analysis of the possible causes of product market malfunctioning in the EU: First results for manufacturing and service sectors, published as: European Economy, Economic Papers No. 336, August 2008 (European Commission, DG ECFIN).

Kalotai, K. & Hunya, G. (2000): Privatization and FDI in Central and Eastern Europe, in: Transnational Corporations 9 (1), pp. 1377-1398.

Krieger-Boden, C. (1995): Neue Argumente für Regionalpolitik? Zur Fundierung der Regionalpolitik in älteren und neueren regionalökonomischen Theorien, in: Die Weltwirtschaft, No. 2, pp. 193-215.

Krugman, Paul (1980): Scale Economics, Product Differentiation, and the Pattern of Trade, in: American Economic Review, Vol. 70, pp. 469-79.

Krugman, Paul (1991a): Geography and Trade, lecture at the Catholic University of Leuven, Leuven University Press & MIT Press, 1991.

Krugman, Paul (1991b): Increasing Returns and Economic Geography in: Journal of Political Economy, Vol. 99, No. 3, 1991.

Krugman, Paul (1992): A dynamic spatial model, NBER working paper No. 4219.

Krugman, Paul (1993): On the number and location of cities, in: European Economic Review, No. 37, pp. 293-298.

Krugman, Paul (1994): Complex landscapes in economic geography, in: American Economic Review, No. 84, pp. 412-416.

Krugman, Paul (1999): Was It All In Ohlin?, October 1999, http://web.mit.edu/krugman/www/ohlin.html.

Krugman, P. & Venables, A. J. (1996): Integration, specialization, and adjustment in: European Economic Review, No. 40, pp. 959-967.

Lammers, K. & Stiller, Silvia (2000): Regionalpolitische Implikationen der neuen ökonomischen Geographie, HWWA Discussion Paper No. 85, 2000.

Landesmann, M. & Stehrer, R. (2002): The CEECs in the enlarged Europe: convergence patterns, specialization and labour market implications, The Vienna Institute for International Economic Studies, July 2002.

Landesmann, M. & Stehrer, R. (2003): Potential switchovers in comparative advantage: Patterns of industrial convergence, Flowenla Discussion Paper No. 18, HWWA, 2003.

Livas-Elizondo, Raul & Krugman, Paul (1996): "Trade policy and the Third World metropolis", in: Journal of Development Economics, Elsevier, vol. 49, 1996, pp. 137-150.

Ludema, R. D. & Wooton, I. (1997): Regional Integration, Trade, and Migration: Are Demand Linkages relevant in Europe? CEPR Discussion Paper, No. 1656.

Martin, Ph. & Ottaviano, G. I. P. (2001): "Growth and Agglomeration", International Economic Review, Vol. 42, pp. 947-968.

Mafioli, Alessandro (2003): The Emerging Economic Geography in Hungary, in: Traistaru, Nijkamp & Resmini (2003): The Emerging Economic Geography in EU Accession Countries, Ashgate Publishing Ltd, 2003.

Midelfart-Knarvik, K. H. & Overman, H. G. & Redding, S. J. & Venables, A. J. (2000): The Location of European Industry in: Economic Papers No. 142, April 2000.

Monfort, Philippe (2009): Regional Convergence, Growth and Interpersonal Inequalitics across the EU, Working paper in context of the Barca (2009) Report; DG Regional Policy, European Commission, Brussels.

Nagy, Imre (2001): Cross-Border Co-operation in the Border Region of the Southern Great Plain of Hungary, Centre For Regional Studies, Hungary, Discussion Papers, 2001.

Nagy, Imre (2002): Hungary's Seven Border Regions, in: Journal of Borderlands Studies, Ed.: J. M. Patrick & H. v Houtum & M. v d. Velde, Sheridan Books, INC. Summer, 2002.

Nemes-Nagy, József (2000): The new regional structure in Hungary, in: Petrakos, G., Maier, G. & Gorzelak, G. (2000): Integration and Transition in Europe, Routledge, London and New York, pp. 170-186.

Niebuhr, Annekatrin & Schlitte, Friso (2008): EU Enlargement and Convergence - Does Market Access Matter, HWWI Research Paper 1-16, Hamburg, 2008, 24 p.

Niebuhr, Annekatrin. & Stiller, Silvia (2002): Integration Effects in Border Regions - A Survey of Economic Theory and Empirical Studies, HWWA Discussion Paper No. 179, 2002.

Nijkamp, P. & van Hemert, P. (2007): Going for Growth - A Theoretical and Policy Framework, Papers DYNREG no. 14, Economic and Social Research Institute (ESRI).

Ottaviano, G., Tabuchi, T. & Thisse, J.-F. (2002): Agglomeration and Trade Revisited, International Economic Review, Vol. 43, No. 2, May 2002.

Overman, H. G. & Redding, S. & Venables, A. J. (2001): The Economic Geography of Trade, Production, and Income: A Survey of Empirics, ESRC Discussion paper No. 508.

Overman, H. G. & Rice, P. & Venables, A. J. (2008): Economic Linkages Across Space, CEPR Discussion paper No. 6786.

Perroux, F. (1970): A note on the concept of growth poles, in: McKee, D. Dean, R. & Leahy, W. (ed.s): Regional economics theory and practice, Free Press, pp. 93-103.

Petrakos, G., Maier, G. & Gorzelak, G. (2000): Integration and Transition in Europe, Routledge, London and New York.

Porter, Michael E. (1990): The Competitive Advantage of Nations, London, New York.

Pratten, C. (1988): A Survey of the Economies of Scale, in: Commission Of The European Communities: Research on the "Cost of Non-Europe", Volume 2, Studies on the Economics of Integration, Luxembourg.

Puga, Diego (1999): The rise and fall of regional inequalities in: European Economic Review 43, pp. 303-334, Elsevier, 1999.

Puga, Diego (2002): European regional policies in light of recent location theories in: Journal of Economic Geography 2, pp. 373-406.

Puga, Diego & Venables, A. (1997): Preferential Trading Arrangements and Industrial Location, in: Journal of International Economics, Vol. 43, pp. 347-368.

Rechnitzer, János (2000): The Features of the Transition of Hungary's Regional System, Centre for Regional Studies of the Hungarian Academy of Sciences Discussion Paper No. 32, 2000.

Reichenbach, Horst, Emmerling, T., Staudenmyer, D., & Schmidt, S. (1999): Integration: Wanderung über europäische Gipfel, Nomos-Verlag, Baden-Baden, 243 p.

Rodrik, D. (2005): "Growth Strategies", in: Aghion, P. and Durlauf, S.N. (eds.), Handbook of Economic Growth, North Holland, Elsevier Academic Press, Vol. 1A, pp. 967-1014.

Rodrigues-Posé, A. & Fratesi, U. (2004): Between Development and Social Policies : The impact of European Structural Funds in Objective 1 Regions. Journal of Regional Studies, No. 38, pp. 97-113.

Romer, P. (1987): Growth based on Increasing Returns due to Specialization, American Economic Review, Vol. 77, pp. 56-62.

Sapir, André (1996): The Effects of Europe's Internal Market Program on Production and Trade: A First Assessment in: Weltwirtschaftliches Archiv, Vol. 132 (3), 1996.

Samuelson, Paul (1964): Theoretical Notes on Trade Problems, in: Review of Economics and Statistics, vol. 23.

Schmutzler, A. (1999): The New Economic Geography in: Journal of Economic Surveys Vol. 13, No. 4, Blackwell Publishers Ltd.

Sdogati, F. & Baldone, S. & Tajoli, L. (2002): EU Enlargement to the CEECs: Trade Competition, Delocalisation of Production, and effects on the Economies of the Union, Franco Angeli, Milano, 2002.

Stierle-von Schütz, U. & Stierle, M. H. (2004): An Empirical Analysis of Regional Specialization and Sectoral Concentration in an enlarged EU, mimeo.

Stirböck, Claudia (2001): Agglomeration Tendencies in EU Regions: Where Does Capital Go?, ZEW Discussion Paper No. 01-28, Mannheim.

Straubhaar, Thomas (1998): Wirtschaftliche Konvergenz: Was? Wie? Wozu?, in: Fischer, Peter A. & Straubhaar, Thomas (1998) (eds.): Ökonomische Konvergenz in Theorie und Praxis, Veröffentlichungen des HWWA, Band 41, Nomos Verlagsgesellschaft, Baden-Baden, 1998.

Straubhaar, Thomas (2004): EU-Erweiterung: Überschätzte ökonomische Effekte, in: Wirtschaftsdienst - Zeitschrift für Wirtsdchaftspolitik, 84. Jahrgang, Heft 4, 2004, pp. 4-5.

Szanyi, Miklos (2005): Competitiveness and Industrial Renewal Through International Production Relocation: Paper presented at the conference "Relocation of production and jobs to CEE countries - who gains and who loses?" HWWA Hamburg, 16 - 17 Sept. 2005.

Tajoli, L. (2003): EU-CEECs convergence in trade structures: Does international fragmentation of production matter?, Flowenla Discussion Paper No. 24, 2003.

The Hungarian Economy (2002): The first year of the Széchenyi Plan; Ten-year industrial park programme, Budapest, 1/2002.

Thisse, J.-F. (2000): Agglomeration and regional imbalance: Why? And is it bad?, EIB Papers No. 52, pp. 47-68.

Tondl, G. & Vuksic, G. (2003): What Makes Regions in Eastern Europe Catching Up? The Role of Foreign Investment, Human Resources and Geography, ZEI-Working Paper, B12, 2003.

Traistaru, I. & Nijkamp, P. & Longhi, S. (2002): Regional Specialization and Concentration of Industrial Activity in Accession Countries, ZEI Working Paper B 16, 2002.
Traistaru, I. & Nijkamp, P. & Resmini, L. (2003): The Emerging Economic Geography in EU Accession Countries, Ashgate Publishing Ltd, 2003.

Vadász, Zsuzsa N. (2000): Customs-free Zones in the Lead, in: The Hungarian Economy, 2/2000, pp. 16-18.
Venables, Anthony J. (1996): Equilibrium Locations of Vertically Linked Industries, in: International Economic Review, Vol. 37, No. 2, May 1996, pp. 341-359.

Wagener, Hans-Jürgen & Eger, Thomas, & Fritz, Heiko (2006): Europäische Integration. Recht und Ökonomie, Geschichte und Politik, München, Verlag Vahlen, 641 p.
Wandel, Cordula (2004): Höheres Wirtschaftswachstum für Europa? Eine Zwischenbilanz der Lissabon-Strategie, in: integration, 27. Jhg., 1-2/04, Nomos Verlag, Baden-Baden, pp.147-155.

SCHRIFTEN ZUR WIRTSCHAFTSTHEORIE UND WIRTSCHAFTSPOLITIK

Herausgegeben von Klaus Beckmann, Michael Berlemann, Rolf Hasse, Jörn Kruse, Franco Reither, Wolf Schäfer, Thomas Straubhaar, Klaus W. Zimmermann

Band 1 Lars Bünning: Die Konvergenzkriterien des Maastricht-Vertrages unter besonderer Berücksichtigung ihrer Konsistenz. 1997.

Band 2 Andreas Henning: Beveridge-Kurve, Lohnsetzung und Langzeitarbeitslosigkeit. Eine theoretische Untersuchung unter Berücksichtigung des Insider-Outsider-Ansatzes und der Entwertung des Humankapitals. 1997.

Band 3 Iris Henning: Die Reputation einer Zentralbank. Eine theoretische Untersuchung unter besonderer Berücksichtigung der Europäischen Zentralbank. 1997.

Band 4 Rüdiger Hermann: Ein gemeinsamer Markt für Elektrizität in Europa. Optionen einer Wettbewerbsordnung zwischen Anspruch und Wirklichkeit. 1997.

Band 5 Alexander Tiedtke: Japan und der Vorwurf des Trittbrettfahrerverhaltens in der US-amerikanisch-japanischen Allianz. 1997.

Band 6 Wolfgang Grimme: Ordnungspolitisches Konzept der Regionalpolitik. Darstellung der Defizite und des Reformbedarfs der Regionalpolitik am Beispiel Mecklenburg-Vorpommerns. 1997.

Band 7 Christian Ricken: Determinanten der Effektivität der Umweltpolitik. Der nationale Politikstil im Spannungsfeld von Ökonomie, Politik und Kultur. 1997.

Band 8 Christian Schmidt: Real Convergence in the European Union. An Empirical Analysis. 1997.

Band 9 Silvia Marengo: Exchange Rate Policy for MERCOSUR: Lessons from the European Union. 1998.

Band 10 Jens Kleinemeyer: Standardisierung zwischen Kooperation und Wettbewerb. Eine spieltheoretische Betrachtung. 1998.

Band 11 Stefan M. Golder: Migration und Arbeitsmarkt. Eine empirische Analyse der Performance von Ausländern in der Schweiz. 1999.

Band 12 Stefan Kramer: Die Wirkung einer Internationalisierung des Yen auf die japanischen Finanzmärkte, die japanische Geldpolitik und die Usancen der Fakturierung. 1999.

Band 13 Antje Marielle Gerhold: Wirtschaftliche Integration und Kooperation im asiatisch-pazifischen Raum. Die APEC. 1999.

Band 14 Tamim Achim Dawar: Deutsche Direktinvestitionen in Australien. Eine Evaluation der theoretischen Erklärungsansätze und der Standortattraktivität des Produktions- und Investitionsstandortes Australien. 1999.

Band 15 Hans-Markus Johannsen: Die ordnungspolitische Haltung Frankreichs im Prozeß der europäischen Einigung. 1999.

Band 16 Annette Schönherr: Vereinigungsbedingte Dimensionen regionaler Arbeitsmobilität. Wirkungen unter analytisch einfachen Bedingungen und potentielle individuelle Migrationsgewinne in Deutschland nach der Vereinigung. 1999.

Band 17 Henrik Müller: Wechselkurspolitik des Eurolandes. Konfliktstoff für die neue währungspolitische Ära. 1999.

Band 18 Lars H. Wengorz: Die Bedeutung von Unternehmertum und Eigentum für die Existenz von Unternehmen. Eine methodenkritische Analyse der Transformation des Wirtschaftssystems in Russland. 2000.

Band 19 Eckart Bauer: Konzeptionelle Grundfragen eines Kinderleistungsausgleichs im Rahmen einer umlagefinanzierten zwangsweisen Rentenversicherung. 2000.

Band 20 Hubertus Hille: Enlarging the European Union. A Computable General Equilibrium Assessment of Different Integration Scenarios of Central and Eastern Europe. 2001.

Band 21 Tobias Just: Globalisierung und Ideologie. Eine Analyse der Existenz und Persistenz von Partisaneffekten bei zunehmender Internationalisierung der Märkte. 2001.

Band 22 Simone Claber: Großbritannien und die Europäische Integration unter besonderer Berücksichtigung ordnungspolitischer Aspekte. 2002.

Band 23 Silvia Rottenbiller: Essential Facilities als ordnungspolitisches Problem. 2002.

Band 24 Peggy Dreyhaupt von Speicher: Die Regionen Polens, Ungarns und der Tschechischen Republik vor dem EU-Beitritt. Interregionale Disparitäten, Bestimmungsfaktoren und Lösungsansätze. 2002.

Band 25 Gerhard Rösl: Seigniorage in der EWU. Eine Analyse der Notenbankgewinnentstehung und -verwendung des Eurosystems. 2002.

Band 26 Jörn Quitzau: Die Vergabe der Fernsehrechte an der Fußball-Bundesliga. Wohlfahrtsökonomische, wettbewerbspolitische und sportökonomische Aspekte der Zentralvermarktung. 2003.

Band 27 Małgorzata Stankiewicz: Die polnische Telekommunikation vor dem EU-Beitritt. 2003.

Band 28 Sarah Schniewindt: Einführung von Wettbewerb auf der Letzten Meile. Eine ökonomische Analyse von Netzinfrastruktur und Wettbewerbspotential im Teilnehmeranschlussbereich. 2003.

Band 29 Jens Bruderhausen: Zahlungsbilanzkrisen bei begrenzter Devisenmarkteffizienz. Ein kapitalmarkttheoretischer Ansatz. 2004.

Band 30 Philip Jensch: Einkommensteuerreform oder Einkommensteuerersatz? Alternative Ansätze einer Reform der direkten Besteuerung unter besonderer Berücksichtigung steuerpraktischer Gesichtspunkte. 2004.

Band 31 Karsten J. Adamski: Mikroanalyse eines Grundrentenkonzeptes der Alterssicherung. Eine empirische Studie zur Wirkung einer Grundrente auf Basis des Sozioökonomischen Panels. 2004.

Band 32 Sven Schulze: Anreizwirkungen und Arbeitsmarkteffekte der Ausgestaltung einer Arbeitslosenversicherung. 2004.

Band 33 Alkis Henri Otto: Makroökonomische Effekte der Direktinvestitionen. 2005.

Band 34 Stefan Hardege: Informationstechnologische Entwicklung und der Schutz von Verfügungsrechten für Informationsgüter. Eine ökonomische Analyse zur Ausgestaltung des Urheberrechts. 2006.

Band 35 Christoph Kimmel: Vermögenspreisinflation als wirtschaftspolitische Herausforderung. 2008.

Band 36 Axel Czaya: Das Europäische Normungssystem aus der Perspektive der Neuen Institutionenökonomik. 2008.

Band 37 Jana Brandstätter: International divergierende demographische Entwicklungen und internationale Kapitalbewegungen. 2008.

Band 38 Annette Olbrisch: Die Zinsmarge und ihre Determinanten. Eine theoretische und empirische Analyse unter besonderer Berücksichtigung von Protektion im Bankensektor. 2009.

Band 39 Hien Phuc Nguyen: National Competitiveness of Vietnam: Determinants, Emerging Key Issues and Recommendations. 2009.

Band 40 Heiko Geruschkat: Zur Ökonomie politischer Systeme. 2010.

Band 41 Reto Schemm-Gregory: Europa als ein Club voller Clubs. Eine clubtheoretische Betrachtung des politischen Systems der Europäischen Union. 2010.

Band 42 Cordula Wandel: Industry Agglomerations and Regional Development in Hungary. Economic Processes during European Integration. 2010.